The German-Speaking World

A Practical Introduction to
Sociolinguistic Issues

Second edition

**Patrick Stevenson, Kristine Horner,
Nils Langer and Gertrud Reershemius**

Routledge
Taylor & Francis Group

LONDON AND NEW YORK

Second edition published 2018
by Routledge
2 Park Square, Milton Park, Abingdon, Oxon OX14 4RN

and by Routledge
711 Third Avenue, New York, NY 10017

Routledge is an imprint of the Taylor & Francis Group, an informa business

First edition published by Routledge 1997

British Library Cataloguing-in-Publication Data
A catalogue record for this book is available from the British Library

Library of Congress Cataloging-in-Publication Data
Names: Stevenson, Patrick, 1954– author.
Title: The German-speaking world : a practical introduction to
    sociolinguistic issues / Patrick Stevenson, Kristine Horner,
    Nils Langer and Gertrud Reershemius.
Description: Second edition. | New York : Routledge, 2018. |
    Series: Routledge language in society | Includes bibliographical
    references and index.
Identifiers: LCCN 2017013808| ISBN 9781138858398 (hardback) |
    ISBN 9781138858428 (pbk.) | ISBN 9781315718026 (ebook)
Subjects: LCSH: German language—Social aspects. |
    German language—Europe, German-speaking. |
    German language—Dialects. | Sociolinguistics.
Classification: LCC PF3073 .S773 2018 | DDC 306.442/31—dc23
LC record available at https://lccn.loc.gov/2017013808

ISBN: 978-1-138-85839-8 (hbk)
ISBN: 978-1-138-85842-8 (pbk)
ISBN: 978-1-315-71802-6 (ebk)

Typeset in Times New Roman
by Apex CoVantage, LLC

Visit the eResources: www.routledge.com/9781138858428

The German-Speaking World

The German-Speaking World is an accessible textbook that offers students the opportunity to explore for themselves a wide range of sociolinguistic issues relating to the German language and its role in the world.

This new, second edition has been fully revised to reflect the many political and social changes of the last 20 years, including the impact of technology on language change. It continues to combine text with practical exercises and discussion questions to stimulate readers to think for themselves and to tackle specific problems.

Key features of this book:

- Informative and comprehensive: covers a wide range of current issues.
- Practical: contains a variety of graded exercises and tasks, plus an index of terms.
- Topical and contemporary: deals with current situations and provides up-to-date illustrative material.
- Thought-provoking: encourages students to reflect and research for themselves.

The German-Speaking World is the ideal textbook for undergraduate students who have a sound practical knowledge of German but who have little or no knowledge of linguistics or sociolinguistics.

Patrick Stevenson is Professor of German and Linguistics at the University of Southampton, UK.

Kristine Horner is Reader in Luxembourg Studies and Multilingualism at the University of Sheffield, UK.

Nils Langer is Professor of North Frisian and Minority Research at the University of Flensburg, Germany.

Gertrud Reershemius is Professor of Linguistics and Language Contact at Aston University, UK.

Routledge Language in Society

www.routledge.com/Routledge-Language-in-Society/book-series/SE0025

The **Routledge Language in Society** series provides the basis for a typical one-semester course. It combines a review of current sociolinguistic themes and relevant reading with a range of practical tasks exploring particular topics, and a selection of readings illustrating the sociopolitical significance of language-related issues. The focus encourages students to engage directly with important linguistic issues in a variety of ways. The outcome of this process is that students have a greater knowledge of, and sensitivity to, sociolinguistic problems and are able to observe and explore these problems when they have the opportunity to experience them at first hand.

EXISTING TITLES

The French-Speaking World
Rodney Ball and Dawn Marley

The German-Speaking World
Patrick Stevenson, Kristine Horner, Nils Langer and Gertrud Reershemius

The Spanish-Speaking World
Clare Mar-Molinero

Contents

Preface to the second edition

A great deal has happened in the 20 years since the first edition of this book was written. Both the German language itself and the contexts in which it is used have changed, in some respects quite dramatically. On the one hand, some topics that were particularly salient at that time now appear of marginal or purely historical interest, while new phenomena and topics have arisen that need to be addressed. On the other hand, many issues and questions covered in the original text continue to be relevant today, but their discussion needs to take account of contemporary conditions. In particular, of course, technological changes have meant both that language is used differently now, in a vast range of digital media and platforms, most of which didn't exist in the mid-1990s, and that linguistic research can be undertaken with great ease online, as well as through the more conventional means in physical libraries.

This new edition retains the basic structure of its predecessor, in that it consists of 12 chapters divided into three parts dealing respectively with the position of German in the world, particular aspects of language use and sociolinguistic controversies. Some passages have been carried over, updated where necessary, but much of the text is completely new. There are two main reasons for this. First, it became clear in the process of considering how best to revise the book that more radical changes were needed than simply, for example, replacing out of date statistics or adding references to new sources. Second, reviewers and users of the original edition had suggested that a more uniform and consistent structure for each chapter would make the book easier to use.

The most significant change in terms of the composition of the new edition is that it has been written not by an individual author but by a team. Again, this was, in part, due to the rapid expansion of the field of sociolinguistics over the last 20 years; each author brought their own expertise to bear on a particular set of topics. A collaborative approach to writing a textbook also seemed appropriate in that the combined classroom experience of colleagues working in different institutions was likely to bring a broader range of insights into what would appeal to students and how to make the book as flexible and adaptable as possible.

Patrick Stevenson, author of the first edition, acted as 'project manager' and editor of the entire text of this second edition. Individual chapters were written by Kristine Horner (Chapters 1, 2, 9 and 12), Nils Langer (Chapters 4, 5, 10 and 11) and Gertrud Reershemius (Chapters 3, 6, 7 and 8). Imogen Cobden, who was studying German at the University of Southampton while the book was in preparation, revised the list of keywords, the index, and the bibliography.

Figures

Maps

Tables

Phonetic symbols

A complete list of the symbols in the International Phonetic Alphabet (IPA) can be found on the website of the International Phonetic Association: www.internationalphoneticassociation. org/content/ipa-chart.

Detailed descriptions of the phonetics and phonology of German, with helpful examples, are in Fagan (2009), Chapter 1, and Johnson and Braber (2008), Chapter 4.

Here we list only those symbols that are used in this book, in each case with an example from (standard) German.

[a]	Stadt
[a:]	Staat
[ɛ]	elf
[ɪ]	Liste
[i:]	bieten
[ç]	Mädchen
[d]	du
[k]	kann
[p]	Panne
[pf]	Pfanne
[r]	rot
[s]	fast
[ʃ]	Fisch
[t]	Tisch
[ts]	Zeit
[x]	doch
[z]	sein

Acknowledgements

We would like to thank our editor at Routledge, Sam Vale Noya, for her encouragement and support throughout the process of producing this new edition of the book. We are also grateful to Imogen Cobden for her help in revising the list of keywords, the index and the bibliography and to Rosie Bailey Stevenson for helping with the design and creation of some of the figures.

Thanks are due to the following publishers and individuals for permission to use material (maps, photographs, figures, cartoons and extracts), the full sources of which are recorded either in the bibliography or where the items appear in the text:

Mary Allison; Mohamed Amjahid; Bergedorfer Buchdruckerei von Ed. Wagner GmbH; Bibliographisches Institut GmbH; Jenny Carl; Katherine Clark; dtv Verlagsgesellschaft mbH & Co. KG; Anna Havinga; Knud Kamphues; Felecia Lucht; Robert Möller and Stephan Elspaß; Lucian Rothe; Robert Sedlaczek; Spiegel Online GmbH; Axel Springer Syndication GmbH; Verein Deutsche Sprache e.V.; Wiener Zeitung.

All possible efforts have been made to obtain copyright approval for all material that has been reproduced here.

Introduction

THE AIM OF THIS BOOK is to offer students the opportunity to explore for themselves a wide range of sociolinguistic issues in relation to the German language. It is intended principally for undergraduate students of German who have a reasonably advanced knowledge of the language, but who may have little or no knowledge of linguistics in general or sociolinguistics in particular. Relevant theoretical concepts are introduced where necessary and helpful, but the emphasis throughout is on encouraging readers to think for themselves and to tackle specific problems. To this end, each chapter is punctuated with short reflective tasks and questions designed to stimulate readers to pause and think about specific issues raised in the text, and concludes with a number of proposed research activities and annotated suggestions for further reading.

The book has been written with a typical semester-length course in mind, and it could therefore be worked through as the principal course text. However, although there is a progression within each chapter and through the three parts, it is hoped that the structure of the book is sufficiently flexible to allow it to be used in various ways to suit particular needs. For example, individual parts or chapters can be selected to complement other material, and students or tutors can decide for themselves which tasks to attempt. The tasks at the end of each chapter are graded in terms of the time required to tackle them (see the description of 'How to use this book' in the next section) and can be adapted to meet readers' interests.

Part 1 takes as its starting point the question of what we mean by 'German-speakers' and 'the German-speaking world'. The three chapters in this first part of the book invite readers to investigate and reflect on fundamental 'macro-sociolinguistic' issues about the status and function of the German language in relation to its speakers, the enduring importance of the relationship between language and national identity and the changing position of the German language in the wider world.

Part 2 aims to encourage readers to explore social and regional variations in German from a 'micro-sociolinguistic' perspective. In other words, the focus shifts from the role of the language as a whole in national and international contexts to the forms and functions of individual features and varieties, in the past and in the present. This involves, for example, identifying distinctive features of regional speech varieties, tracing the emergence of standard German and analysing ways in which the contemporary language is changing, investigating the impact on language use of increased social diversity and digital technologies, and exploring visual representations of language.

Part 3 shifts the focus again, this time to a consideration of broader social impacts of the German language. These final chapters focus on people's attitudes towards the language and their perceptions of how it is changing, on controversies about language in education in increasingly diverse societies and on debates about proficiency in 'national' languages as a requirement for acquiring citizenship.

A particular challenge confronting anyone writing about German is how to refer to 'Germany'. This issue is tackled explicitly in Chapter 1, and readers are invited to reflect on its historical and contemporary complexity. In the interests of readability, however, a pragmatic solution has been adopted in the writing of the book. With reference to the periods before 1949 and after 1990, the simple name Germany is used, in spite of the fact that it refers to very different geopolitical entities at different times. For the period 1949–1990, either the formal designations German Democratic Republic (GDR) and Federal Republic of Germany (FRG) are used or (depending on context and for ease of expression) the informal East and West Germany.

One final point: this book is not intended as an introduction to sociolinguistics as such. Where concepts and terminology are used that might be new to readers, they are either briefly explained or used as the basis of tasks requiring readers to find out for themselves what the terms mean. The most important concepts are given in **bold** the first time they appear in each chapter, and they are briefly defined in a list of keywords at the end of the book, which provides a simple guide to the way they are used here. However, a fundamental purpose of the book is to demonstrate that there are few, if any, hard and fast answers to sociolinguistic questions and to encourage readers to reach their own conclusions. Therefore, the list of keywords does no more than provide a quick source of reference and act as an *aide-mémoire*.

* * *

The suggestions for further reading at the end of each chapter are usually quite specific and are intended to direct readers to useful material on particular points. However, it might be useful to consult some or all of the following books, which provide a wealth of background reading, useful information and explanations of important points, both in general terms and specifically in relation to German.

Crystal, David (2010) *The Cambridge Encyclopaedia of Language*, Cambridge: Cambridge University Press.
Crystal, David (2008) *A Dictionary of Linguistics and Phonetics*, Oxford: Blackwell.

These are excellent general reference books, which should provide answers to any questions on linguistic terminology and concepts used in the description and analysis of language.

Holmes, Janet (2013) *An Introduction to Sociolinguistics*, London: Routledge.
Mesthrie, Rajend, Joan Swann, Ana Deumert and William L. Leap (2009) *Introducing Sociolinguistics*, Edinburgh: Edinburgh University Press.
Meyerhoff, Miriam (2011) *Introducing Sociolinguistics*, London: Routledge.
Wardhaugh, Ronald and Janet M. Fuller (2015) *An Introduction to Sociolinguistics*, Oxford: Blackwell.

Amongst the many introductory textbooks on general sociolinguistics, these four are perhaps the most accessible, and they offer a wide range of illustrations and practical activities.

Fagan, Sarah (2009) *German: A Linguistic Introduction*, Cambridge: CUP.
Johnson, Sally and Natalie Braber (2008) *Exploring the German Language*, Cambridge: CUP.

Both of these textbooks offer a broad survey of topics in German linguistics, including chapters on sociolinguistic issues, with plentiful useful examples. Johnson and Braber offer a lively and very readable introduction and provide practical exercises and suggestions for further reading; Fagan goes into greater depth and – despite the title – writes for the more advanced reader.

Durrell, Martin (2003) *Using German: A Guide to Contemporary Usage*, Cambridge: CUP.

A practical and very helpful guide to structures and styles of contemporary German, including chapters on contemporary change and regional variation.

Salmons, Joseph (2012) *A History of German: What the Past Reveals About Today's Language*, Oxford: OUP.
Stedje, Astrid (2007) *Deutsche Sprache gestern und heute*, Stuttgart: utb.

For those who want to delve more deeply into the history of the German language, Salmons gives a comprehensive and scholarly but readable account, while Stedje offers a very accessible illustrated survey of the historical development of German from its origins to the present day.

In addition to these book publications, you will of course find many useful sources online. A good place to start for the most up-to-date developments and information on current research is the Institut für Deutsche Sprache (www.ids-mannheim.de).

How to use this book

Each chapter is written in such a way as to give the reader an introduction to and overview of a particular topic and also to encourage the reader to think actively about the topic and to look for ways to find out more. This is done in two ways. First, the text is interrupted at various points by short, simple questions that are designed to make the reader pause and reflect on specific aspects of the topic and that can normally be answered without consulting other sources (or at most with a quick internet search). Second, at the end of each chapter there is a list of tasks and activities that invite the reader either to reflect on what they think they have learned ('reflective tasks') or to undertake some further research in order to explore particular issues in greater depth. Some of these are fairly straightforward and can be carried out individually ('research tasks'); others require rather more time and effort and lend themselves to group work ('project ideas'). There could be many different outcomes of these various activities: for example, group discussions in class; presentations; posters, reports, essays or even dissertations; individual or collaborative blogs.

Each chapter draws heavily on a wide range of sources, but for ease of reading these are cited within the text only when they are referred to explicitly and at greater length. The Bibliography lists all relevant sources consulted by the authors and provides a good starting point for research on the tasks and activities. The 'Annotated further reading' section at the end of each chapter offers some initial suggestions for ways of following up on particular topics discussed in the text.

Part 1

The position of German in the world

1 German

Language, people, place

1.1 Introduction

When we say we 'can't see the wood for the trees', we are expressing a need to establish a general picture of something that is more than the sum of its parts. Categorising and classifying things we encounter in everyday life are therefore important steps in the process of imposing some kind of order on the infinite varieties of human experience: they are part of a general strategy of 'making sense of the world' by artificially reducing variation to manageable proportions. For example, it is both conceptually and communicatively more economical if we can classify tulips, roses and daffodils as members of the general category *flower* or Volkswagens, Fords and Nissans as belonging to the category *car* (or *automobile*).

Naming languages is a similar process, but allocating individual varieties to a particular language may be more arbitrary and more complicated than is the case with types of flower or car, and there may be other reasons than convenience or communicative efficiency for doing so. Furthermore, the names themselves are more than mere labels and may reveal a great deal about the relationship between the linguistic forms and their speakers. Consider, for example, the names for English, French and German in Table 1.1. A glance from left to right across the table should reveal at least two interesting points in this respect: firstly, the fact that many different languages use (versions of) the 'same' name to designate English and French; second, the fact that there is, by contrast, no general agreement on how to designate German. European language names are most commonly based either on the names of tribes or peoples (here, for example, Angles and Franks) or on the names of geographical locations; some of the labels used for German follow these two patterns, but others derive not from people or places but from language itself.

- Can you think of any controversies concerning the naming of languages? (You could think, for instance, of the situation in the former Yugoslavia or the relationship between Czech and Slovak; the linguistic dispute in the Republic of Moldova; the two names given to Spanish (español vs. castellano); or the different names given to Chinese.)

Table 1.1 Nationality/language adjectives in a range of languages

English	*Italian*	*Russian*	*German*	*Hungarian*	*Turkish*
English	inglese	anglijskij	englisch	angol	ingiliz
French	francese	francuzskij	französisch	francia	fransız
German	tedesco	nemeckij	deutsch	német	alman

Source: based on Townson 1992: 78

1.2   Historical overview of Germanic languages

From a contemporary **synchronic** perspective, the label *deutsch* has linguistic, ethnic and geographical applications: we may talk of *die deutsche Sprache, die Deutschen, Deutschland*. However, if we consider it **diachronically**, we find that its use to designate a language predates its use in reference to people and places. In other words, the constitution of the ethnic or national group derives from the idea of a 'common' language, and this is what makes the German case particularly significant in the European context (see Chapter 2): any attempt to define the elusive concept of 'Germanness' has to start with the language. However, this creates more problems than it resolves:

> Wenn Helmut Kohl im Laufe der Jahre 1989–1991 wohl hundertmal von der Einheit *des deutschen Volkes* gesprochen hat, dann ist klar, daß dies nur Bürger der alten/ neuen Bundesrepublik Deutschland betrifft, also *die Deutschen*. Und es ist ebenso klar, daß Schweizer, Liechtensteiner, Österreicher usw. zwar Deutsch sprechen, aber keine Deutschen sind. Die semantische Aufgabenverteilung scheint gelöst zu sein.
>
> Trotzdem ist die Sache so einfach nicht. [. . .] Was weithin übersehen wird, ist die Tatsache, daß es sich hier in hohem Maße schlichtweg um ein terminologisches Problem handelt, das unlösbar ist. Hieße die Bundesrepublik Deutschland etwa *Preußen*, dann wären Preußen, Österreich, die Schweiz usw. einfach deutsche oder teilweise deutsche Länder. Dem ist nicht so. Die Realität beschert den deutschsprachigen Ländern außerhalb Deutschlands auch auf weitere Sicht den alten Konflikt zwischen Staatsnation und Sprachnation und die Frage nach dem jeweiligen Deutschsein dieser Staaten. Gerade während der letzten Jahre ist diese Frage angesichts der erreichten Einheit Deutschlands wieder aktuell geworden. Sie wird jedoch – bei verschiedenen Ausgangspunkten – in der Schweiz und in Österreich schon seit einigen Jahren verstärkt diskutiert. In dieser Diskussion führt kein Weg am Faktum der Staatssprache Deutsch vorbei, die dort eben nicht etwa nur Bildungs- oder Verwaltungssprache ist, sondern Volks- und Muttersprache seit Anbeginn.
>
> (Scheuringer 1992: 218–219)

So just when we thought we had identified a neat relationship between 'the German language' and 'the German people', we find that things are actually more complex. Scheuringer's argument, for example, confronts us with a number of questions:

* If 'the German language' is in some sense the cornerstone of 'the German nation', what does this mean for 'the Austrians' or the 75 per cent of Swiss citizens whose first language is German?
* What does it mean for the millions of citizens of other states all over the world who consider German to be their 'mother tongue'? Conversely, what implications does it have for those living in Germany (or Austria) for whom German is a second or foreign language?

Even if we restrict our consideration of the word *deutsch* to the relatively recent past (for example, post-1945), we can see that its multiple uses and connotations provide a key to many of the currents of social and political history in the centre of Europe. The official names of the two German states that existed between 1949 and 1990 were Die Deutsche Demokratische Republik and Die Bundesrepublik Deutschland. While the former was often abbreviated to DDR (in German), both in the GDR itself and in the FRG, even in official contexts, the German abbreviation BRD was never officially sanctioned in West Germany and from the late 1970s was actually prohibited. A university professor, who had used the short form in an official letter, received this stern rebuke from the Bund Freiheit der Wissenschaft (a small group of conservative academics):

> Wie Ihnen sicherlich bekannt ist, ist der Ausdruck „BRD" ein semantisches Kampfmittel der DDR gegen die freiheitliche Bundesrepublik Deutschland. Dieses Kampfmittel wird mit aller Konsequenz auch von den extremistischen Kräften in der Bundesrepublik angewandt, die mit unserer freiheitlichen Grundordnung nichts anzufangen wissen und sie bekämpfen.
>
> (Glück and Sauer 1990: 20; originally cited in *Die Glottomane* 4/1976: 6)

• Why do you think a seemingly innocent abbreviation would be considered threatening?

During the existence of the two Germanies, West Germans had increasingly come to use *deutsch* and *Deutschland* with reference to themselves and their state. Similarly, it was commonplace for many West German organisations and institutions to include the word *deutsch* in their title (Deutscher Gewerkschaftsbund, Deutsche Welle). However, while some organisations in the GDR did so too (Deutsche Reichsbahn), many either concealed it by the consistent use of an abbreviated form of the title (FDJ for Freie Deutsche Jugend, ADN for Allgemeiner Deutscher Nachrichtendienst) or changed their name (Deutsche Akademie der Wissenschaften became Akademie der Wissenschaften der DDR). From 1990, *deutsch* and *Deutschland* rapidly re-established themselves as demonstrative emblems of national unity. For example, a trade magazine for butchers proudly declared: 'Der deutsche Wurstfreund kann seinen Tisch mit über 1500 leckeren Sorten decken. Dafür sorgen Deutschlands gewissenhafte Fleischer. [. . .] Genießen Sie also die Abwechslung und den Geschmack, die der große deutsche Wurstschatz bietet' (Glück 1992: 153; originally in *Lukullus Fleischer-Kundenpost* 31/1990: 2).

• In the light of what we have said previously, what do you think was the political significance of the gradual disappearance of the word *deutsch* from public discourse in the GDR? Consider, for example, the wording of the following extracts from different versions of the GDR constitution:

Preamble

Von dem Willen erfüllt, die Freiheit und Rechte des Menschen zu verbürgen, [. . .] hat sich das deutsche Volk diese Verfassung gegeben.

(1949 version)

Erfüllt von dem Willen, seine Geschicke frei zu bestimmen, [. . .] hat sich das Volk der Deutschen Demokratischen Republik diese sozialistische Verfassung gegeben.

(1974 version)

Article 1, clause 1

Deutschland ist eine unteilbare demokratische Republik.

(1949 version)

Die Deutsche Demokratische Republik ist ein sozialistischer Staat deutscher Nation.

(1968 version)

Die Deutsche Demokratische Republik ist ein sozialistischer Staat der Arbeiter und Bauern.

(1974 version)

1.3   The problem of definitions: what is German, who are German-speakers?

Much of the discussion in the previous section took for granted the existence of a discrete set of linguistic forms that can readily be subsumed under the label *the German language*. As with many other abstract concepts (goodness, happiness, beauty), the prevailing view of this notion is based on a paradox: we readily accept that there is such a thing, that it is somehow self-evident, and yet cannot find any convincing way of defining it. In other words, we are generally confident of being able to identify whether a stretch of speech is German or not, but we have no watertight and universally agreed criteria for reaching such judgements.

- Sometimes, it might not be so straightforward to decide what is German and what is not. Try reading the following four sentences aloud (they are represented in 'normal' script rather than in phonetic transcription for ease of reading): do they *look* German, do they *sound* German, *are* they German?[1]

1   Dat Book is so anleggt, dat't för de tokaamen 10 Johr bruukt warden kann.
2   M'r han ken finanzielli Understetzung. D'abonnements allein helfen uns de Zittung ze bezahle.
3   Die erschte settler fon Levnon County, echssept's weschtlich dehl, ware's menscht fon Deitschland.
4   Die yugnt-delegatn af der velt-konferents far yidish un yidisher kultur deklarirn tsu der yidisher yugnt fan der velt az die yidishe shprakh un kultur senen an integraler un neytiker teyl fun undzer lebn vi yidn baym haintikn tog.

However, while the search for an adequate definition of German may ultimately be hopeless, the quest for a solution is a necessary part of understanding the problem: if we cannot delimit German, we cannot hope to find satisfactory answers to any further questions to do with its status and use, the number of its speakers, its geographical spread and so on. The nearest thing there is to a consensus on this issue is that it can best be resolved by combining objective and subjective criteria: in particular, the principle of linguistic relatedness on the one hand, and individual speakers' perceptions on the other. In other words, two linguistic **varieties** may be considered to be versions of the same language if they can be shown to be closely related (in grammar, vocabulary, etc.) and are felt by their speakers to belong to the same language. As a means of forging a link between these two criteria, the concept of ***Überdachung*** has been proposed, according to which two linguistic varieties are accommodated under the 'umbrella' of a single **standard** language variety. For instance, linguistic varieties spoken on either side of the Dutch-German border sound very similar, but their users will consider that they are speaking forms of Dutch and German, respectively, and will acknowledge standard Dutch and standard German as their respective points of reference, as the authoritative forms of their language.

However, this temptingly simple approach is not without its problems, especially since it appears to gloss over the controversial nature of the concept *standard German*. One of the problems, which is fairly easily disposed of, is the common misconception that the 'standard' form of any language is its 'original, uncorrupted state', from which all other forms have subsequently deviated. Far from being a naturally occurring phenomenon, it is always the result of relatively recent and deliberate intervention in the 'natural' development of the language. The earliest serious attempts to standardise German resulted in the publication of dictionaries and grammars in the seventeenth century. These scholarly works were intended to 'fix' the form of the language, to represent a definitive account of what constitutes 'correct German'. However, if you compare what is contained in these reference works with what can be found in current ones, you will immediately notice differences at every linguistic level (see Chapter 5 for a detailed discussion of the standardisation of German).

- What does this suggest about the process of standardisation, and what implications does this have for the way we think about the 'standard' forms of languages?

The issues raised by the previous question are another illustration of the importance of diachronic perspectives on language. However, a synchronic study of different dictionaries and grammars (that is, ones published around the same time) will also reveal another set of problems for the attempt to incorporate the concept of standard language into the project of delimiting the language as a whole. Just as at any historical moment in the last 200 years we can find 'German-speakers' rallying round several different 'national' flags, so we would find competing representations of 'standard German' that differ from each other sufficiently to provoke a debate on whether there is (at the time in question) one single form of standard German or whether there are in fact two or three, or even four.

At first glance, the concept of a standard form seems to imply something absolute, so we may well ask how there can be more than one 'standard German'. On the other hand, we have seen that a historical analysis of the concept forces us to see it as a relative rather than an absolute notion; therefore, on the synchronic level it may not necessarily be contradictory to talk of several co-existent (and overlapping) standard varieties. To account for this, German is sometimes referred to as a **pluricentric** language.

- All of the following words would be considered 'standard German', but what is the difference in the status of those in the left- and right-hand columns?

der Advokat	der Rechtsanwalt
Jänner	Januar
die Jause	der Imbiss
die Marille	die Aprikose
der Rauchfang(kehrer)	der Schornstein(feger)
das Morgenessen	das Frühstück
die Gschwellti	die Pellkartoffeln
das Sackgeld	das Taschengeld
das Spital	das Krankenhaus
das Billett	die Fahrkarte

The conundrum of what constitutes the German language is clearly difficult to resolve, but even if we can decide on a working definition it is not a simple matter to establish who to count as German-speakers. By now it should be clear that there is no straightforward equation between language and nationality or language and citizenship (a question we return to in Chapter 12), but just how far do you spread the net to capture everyone who arguably belongs in this category? One recent study comes to the conclusion that the total number of German-speakers throughout the world could be anywhere between 143.5 million and 248.5 million, depending on which criteria you adopt (Ammon 2015: 179). Even if we take a narrower focus and base our findings entirely on published surveys, a great deal of care needs to be taken in interpreting the results. For example, on their own, the figures in Table 1.2 have no particular value: we cannot begin to evaluate or comment on them unless we know exactly how the individual totals were arrived at. We would need to know, for example, what is meant by 'speakers of German as a first or second language', what sources the figures derive from and what questions were asked in order to determine the figures.

• What further details would we need to best interpret the figures given in Table 1.2?

If the tasks of delimiting the language and counting its speakers (or perhaps we should now say its users) are fraught with difficulty, it would not be surprising to find that the seemingly uncontroversial **generic** label *the German-speaking countries* is actually less straightforward than it might appear. The main problem with the term is that it seems to be an 'either-or' category, which does not correspond to the observable reality: for example, Germany and Austria are surely German-speaking countries, and yet their resident populations include speakers of many other languages; conversely, there are substantial German-speaking populations in, for example, the UK, Canada and Brazil, and yet no one would seriously suggest calling them German-speaking countries. However, it is not merely a question of which countries to include in the list: what is more important is the status and function of German in different countries. In other words, the interesting sociolinguistic issue is the relative significance of the German language in different parts of the world, the spatial distribution of its influence (see Chapters 2 and 3, where we deal with these points in more detail).

In order to investigate this question it is necessary to discuss some key terms. The terminology in this area is often confusing, and the use of certain terms is far from consistent, but there are a number of key concepts which are commonly encountered in the literature and which can be defined in a way that is useful for our purposes:

Amtssprache. It is sometimes necessary to distinguish between official status and official function, as there are cases where a language may have one but not the other. However, this distinction is not relevant in situations where German is an official language.

Table 1.2 Speakers of German as a first and second language in the areas where German is an officially recognised language

Country/area	German-speakers
Germany	81,102,768
Austria	8,234,060
Liechtenstein	36,107
Switzerland	5,705,847
Italy (South Tyrol only)	438,041
Eastern Belgium	72,878
Luxembourg	407,200
Total	95,956,901

Source: based on Ammon 2015: 170

Nationale bzw. regionale Amtssprache. A language may have official status and/or function at either national or regional level, and this is an important distinction as far as German is concerned.

Solo-offizielle bzw. ko-offizielle Amtssprache (or, sometimes, *alleindominante bzw. ko-dominante Amtssprache*). On both national and regional levels, an official language may be the only language that is accorded this position or it may share it with one or more other languages.

Nationalsprache. The use of this term tends to be determined ideologically, but in general it can be said to relate to symbolic rather than instrumental functions that a language can perform. In some cases, a particular language may be both a national and an official language, but in principle the two categories are independent of each other.

- Map 1.1 shows where German has the status and function of an official language at national and regional levels: using the terminology given previously, try to characterise the position of German in each of these countries more precisely.

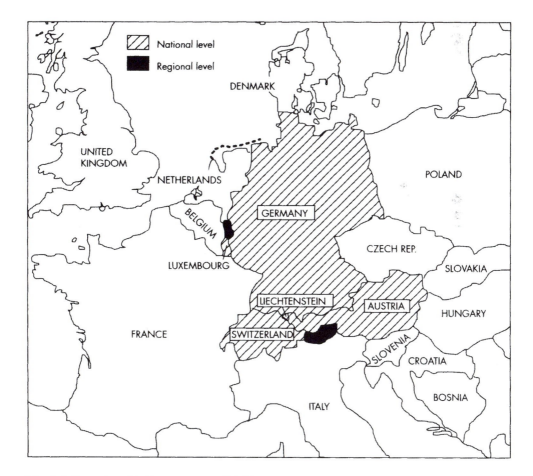

Map 1.1 Countries with German as an official language
Source: Stevenson 1995: 32

1.4   The presence of German outside of German-speaking countries

Now that we have discussed issues around defining the German language and identifying German-speaking countries, this final section focuses on the presence of German outside of what are commonly referred to as German-speaking countries. There are two main reasons why German-speakers and, more broadly, the German language can be found beyond the borders of German-speaking countries. The first reason is that political borders in central Europe have shifted multiple times over the course of history: this has been in connection with the fall of empires and the rise of the nation-state over the course of the long nineteenth century, the two World Wars and ensuing Cold War in the twentieth century and, finally, the post-Cold War period. The second reason why we find German outside of German-speaking countries is closely connected to the first: the emigration of hundreds of thousands of German-speakers for economic and religious reasons both to eastern Europe and beyond and to other parts of the world at various points in time over the last three centuries.

• In the place where you live, or in places where you have travelled, have you heard languages spoken other than those recognised by the state? Which languages are/were spoken there and in what contexts?

Aside from the German-speaking countries, two parts of the world where German-speakers have been most numerous are in certain regions of central and eastern Europe and in North America. There are various differences in the status and function of German in these contexts, with one being the distinction that is sometimes made between **autochthonous** and **allochthonous** minorities, or regional and immigrant minorities, even if this distinction proves to be problematic in practice. In parts of central Europe, ethnic Germans form an autochthonous minority and a number of countries including the Czech Republic, Hungary, Poland and Slovakia recognise the German language, albeit to varying degrees, in line with stipulations of the European Charter for Regional or Minority Languages (see Chapter 11). The German language forms an important part of the history of these central European countries, and multilingual contact zones on present-day political borders with Germany and/or Austria are sites where questions of identity and belonging can be explored (see also Chapter 9). Identity is a relatively flexible concept in that it can fluctuate over time and can even shift according to context at one point in time. This is because it involves both how we see ourselves and how others see us. The role of language in identity formation is often described as 'contingent' since it cannot be taken for granted, even if it often plays a crucial role in how people are socially positioned.

Consider the following passage from an interview with Szilvia (pseudonym) in Sopron, Hungary, which lies less than 20 kilometres from the Austrian border:

> Sie war Wienerin die Oma und der Grossvater war eben ein Soproner Handwerker und so haben sie hier gelebt und auch meine Mutter entstammt einer Ruster Familie. Rust ist am Neusiedler See und jetzt gehört Rust zu Österreich und in diesen Familien ist es absolut egal ob Deutsch oder Ungarisch gesprochen wird. Sogar die Grossmutter hat kein einziges ungarisches Wort gesprochen sondern nur Deutsch und so haben wir Deutsch gelernt [. . .] Ich habe auch eine Schwester dann wären wir wahrscheinlich im Handwerk tätig wie alle in der Familie und dass wir eben das nicht weitergeführt haben dafür haben wir aber die Sprache und so- ich sage immer, 'das Diplom in die Wiege gelegt bekommen'.
>
> (Stevenson and Carl 2010: 143)

In this biographical narrative, Szilvia explains how the German language was passed down by her grandmother and also how German is significant for her profession. In this way, the use of German shifted from the personal sphere of the family to play an instrumental function in Szilvia's life as her skills in the language led to employment opportunities. In recent years, the German language has once again taken on a degree of instrumental value in parts of central Europe, as illustrated by the images from present-day Sopron in Figures 1.1 and 1.2 (Carl 2014: 258–260).

- Why do you think the use of German is so prominent on the signs in Figures 1.1 and 1.2? Which languages do you think were used on related signage in Sopron some 50 years ago and why?

If we now investigate the use of German in other parts of the world, this can provide us with some interesting points of contrast to its use in European contexts. While there was a significant level of immigration of German-speakers to countries such as Argentina, Australia, Canada and the United States, there has not been any official recognition of the German language in these countries. It is estimated that the initial German-speaking immigrants arrived in (what would become) the United States in the early seventeenth century. It is difficult to pinpoint the number and date of first arrivals due to the absence of a German state and the broad range of Germanic language varieties that were spoken at the time: both factors make it difficult to discern who could be counted as a German-speaker. The peak of German-speaking immigration to the United States was in the nineteenth century, and it tapered off in the twentieth century, with the exception of some further arrivals in the aftermath of the Second World War.

Research on the German language in the United States is often framed in terms of **language maintenance** and **language shift**. Rather than pointing to just one factor contributing to the decline in use of German in the United States, for example, in connection with the World Wars and negative stereotyping of Germans and the German language, we should take into account multiple factors that lead to the continued use or disuse of the language, which

Figure 1.1 Advertisement for dental clinic, Sopron, Hungary
Photo: Jenny Carl

Figure 1.2 Menu board outside café, Sopron, Hungary
Photo: Jenny Carl

is often a gradual process rather than an abrupt one. Consider the rise and fall in the production of German language newspapers as an example: the pattern portrayed in Figure 1.3 can best be explained by various changes in societal and economic structures that affected the overall publishing industry and the fate of many small-scale newspapers. For example, larger newspapers benefitted from new printing technologies, while the smaller newspapers could not afford to invest in these technological advances. Moreover, some smaller newspapers, such as the *Watertown Weltbürger*, transferred ownership from a locally operated company to a conglomeration in the early twentieth century and were later phased out.

While the use of German was widespread in certain parts of the United States until roughly the early twentieth century, especially in the upper midwestern region of the country where German-speaking immigrants settled in largest numbers, it has gradually fallen into decline in everyday use from the turn of the twentieth century to the present. However, it is notable that the symbolic use and public display of German persists in some places (see

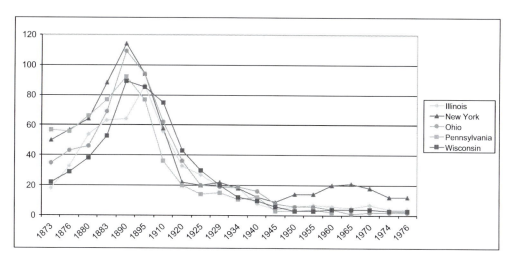

Figure 1.3 Number of German language publications in the US, 1873 to 1976

Source: Lucht et al. 2011; following Arndt and Olson 1976: 805–806, and Lucht 2007, cited in Lucht et al. 2011

Figure 1.4 Mural, University of Wisconsin-Madison Memorial Union

Source: Mary Allison

Figure 1.5 Mural, University of Wisconsin-Madison Memorial Union
Source: Mary Allison

Chapter 9). Thus, for instance, the images in Figures 1.4 and 1.5 can be found in areas that are frequented by students at the University of Wisconsin-Madison Memorial Union.

• Why do you think it was decided to display a language other than English in a university setting in the United States? What might this suggest about the link between language and identity?

1.5   Conclusion

This opening chapter has raised more questions than it has provided answers. This is partly deliberate, as it is your job to find answers, and partly inevitable, as many of the fundamental questions at issue here defy all attempts to reach a definitive position. However, to make subsequent discussion possible, it is necessary to establish some working generalisations. For example, in spite of our scepticism about the validity and appropriateness of the term we can still use the label *the German-speaking countries* as a convenient fiction, a shorthand device for referring to Germany, Austria, Switzerland, Liechtenstein and Luxembourg on the basis that German is the, or an, officially recognised language of the state in each case. The final section of the chapter explored the status and function of the German language beyond the borders of the German-speaking countries to highlight the ways in which the language is used in contexts where it has limited or no official recognition. The next two chapters develop the theme of the status and function of the German language today, first in relation to national identity in German-speaking countries and then in terms of the consequences of globalisation.

Tasks and suggestions for research

Reflective tasks

1   What historical and contemporary factors pose challenges to attempts to determine the precise numbers of German-speakers in given places?
2   Shortly after the (re)unification of Germany in 1990 German embassies issued a press release announcing that the official title of the (new) state was (still) Bundesrepublik Deutschland, but that it was acceptable to refer to it informally simply as Deutschland. Why do you think they did this and why should it matter?

Research tasks

1   Find out what you can about the **etymology** of the word *deutsch*.
2   Look up the entries for *deutsch* and *Deutschland* in a number of different dictionaries published at different times (and if possible in different countries) over the last 100 years: what contrasts and changes do you find? If possible, also explore the ambiguities of the terms *westdeutsch*, *ostdeutsch* and *mitteldeutsch*, and consider them in relation to the older terms *großdeutsch* and *kleindeutsch*.
3   Explore the use of other terms (at what times and by whom?) to designate the two German states that existed from 1949 to 1990, and try to discover why the publishers of the *Bild-Zeitung* considered it newsworthy to make the solemn proclamation in August 1989 that they had finally decided 'DDR ohne Anführungszeichen zu schreiben' (see Glück 1992: 144).

Project idea

Choose one country where German is a minority language. Find out when German-speakers immigrated there and why. Is the German language still maintained there and, if so, in what contexts? Is there institutional support for the use of German?

Note

1   The four sentences are examples of *Niedersächsisch* (Low Saxon), *Elsässisch* (Alsatian), *Pensilfaanisch* (Pennsylvania Dutch – i.e. Deutsch) and *Jiddisch*, respectively. They are taken from Kloss (1978: 102, 133, 139, 196).

Annotated further reading

Ammon (2015) is an authoritative source on the number and distribution of German-speakers.
Barbour and Stevenson (1990/1998), Chapter 1, discuss all of the issues raised here in greater depth.
Clyne (1995), Chapter 2, explains the idea of German as a pluricentric language.
Glück and Sauer (1990), pp. 1–22, review the use of the word *deutsch*, and alternative ways of referring to institutions in the GDR and the (pre-1990) Federal Republic.
Johannessen and Salmons (2015) provide a comprehensive account of the Germanic heritage languages in North America.
Scheuringer (1992) gives a critical account of the relationship between 'speaking German' and 'being German' in Switzerland and Austria.
Stevenson and Carl (2010) show the historical and contemporary importance of language for German-speaking minorities in central Europe.
Townson (1992), Chapter 3, especially pp. 77–80, gives a detailed overview of the origins of the term *deutsch*.

2 Language and national identity

2.1 Introduction

One of the deepest layers of identity that many people feel strongly about, particularly in Europe, is national identity. Yet, notions of national identity are somewhat ambiguous since they could refer to citizens of a political state (for example, Germans as citizens of Germany) or members of a national group (for example, people who feel that they are members of the German nation, regardless of their citizenship). Indeed, the concepts of *state* and *nation* are frequently used interchangeably in popular discourse, although they are not one and the same thing. The state is more straightforward to define than the nation because the state is aligned with geopolitical borders that appear on world maps and the people who reside in that space are subject to the laws of that state. Conversely, the idea of the nation is rather complex, and there is no generally accepted, universal definition for this concept.

Nevertheless, some common themes arise when attempting to define the nation. According to Guibernau (1996), a nation is a group of people who perceive themselves as sharing certain elements, including the following:

> common descent
> common historical memories
> common culture
> homeland
> desire for political self-determination

The word *perceive* is a key aspect in definitions of the nation because it emphasises the fact that some characteristics or features are not automatically shared, but rather come to be regarded as if they were. Depending on the socio-historical context, different elements can and will be foregrounded as key symbols of nationhood. Language often functions as one of these key symbols, and **language ideologies**, or deeply ingrained and institutionally supported beliefs about language and the way that language and society should be organised, have the potential to influence our broader world views.

- Can you think of some common beliefs that people have about language?
- Can you also think of beliefs that concern the links between language and society?

One of the most widespread language ideologies is the *one nation, one language ideology*, which directly equates a language with a nation on the basis that the linkage between these concepts is natural, timeless and indisputable (see also Chapter 12). Another widespread language ideology is the *standard language ideology*, the idea that there exists a fixed, unchangeable and homogeneous **variety** of a language, which tends to be regarded as the most highly valued variety in a particular society (see Chapter 5). The following sections explore how various factors, including language ideologies, influence the status and function of German as well as the link between language and national identity in Germany, Austria, Switzerland and Luxembourg.

2.2   The role of language in German and Austrian national identities

Germany only became a political entity, in the sense that we know it today, when many of the German-speaking territories in central Europe were united following the end of the Franco-Prussian War in 1871, forming a sovereign state based on the idea of a German nation: a *nation-state*. The rise of the nation-state in Europe as a predominant model for the organisation of social, political and economic life became prominent during the 'long nineteenth century' (between the start of the French revolution in 1789 and the outbreak of the First World War in 1914). Scholars often refer to the way that the nation was conceived during that period as either a *Kulturnation* (ethnic nation based on a sense of shared culture) or a *Staatsnation* (civic nation based on the will to sovereignty); Germany is often considered to be a prime example of the former, in contrast to France as an example of the latter.

The idea of the German language as a common bond, uniting the German people, emerged as a powerful force in focusing an otherwise rather disparate sense of nationhood. Consider the link that Jacob Grimm makes between *Volk* and *Sprache*, as well as the date of the original quotation:

> Lassen Sie mich mit der einfachen frage anheben: Was ist ein volk? Und ebenso einfach antworten: ein volk ist der inbegriff von menschen, welche dieselbe sprache reden. Das ist für uns Deutsche die unschuldigste und zugleich stolzeste erklärung.
>
> (Grimm 1847: 11, cited in Stevenson 2002: 23)

- In addition to their groundbreaking work on the German language, the brothers Jacob and Wilhelm Grimm are, of course, also renowned for gathering and compiling a large collection of *Märchen*. What connections might there be between these two enterprises, especially in the context of the mid-nineteenth century?

Such sentiments allowed the German language to serve as the principal unifying element of the newly formed German state, with language being cast as the soul of the nation and thus making the new political unity appear to follow the natural progression of things. However, when the German state was founded, it was not on the basis of a 'perfect match' between language and territory. On the one hand, not all German-speaking lands were included (the most obvious exclusion, of course, was Austria). On the other hand, even the territory of the new Germany wasn't linguistically uniform as it included speakers of other **autochthonous** languages, such as Sorbian and Frisian (see also Chapter 11). As a result of the drive towards a unified nation-state, underpinned by the one nation, one language ideology, the speakers of these languages came to be perceived as linguistic minorities and gradually shifted to the use of German, even if Sorbian and Frisian continued to be spoken to a limited degree (see also Chapters 9 and 11 on bilingualism and language use along the borders of Germany).

So while the idea of a common language was a fundamental component of the nineteenth-century project of creating unified nation-states across Europe, it was clearly not unproblematic. This issue emerged very clearly in the aftermath of the Second World War. If 'the German language' was a key defining feature of 'the German nation', what role could it play in the post-war formation of not one but two new German states – the GDR, or East Germany, and the FRG, or West Germany? And how could Austria also lay claim to a German-speaking heritage without appearing to be subservient to its northern neighbour(s)?

Invoking the legacy of Jacob Grimm and other proponents of the *Sprachnation*, the 'linguistic nation', political commentators in both the GDR and the FRG asserted their state's right to the inheritance of the cultural traditions articulated in the German language, which they simultaneously accused each other of defiling. For many years, a kind of linguistic and cultural Cold War was conducted with greater or lesser intensity in academic journals and newspapers of all kinds on the question, 'Gibt es zwei deutsche Sprachen?' By the late 1980s, however, the general view was that beyond a limited set of **lexical** items and certain **semantic** contrasts, the substance of the German language had not been affected by the political division of Germany and, as most of the differences that could be identified were generally confined to formal, official contexts (politics, economics, state institutions, etc.), they had little impact on everyday language.

The logical conclusion from this argument was that these differences would evaporate, should the 'need' for them disappear. It was therefore ironic that just as the debate had virtually been laid to rest with the (re)unification of Germany in 1990, the opportunity to test this conclusion arose and differences were revealed: not so much in the structure of the language as in the ways in which it was used (ways of speaking, of interacting, of interpreting others) and in the unexpectedly profound imprint of 'official' language on everyday usage. Consider the following text as an example:

> Es ist also verdächtig oder sogar 'out', hier im Osten weiter von der 'Kaufhalle', von 'viertel acht' oder vom 'Kollektiv' zu reden. Ich möchte statt der im MZ-Beitrag ange-führten Belanglosigkeiten dieses in meinen Augen Sprachterrors einmal ein paar wes-entliche neue Vokabeln nennen, die hier hereingebrandet sind: Massenarbeitslosigkeit, Ministergeldskandale, abwickeln, feuern, Obdachlose, Aussteiger, Reps, Rauschgift-szene, Kinderfeindlichkeit, gegauckt werden.
>
> (reader's letter in *Mitteldeutsche Zeitung*,
> 26 February 1994; cited in Kühn 1995: 331)

- What lexical and semantic differences between the forms of standard German that developed in the FRG and the GDR between 1949 and 1989 are flagged up here?
- In what ways do these linguistic differences link to broader ideological debates?

Multiple and interrelated language debates have been taking place in the decades following German reunification. Some of these debates focus on the role of the global spread of English and linguistic purism (see Chapters 3 and 10), whereas others deal with migration and the linguistic 'integration' of **allochthonous** minorities (see Chapters 7, 11 and 12). These language debates illustrate how language policies and practices continue to be shaped by the nation-state model well into the early twenty-first century.

As is the case in Germany, the default language in Austria is German even if Austrian German varieties exhibit certain **phonological**, lexical and grammatical differences from the German that is spoken in Germany. In this way, Austrian German constitutes one means of marking group boundaries between Austria and Germany and thus plays a role in construct-ing national group membership (see Chapter 5). However, like Germany, Austria is home

Table 2.1 The 2001 population in Austria according to '*Umgangssprache*' or spoken language

Bevölkerung 2001 nach Umgangssprache	
Insgesamt	8,032,926
Ausschließlich Deutsch	7,115,780
Sprachen der anerkannten österreichischen Volksgruppen	119,667
Sprachen des ehemaligen Jugoslawien und der Türkei	534,207
Englisch, Französisch, Italienisch	79,514
Sonstige europäische Sprachen	116,892
Afrikanische Sprachen	19,408
Asiatische Sprachen	47,420
Andere Sprachen, unbekannt	38

Source: Statistik Austria 2007, cited in Busch 2013: 97; 2016: 5–6

to many autochthonous and allochthonous minorities for historical as well as contemporary reasons alike (see Chapter 9). Have a look at the figures in Table 2.1 based on the 2001 Austrian census.

- Which languages are mentioned by name and which ones are not?
- Why do you think that languages are categorised and grouped here in this way?

These figures shed light on how statistical offices process large amounts of census data. As noted in Chapter 1, it is important to ask questions about statistics rather than take them at face value. For example, we might like to know how the questions on the census were formulated or how speakers were later assigned to language categories as represented in Table 2.1. Busch (2016) explains how this processing of statistical data in Austria has developed historically and is linked to the nation-state model. Despite the fact that various forms of **individual multilingualism** exist in Austria, and that limited rights and entitlements are granted to certain minority languages and their speakers, language policies appear to be hierarchical and prioritise German over other languages, thus orienting to the one nation, one language ideology (see also Chapter 12). The following section explores language and national identity in European countries that are not only multilingual in practice but also have explicitly formulated multilingual policies at the level of the state.

2.3   Languages and national identity in Switzerland and Luxembourg

As we have seen, the relationship between language and national identity in Germany and Austria is constructed solely in terms of the *German* language, which involves the erasure or blocking out of certain aspects of the multilingual reality in these countries. We will now look at the status and function of German, as well as the link between languages and national identity, in Switzerland and Luxembourg. **Societal multilingualism** comprises a visible part of everyday public life in these countries, which can be observed by looking at images from train stations in Switzerland and Luxembourg, respectively (see Figures 2.1 and 2.2).

- Which languages are prominent on these signs?
- Do all signs in Switzerland and Luxembourg use the same set of languages?

Figure 2.1 Sign at the train station in Biel/Bienne, Switzerland
Photo: Kristine Horner

Figure 2.2 Sign at the train station in the capital city of Luxembourg
Photo: Kristine Horner

Luxembourg and Switzerland not only formally acknowledge the co-existence of several different languages, they effectively define themselves as multilingual states. Indeed, specific forms of multilingualism are considered to be a key component of national identity in these countries. In the case of Luxembourg, the 1984 Language Law recognises three languages: Luxembourgish, French and German. Luxembourgish is designated as the **national language**, French is the legislative language and all three languages function (in theory) as administrative languages. If you take another look at the sign from the train station in Luxembourg in Figure 2.2, you'll observe that it is written in French and German but not in Luxembourgish. Luxembourgish has traditionally been a predominantly oral means of communication, but it has become more widespread as a written medium over the past few decades. There is growing momentum to promote Luxembourgish, and citizenship applicants are even required to demonstrate proficiency in the language (see Chapter 12).

In Switzerland, the status of the four officially recognised autochthonous languages of the country, German, French, Italian and Romansh, was enshrined in Article 116 of the constitution, which stated:

1   Das Deutsche, Französische, Italienische und Rätoromanische sind die National-
    sprachen der Schweiz.
2   Als Amtssprachen des Bundes werden das Deutsche, Französische und Italienische
    erklärt.

In a referendum in March 1996, 76 per cent of those who voted were in favour of the following revised version of Article 116:

1   Deutsch, Französisch, Italienisch und Rätoromanisch sind die Landessprachen der
    Schweiz.
2   Bund und Kantone fördern die Verständigung und den Austausch unter den Sprachge-
    meinschaften.
3   Der Bund unterstützt Massnahmen der Kantone Graubünden und Tessin zur Erhaltung
    und Förderung der rätoromanischen und der italienischen Sprache.
4   Amtssprachen des Bundes sind Deutsch, Französisch und Italienisch. Im Verkehr mit
    Personen rätoromanischer Sprache ist auch das Rätoromanische Amtssprache des
    Bundes. Das Gesetz regelt die Einzelheiten.

Following further revisions in 1999, the current formulation of the constitution stipulates in Article 70:

1   Die Amtssprachen des Bundes sind Deutsch, Französisch und Italienisch. Im Verkehr
    mit Personen rätoromanischer Sprache ist auch das Rätoromanische Amtssprache des
    Bundes.
2   Die Kantone bestimmen ihre Amtssprachen. Um das Einvernehmen zwischen den
    Sprachgemeinschaften zu wahren, achten sie auf die herkömmliche sprachliche Zusam-
    mensetzung der Gebiete und nehmen Rücksicht auf die angestammten sprachlichen
    Minderheiten.
3   Bund und Kantone fördern die Verständigung und den Austausch zwischen den
    Sprachgemeinschaften.
4   Der Bund unterstützt die mehrsprachigen Kantone bei der Erfüllung ihrer besonderen
    Aufgaben.

5   Der Bund unterstützt Massnahmen der Kantone Graubünden und Tessin zur Erhaltung
     und Förderung der rätoromanischen und der italienischen Sprache.

•   What do you think these constitutional changes were intended to achieve? Consider
     how the terms *Amtssprache*, *Nationalsprache* and *Landessprache* are used in these
     legal texts.
•   Who is being referred to (in the current Article 70, paragraph 2) as 'Sprachgemein-
     schaften' and 'die angestammten sprachlichen Minderheiten'?

   At this point, it is useful to focus on certain differences between Luxembourg and Switzerland. First, while the language legislation in Switzerland derives directly from the fact
that the autochthonous population of the country is composed of four ethnolinguistic communities, trilingualism in Luxembourg is based on the long-standing tradition of using German, French and Luxembourgish, which gradually came to be acknowledged as a language
in its own right over the course of the twentieth century (see also Chapter 1 on naming languages). Second, while there are no territorial limitations on the status of the three languages
in Luxembourg, 22 of the 26 cantons and half-cantons in Switzerland are officially monolingual. That is to say, according to the so-called territorial principle, each canton has the right
to declare which language (or languages) will have official status within its territory. This is
what gives rise to the impression that there are discrete 'language areas' in Switzerland, as
the cantons in which each language has official status are adjacent to each other and therefore appear to form a territorial entity (see Map 2.1). This means that the use of German and
French in Figure 2.1 is not found uniformly on signs in all Swiss train stations; rather, it so
happens that Biel/Bienne is located in the bilingual canton of Bern/Berne.

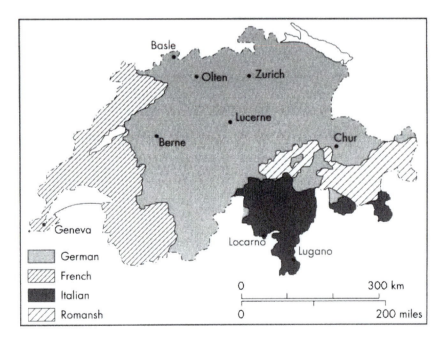

Map 2.1 Language areas in Switzerland

The de facto, if not de jure, division of Switzerland into discrete 'language areas' inevitably highlights both the presence of different ethnolinguistic groups and the considerable differences in their size. However, one of the major arguments that is often advanced as an explanation of the fact that the tensions between these groups do not escalate into open conflict is that the language boundaries do not coincide with any other significant divisions or 'cleavages'. According to this argument, all other cleavages (such as more rich/less rich, Protestant/Catholic, urban/rural) cut across the language divide and therefore reduce its significance. In Luxembourg, on the other hand, there are no discrete language areas, but there is a degree of language conflict linked to shifts in long-standing patterns of language use, with French nowadays becoming more widely used as a spoken language in the public sphere, whereas this had previously been more dominated by the use of Luxembourgish (historically, in the nineteenth century, referred to as *ons Däitsch*, 'our German'). A key question in the study of individual language choice in multilingual communities is therefore to what extent individual choices are constrained by norms or patterns of language use that are widely shared throughout the community, or whether they are more a matter of personal preferences.

It is often claimed that stable societal multilingualism is most likely to be found where each of the individual languages, or even each of the language varieties, is assigned to particular functions. In other words, an unwritten social convention determines which language will normally be used in which circumstances: a phenomenon referred to as **diglossia**. According to the original conception, languages (or, more strictly, 'language forms') that are in a diglossic relationship in a particular speech community are said to be in **complementary distribution**: A is always and only used in one set of domains (for example, classroom, church, workplace), while B is always and only used in another set (for example, home, bar, club). The former was often referred to in academic literature as the H variety (for 'high language') and the latter as the L variety (for 'low language'), but this terminology has been problematized in recent research due to the hierarchy that this presupposes.

- To what extent does the 1984 Language Law in Luxembourg, which was discussed previously, map out the three designated languages onto particular functions?

The German-speaking part of Switzerland is often considered to be a prime example of diglossia due to the widespread spoken use of non-standard German varieties, usually referred to as *Schwyzertüütsch* (Swiss German), for spoken functions and the use of **standard German**, often referred to as *Schriftdeutsch*, for written functions. Watts (1999) points out that Swiss German has served as the most powerful marker of local Swiss identity at least since the Second World War, and its symbolic value is perceived to be much higher than that of standard German in all domains except the written medium. Indeed, many Swiss Germans look upon Swiss German as their mother tongue, while they refer to *Schriftdeutsch* as their first foreign language. Watts reaches the interesting conclusion that there is no danger of the Swiss German varieties dying out and that it is the oral forms of language which guarantee survival, not the written forms. In fact, Switzerland might even contradict the widespread belief that only a written standard variety can guarantee the survival of a language.

At the same time, however, the Swiss German varieties are sometimes regarded as obstacles to communication in the other parts of Switzerland. The final section of this chapter focuses on the ways in which this state of affairs has led to challenges and reforms in the Swiss multilingual education system, which in turn has implications for questions of language and national identity.

2.4   Contemporary challenges to language and national identity links

While there is no common 'Swiss' language, linguistic pluralism is one of the most prominent features of Switzerland's national 'image'. In the education system, the Swiss traditionally acquire literacy skills in the official language of their canton as their first language (L1)
and learn another language of Switzerland as their second language (L2). Thus, for instance,
in the German-speaking part of Switzerland, the schoolchildren traditionally use German
as the L1 and study French as the L2. Conversely, the French Swiss usually use French as
the L1 and learn German as their L2, yet they often find it easier to communicate with the
German Swiss in English (usually learned as their third language [L3]). This is because they
have been taught standard German, which many German Swiss consider to be a written
language, and the latter prefer to use Swiss German varieties which, however, are difficult
for the French Swiss to understand. So, it is not surprising that English thrives in such a situation, especially in combination with its utility in the global marketplace (see Chapter 3).

Yet, it was not in French-speaking Switzerland but in the heartland of German-speaking
Switzerland that an initiative was first taken that upset the Swiss language-in-education
policy balance. In 1998, the canton of Zurich introduced English (instead of French) as
the first foreign language in its primary schools, thus giving priority to English over the
languages of Switzerland. This caused controversy leading to a major language ideological
debate, frequently referred to as the *Sprachenstreit* 'language dispute/debate', which split
proponents into arguing for or against reforms to language-in-education policy involving
the use of English.

- What kinds of argument do you think are used to support and refute the claim that
  the increased use of English and/or teaching of English at an earlier age poses a threat
  to Swiss national identity?

Another ongoing debate in German-speaking Switzerland is the use of Swiss German varieties or standard German as the medium of instruction in preschool education. This is linked to
the question of whether Swiss German or standard German is the language of 'integration'. In
the canton of Zurich, for instance, the medium of instruction in kindergarten until 2000 was
largely Swiss German. However, after the publication of the rather unsatisfactory results of
the first Programme for International Student Assessment (PISA) tests in 2001 (see also Chapter 11), more emphasis was put on standard German, though in practice many teachers and
students continued to use a lot of **code-switching** between the two varieties. Ten years later, on
15 May 2011, the wheel had turned again, with the adoption, by popular vote, of the initiative
'JA zur Mundart im Kindergarten' (YES to dialect in preschool education). According to the
manifesto of this initiative, Swiss German is to be used as the default medium of instruction
in preschool education, with the double aim of helping children to become 'zweisprachig in
der einen Sprache' (bilingual in one language; Schwarzenbach 2011: 4) and enabling migrant
children to 'integrate' into Swiss society in the best possible way.

If possible, you could have a look at the website of the 'JA zur Mundart im Kindergarten'
campaign: http://mundart-kindergarten.ch, and think about the following questions:

- What strikes you about the website from a visual point of view?
- Consider how some of the arguments in favour of *Mundart* have been formulated.

Despite these ongoing debates about language-in-education policy in German-speaking
Switzerland, the school system has been relatively successful both in building on students'

Swiss German varieties and in developing in students a high level of proficiency in standard German. A major reason for this may well be that the Swiss German varieties are positively valued throughout society and that they are used by speakers of all social classes.

2.5   Conclusion

In this chapter, we have explored the role of language in relation to national identity in the German-speaking countries. We first noted how the key concepts of state, nation and language ideologies can be helpful in this process. We then looked at how the German language has played an important role in the construction of national identity in Germany and Austria, which have traditionally conceived themselves as monolingual states. By way of contrast, we examined how national identity is constructed with reference to societal multilingualism in Switzerland and Luxembourg, and we also discussed how everyday life in these countries is shaped by the use of more than one language. Finally, we discussed how shifts at the global level, such as the global spread of English and migration, intersect with and sometimes challenge long-standing local practices with reference to language-in-education policy. We also considered how links between language and national identity can fluctuate over time and how people attempt to maintain them in the face of major societal changes. The following chapter develops this theme further by discussing the changing place of the German language in the wider world.

Tasks and suggestions for research

Reflective tasks

1   What role does language play in your own sense of identity? Do you feel a strong link with one (or more) particular language(s)?
2   Provide examples of situations in which multilingualism is considered to be an asset and also when it tends to be considered problematic. Why do you think there are differing views on multilingualism that can vary from one situation to the next?

Research tasks

1   Many nationalist movements aspire to nation-state congruence: in other words, they are based on the belief that all citizens of a territory or state should also be members of one nation (constructed as the *Staatsnation* or *Kulturnation*). In what ways can such movements invoke ideas about language to promote forms of social inclusion or, conversely, lead to forms of social exclusion?
2   The relationship between Swiss standard German and *Schwyzertütsch* is often cited as a classic example of diglossia: how appropriate does this seem to be today?
3   The term *triglossia* is sometimes used to describe the sociolinguistic situation in Luxembourg: what evidence can you find to support or cast doubt on the validity of this description?

Project ideas

1   Find out what constitutional or other legislative measures exist in relation to autochthonous and allochthonous minorities in either Germany or Austria. Gather details on

the ways that one minority group is supported and, if possible, investigate what current debates are taking place around these measures.

2   Critically examine a contemporary debate about language in Switzerland or Luxembourg. For example, you may wish to explore current issues around language-in-education policy with regard to either societal multilingualism, the role of Swiss German or Luxembourgish, respectively, or the position of English.

Annotated further reading

Barbour and Carmichael (2000) offer a critical analysis of the link between language and national identity in different European countries.

Busch (2013), Chapter 2, discusses language policy, language ideologies and the categorisation of languages and their speakers.

Busch (2016) provides a critical discussion on the role of statistics in documenting languages and the number of speakers, based on the example of Austria.

Dailey-O'Cain (2000) deals with the concept of standard language ideology with specific reference to internal German migration following reunification.

Gardt (2000) considers ethnolinguistic nationalism in Germany from a historical perspective.

Horner and Weber (2008) provide a comprehensive overview of the contemporary language situation in Luxembourg.

Newton (1996) is an edited collection that includes detailed historical information on the development of Luxembourgish and movements to promote the language.

Stevenson (2002) provides a detailed historical account of the relationship between language and social conflict in Germany with a focus on German reunification.

Stotz (2006) gives an overview of the introduction of English as the first foreign language in Swiss schools.

Watts (1999) discusses the ideology of dialect with reference to the case of Swiss German.

3 German in the globalised world of the twenty-first century

3.1 Introduction

Shortly after he became Foreign Secretary in 2009, German politician Guido Westerwelle (1960–2016) told a British reporter at a press conference in Berlin that he would not answer any questions in English. He said to the BBC journalist, 'Es ist Deutschland hier' and reminded him that in the UK politicians would not answer questions by foreign journalists in their languages either. His stance sparked off a debate in Germany about whether politicians or other figures living in the public eye are right to refuse to use English in order to strengthen the status of the German language. Most people, however, poked fun at Westerwelle for seemingly not being able to speak English properly.

- You can watch a clip of Westerwelle's famous press conference on YouTube: www.youtube.com/watch?v=laUJzGMUEI4. Do you think he was right to refuse to speak English? Why (not)?

Rightly or wrongly, Westerwelle was attempting to assert the national and international status of the German language. After all, he might have argued, with at least 143.5 million speakers of German worldwide, including first and second language speakers (see Chapter 1), German has a significant place amongst the world's languages. In Europe alone, it is the language with the second largest number of speakers: 33 per cent of Europeans speak English as their first or learned language, followed by 22.4 per cent who speak German (http://languageknowledge.eu/). But what is its role at a global level, beyond the borders of the countries in which it enjoys the status of an official language, and how does it compare with other languages?

We live in an era of accelerated globalisation: characteristics of contemporary globalisation include the increased movement of people (for example, migrant workers, refugees, students, tourists, etc.) around the world and increasingly sophisticated means of electronic communication, which in turn creates the ability to reach ever-growing audiences worldwide. Thus we are experiencing today constantly increasing flows of goods, capital, people, ideas and images around the world.

- Globalisation in the twenty-first century is in some ways significantly different from previous manifestations of the phenomenon, but the process itself is not new: can you think of earlier examples?

The newly emerging global networks, economic and social, are only possible when people can communicate with each other, and the dominant vehicle for communication in most parts of the world today – the 'globalising language' – is English. In order to communicate across borders and languages, English has become the **lingua franca** of the modern globalised world.

- What do you understand by the term *lingua franca*?
- Which other languages have served as a lingua franca in the past? And which other ones function in this way today?

So in order to discuss the global position of German today, we need to consider it in the context of an increasingly English-speaking world. In this chapter we will first compare German and English as commodities in the international marketplace. Then we will look at the role of German in business communication and as an academic language, and finally give an overview of institutions, legislation and initiatives that set out to strengthen the status of German in the world.

3.2   English as a Foreign Language (EFL) and *Deutsch als Fremdsprache* (DaF)

In the previous section we introduced the concept of **English as a lingua franca (ELF)**. Although the abbreviations look misleadingly similar, ELF should not be confused with the term **English as a Foreign Language (EFL)**. EFL is the generic name of a 'product' belonging to a branch of the service sector of the British economy that added approximately £1.1 billion of value to the economy in 2014 (www.englishuk.com/uploads/assets/members/newsflash/2015/11_nov/Economic_impact_report_44pp__WEB.pdf; accessed 28 April 2016). *Deutsch als Fremdsprache* (DaF), 'German as a foreign language', plays a less significant part in the national economies of Germany, Austria and Switzerland, but it is nonetheless a major export.

Reasons for learning German as a foreign language may include the following set of generic answers Ulrich Ammon collected when he informally surveyed university students of German from different countries of origin:

Ich lerne Deutsch

1   weil ich in meiner Schule zwei Fremdsprachen lernen musste und es außer Englisch nur Deutsch gab. [. . .]
2   weil ich in Österreich studieren möchte/weil ich in Deutschland arbeiten möchte. [. . .]
3   weil ich in die deutschsprachige Schweiz auswandern möchte. [. . .]
4   weil meine Familie aus Österreich stammt/weil wir Lutheraner sind/weil schon mein Vater Deutsch gelernt hat. [. . .]
5   weil ich die deutsche Kultur schätze/weil mir die deutsche Musik gefällt. [. . .]
6   weil Deutsch eine Herausforderung ist.

(Ammon 2015: 988)

- What motivated you to pick up German? Can you think of other reasons to learn German?

Estimates suggest that in 2010 approximately 14.5 million people worldwide were learning German:

1995	19,511,887
2000	20,167,616
2005	16,718,701
2010	14,500,940

(Ammon 2015: 981)

These figures show a decline in the number of learners since 2000, but according to a comprehensive study conducted by the Goethe-Institut and the German Foreign Office (Deutsch als Fremdsprache weltweit) this trend has since reversed and there were an estimated 15,455,452 learners of German worldwide in 2015.

- Find out comparable numbers for EFL. What do you think might account for the trends in studying EFL and DaF? (Consider, for example, the impact of the global financial crisis in 2008–2009 on employment rates in different countries, especially in southern Europe.)
- Look at Figure 3.1, taken from the Goethe-Institut study, which shows the global distribution of German learners in 2015. How do you think we can explain the proportions in different parts of the world? Choose a country and look up the figures provided by the study in more detail. How many students of German are there in the country of your choice? Which sectors of education are they in?

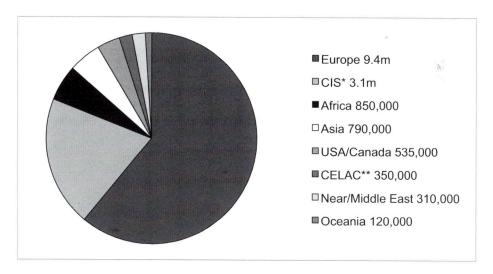

Figure 3.1 Global distribution of learners of German in 2015

*Commonwealth of Independent States (former Soviet Republics)
**Community of Latin American and Caribbean States

Source: Goethe-Institut

Competence in languages such as English and German is an economic resource for individuals living in the 'knowledge societies' of the twenty-first century. It gives the individual speaker access to cultures and societies beyond their own but also to more extensive job markets. Put simply, if you are a speaker of Portuguese and have an excellent command of German, you can apply for work not only in Brazil or Portugal but also in the German-speaking countries. As a German-speaking student from the UK you could apply to universities in Germany or Austria and save a great deal of money since universities in these countries do not currently charge tuition fees. But different languages have different 'market values', with English currently leading the field. It is not only the language of the most powerful economy in the world – the United States – but is also used as a lingua franca in many international domains: for example, in business and higher education, and in diplomacy and tourism.

How can we establish the economic 'value' of the German language? One indicator to measure wealth is to look at the gross national product (GNP) of economies, which is a broad measure of total economic activity and summarises the value of all finished goods and services produced in a year. Consider the data in Figure 3.2, which compares the GNP (in billion US dollars) of the German-speaking countries in 2009 with that of other countries and correlates GNP with the number of speakers (in millions).

- Compare the results for Japanese and Chinese. Which language might have the higher value on the global linguistic market? In what ways has the situation changed since this data was gathered?
- How does the value of the German language appear to compare to that of English and French?
- What are the potential problems with attempts to value languages in this way?

To learn a language is a commitment that costs considerable time and in many cases money. Many language learners see it as an investment in their futures. There are clearly many advantages in speaking German in the twenty-first century, as we saw earlier; however, the question remains whether many potential language learners would consider English their

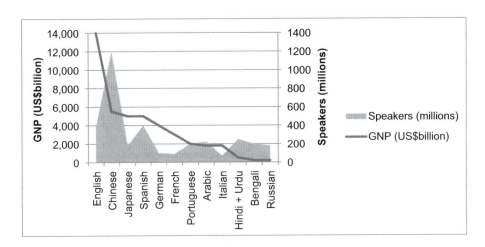

Figure 3.2 The relative strength of the German-speaking economies

Source: based on Ammon 2015: 193

first priority as the dominant lingua franca in a globalised world. Let us now consider one particular domain in which German and English co-exist or compete.

3.3 German in international business communication

The communicative requirements of contemporary life make it necessary for speakers of German to use English in day-to-day situations: German-speakers listen to English pop music lyrics; they see and hear English in many advertisements; even announcements on public transport in larger cities are often bilingual in German and English. They speak English with tourists; many books and articles they read as students are in English; and in many companies the language of the workplace has become English. What, then, is the role of German in international business communication?

We have already noted that the GNP of the German-speaking countries is relatively high. Look at Table 3.1, which indicates the value of the export and import of goods and services in a range of countries.

- Analyse Table 3.1 and think of reasons why differences in export and import in both categories, goods and services, might influence the use of certain languages worldwide in different ways. Keep in mind the business adage that you should 'sell in their mother tongue'.

What languages do German companies actually use with their trading partners worldwide? It's hard to know for sure, but Table 3.2 shows the number of countries for which particular languages are recommended for German trade, according to the Hamburg Chamber of Commerce (Handelskammer) in 2005 (results for 1989 in brackets for comparison).

- What has changed since 1989 and what could be the reasons behind these developments?

Table 3.1 Export and import of goods and services in 2011 (in US$billion)

Goods				Services			
Export		*Import*		*Export*		*Import*	
China	10.4	USA	12.3	USA	13.9	USA	10.0
USA	8.1	China	9.5	UK	6.6	Germany	7.3
Germany	8.1	Germany	6.8	Germany	6.1	China	6.0
Japan	4.5	Japan	4.6	China	4.4	UK	4.3
Netherlands	3.6	France	3.9	France	4.0	Japan	4.2
France	3.3	UK	3.5	Japan	3.4	France	3.5
S. Korea	3.0	Netherlands	3.2	Spain	3.4	India	3.1
Italy	2.9	Italy	3.0	India	3.3	Netherlands	3.0
Russia	2.9	S. Korea	2.8	Netherlands	3.2	Ireland	2.9
Belgium	2.6	Hong Kong	2.8	Singapore	3.1	Italy	2.9
UK	2.6	Canada	2.5	Hong Kong	2.9	Singapore	2.9
Hong Kong	2.5	India	2.5	Ireland	2.6	Canada	2.5

Source: based on Ammon 2015: 411

Table 3.2 Languages recommended for trade by German companies

	Total	*Sole language*	*Co-language*
1 English	137 (122)	52 (64)	85 (58)
2 French	58 (57)	18 (25)	40 (32)
3 German	37 (26)	1 (1)	36 (25)
4 Spanish	28 (26)	16 (17)	12 (9)
5 Russian	23 (1)	–	23(1)
6 Arabic	17 (12)	–	17 (12)
7 Portuguese	13 (8)	–	13
8 Italian	9 (4)	–	9 (4)
9 Dutch	7 (8)	–	7 (8)
10 Chinese	3	–	3

Source: based on Ammon 2015: 438

So far we have been looking at business communication between companies from German-speaking countries and their external partners. Another interesting trend is to see what is going on within companies in Germany, Austria, Luxembourg and Switzerland: which languages do they choose as their day-to-day working languages?

In February 2013, the German tabloid newspaper BILD announced:

> Ob Deutsche Bank, Lufthansa, SAP, Daimler oder auch Adidas – immer mehr deutsche Unternehmen erklären Englisch zu ihrer offiziellen oder zur zweiten Firmensprache. Grund: In zahlreichen deutschen Unternehmen sind die Teams international zusammengesetzt. Doch nicht nur firmenintern ist Englisch wichtig. Martin Wansleben, Hauptgeschäftsführer des deutschen Industrie- und Handelskammertages: „Kaum eine Volkswirtschaft ist international so vernetzt wie die deutsche. Global aufgestellte Unternehmen, aber auch kleinere Betriebe, müssen daher die Sprache der Kunden sprechen."
>
> (www.bild.de/geld/wirtschaft/arbeit/englisch-in-deutschen-unternehmen-28436270.bild.html; accessed 29 April 2016)

Larger and medium-sized companies tend to operate at an international level in the twenty-first century. Communication between different branches can become an issue: it costs money to translate documents and to employ interpreters. It is even more expensive to make a loss due to communication failure. The obvious way out of this dilemma seems to be to establish English as the internal language of communication. However, it is currently not possible to establish how many companies in the German-speaking countries have introduced English as the language of the workplace. Researchers find that companies are hesitant to acknowledge their language policies and are even more reluctant to let linguists analyse their communicative practices (although there are some interesting case studies of anonymised businesses: see 'Annotated further reading').

To sum up our short exploration of German in international business communication we can establish that this is a fluid and rapidly changing area. On the one hand, although the number of learners of German declined in the first decade of this century we can observe a recovery between 2010 and 2015. On the other hand, English seems to be gaining ground against other languages such as German or French, which is due in part to its growing importance as the lingua franca of international business and even as a language of day-to-day communication in companies within the German-speaking countries.

3.4   German as an academic language

Scientific and scholarly exchange has always had a transnational component. Researchers and academics communicate across geographical and linguistic borders, and most of them are able to read and write in more than just their own language. The general tendency today seems to be to establish a lingua franca of academic research. For centuries, Arabic and Latin held this position in Europe. After the European Enlightenment during the eighteenth century, English, French and German replaced Latin as the dominant languages of academic exchange and instruction. German enjoyed considerable prestige as an academic language particularly during the second half of the nineteenth century and the first decades of the twentieth century, so much so that it was even used for this purpose in smaller neighbouring countries such as in Scandinavia or the Netherlands.

The demise of German as an academic language began during the First World War, when the international academic communities decided to boycott German academics and the German language due to many German professors' uncritical and chauvinist stances towards the war. However, the most catastrophic act of self-destruction followed when the Nazis came to power in 1933 and Jewish scholars lost their positions, were forced to emigrate or were deported and murdered. The contributions of the Jewish minority to science and scholarship in Austria and Germany had been immense. The majority of scholars remaining in Austria and Germany either collaborated with the National Socialist (NS) regime or kept quiet, which led to a further loss of prestige for German science and scholarship after the Second World War.

After 1945 German lost its status as an international academic language, although this did not become fully apparent until some decades later. During the 1970s and 1980s the first studies were published that raised awareness of this ongoing trend. However, the advent of modern communication technology, especially email since the late 1980s, has proved to be a game changer. Researchers had always corresponded with each other at a global level, but now they had found a quick and easy means of scholarly exchange, conducted mostly in English. The change from German to English did not happen at the same time or at the same rate in all disciplines, but was marked most dramatically in the natural sciences (see Figure 3.3, adapted from Ammon 2015).

The languages of publication and academic exchange (correspondence or presentations at conferences) are one important part of academic activity. The other is the language of instruction, of learning and teaching at universities. In this area we can also observe a shift towards English: in 2011, 700 undergraduate programmes at German universities were taught in English, mainly in the areas of applied sciences and business studies. Admittedly, this needs to be seen in the context of a total of 14,000 programmes across all universities in Germany, which means that only 5 per cent of programmes are taught in English (Ammon 2015: 626). It will be interesting, however, to observe how this sector will develop over the next 10 to 20 years.

•   English as a Medium of Instruction (EMI) is a growing trend at many universities in non-anglophone countries. What do you think might be the benefits and drawbacks of this in different subject areas (e.g. science, engineering, social sciences, humanities) from the perspective of universities in Germany, Austria, Switzerland or Luxembourg?

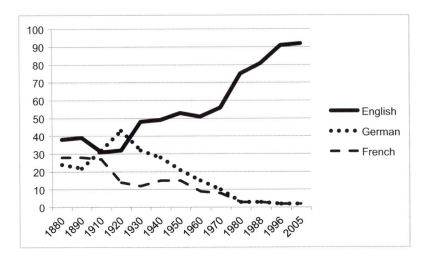

Figure 3.3 Languages of publication in the natural sciences
Source: based on Ammon 2015: 551

3.5   Language promotion and foreign policy

Businesses, institutions and individuals develop their own language policies and practices. But what role can the state play in promoting German across the world? In 2013–2014 the German Foreign Office (Auswärtiges Amt) committed €817.24 million to what it calls 'Pflege kultureller Beziehungen zum Ausland' (maintaining good cultural relations abroad) (www.auswaertiges-amt.de/cae/servlet/contentblob/592080/publicationFile/207398/AA_ im_Ueberblick.pdf). The German Foreign Secretary at the time, Frank-Walter Steinmeier, explains the importance of this task as an aspect of German foreign policy:

> Die Stärkung der Auswärtigen Kultur- und Bildungspolitik ist ein besonderes Anliegen der deutschen Außenpolitik. Gerade angesichts krisenhafter Ereignisse und großer politischer Umwälzungen und Fragestellungen gewinnt die Arbeit im vorpolitischen Raum der Kultur, der Bildung und der Kommunikation an neuer Bedeutung. Mit Kultur- und Bildungsangeboten bereiten wir Boden, auf dem politische Verständigung erst möglich ist.
>
> Dabei gilt es insbesondere mit Blick auf eine Welt, die aus den Fugen geraten scheint, die soziale Kraft von Kultur zu stärken. [. . .] Auf meinen Reisen ins Ausland und in den Gesprächen mit unseren Partnern in der Welt stelle ich immer wieder fest: Auf Deutschland ruhen in der Auswärtigen Kultur- und Bildungspolitik besondere Erwartungen, denen wir gerecht zu werden versuchen.
>
> Hierzu zählt auch die Feststellung, dass sich die Wahrnehmung Deutschlands im Ausland im Vergleich zum Vorjahr deutlich verbessert hat: Deutschland belegt in einer internationalen Studie den ersten Platz und hat ein sehr gutes Image in den Bereichen Qualität der Produkte, Arbeitnehmerfähigkeit, Lebensqualität und Regierungsführung. [. . .]
>
> Der Zugang zu unserer Sprache ist dabei eine entscheidende Grundlage. Deutsch als Fremdsprache hat weltweit einen erfreulichen Aufschwung erlebt. [. . .] Hier gilt es in den nächsten Jahren energisch weiter zu arbeiten, damit sich dieser Trend verstetigt.
>
> (www.auswaertigesamt.de/cae/servlet/contentblob/670488/
> publicationFile/205649/AKBP-Bericht_2013-2014.pdf)

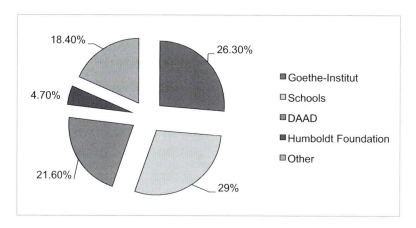

Figure 3.4 Distribution of funding for the German *Mittlerorganisationen*

Source: Auswärtiges Amt on www.auswaertigesamt.de/cae/servlet/contentblob/670488/publicationFile/205649/AKBP-Bericht_2013-2014.pdf

- How does Steinmeier justify the substantial expenditure for the *auswärtige Kultur-politik*?
- What does he mean when he refers to the 'special expectations' that people worldwide appear to have in relation to Germany?

In Germany, there is no single, central institution that is responsible for the linguistic and cultural export drive: it is backed financially by a number of different ministries and implemented by several '*Mittlerorganisationen*' (principally the Goethe-Institut, the Deutscher Akademischer Austauschdienst [DAAD], the Zentralstelle für Auslandsschulwesen and the Alexander von Humboldt Stiftung). Figure 3.4 shows the distribution of funding by the Foreign Office to these organisations.

- Find out what the mission statements of three of these *Mittlerorganisationen* are. Which areas of cultural exchange do they cover and what is the role of German as a foreign language in each of them?

The role of the Goethe-Institut, in particular, has grown considerably since it was founded in 1951. The following newspaper article was published on the occasion of its 60th anniversary in 2011:

> Sechzig Jahre alt wird das Goethe-Institut in diesem Sommer. [. . .] Die Balance zwischen der Öffnung im Zeichen der Globalisierung und der Stärkung der deutschen und europäischen Identität scheint gefunden. Man kann die Karriere des Goethe-Instituts, das seiner Verfassung nach immer noch der private Verein ist, der im Sommer 1951 in München gegründet wurde, durchaus erstaunlich nennen. Der Aus- und Fortbildung ausländischer Deutschlehrer wollte man sich ursprünglich widmen. [. . .] Erst 1959 vereinbarten das Goethe-Institut und das Auswärtige Amt, nach und nach die kulturpolitischen Aktivitäten im Ausland bei dem Münchner Verein zu bündeln. Den Ritterschlag erhielt "Goethe" dann von Willy Brandt, der den von Ralf Dahrendorf

in einer Denkschrift geprägten Begriff von der Kulturpolitik als "dritter Säule" der Außenpolitik zum Programm erhob. Die sozialliberale Ära brachte dem Goethe-Institut eine erste Glanzzeit. Die Bundesrepublik warb um Vertrauen in der Welt, indem sie sich als Musterknabe historischer und gesellschaftspolitischer Selbstkritik aufführte. Die Geschichtswende von 1989/90 rückte Mittel- und Osteuropa in den Fokus der Auswärtigen Kulturpolitik und brachte dem Goethe-Institut zahlreiche Neugründungen in dieser Region. [. . .] Ins Zentrum der Aktivitäten rückte wieder die Vermittlung der deutschen Sprache und eines differenzierten Deutschlandbildes. Mit 3000 Mitarbeitern ist "Goethe" heute ein Kultur-Großunternehmen. Zwei Drittel des [. . .] Etats kommen vom Auswärtigen Amt. Den Rest erwirtschaftet das Institut selbst, vor allem mit Sprachkursen. Die deutsche Sprache erweist sich mehr und mehr als höchst erfolgreicher Exportartikel.

(*Berliner Morgenpost* 6 July 2011)

- Explain what Ralf Dahrendorf and Willy Brandt mean when they refer to the 'third pillar' of German foreign policy.

   In terms of international organisations, the EU is probably the most significant arena for the German language. Within the EU, German is one of 24 official languages. The German Foreign Office summarises its status and linguistic practices within the EU administration like this:

Deutsch ist eine von 24 gleichberechtigten Amts- und Arbeitssprachen der EU. Laut Verordnung Nr. 1 von 1958 gilt das Vollsprachenregime – d.h. die Übersetzung in alle Amts- und Arbeitssprachen – für alle Rechtstexte und das Amtsblatt. Jeder Unionsbürger kann sich schriftlich in einer der 24 Amtssprachen an jedes Organ und jede Einrichtung der EU wenden und muss eine Antwort in derselben Sprache erhalten. [. . .]

   In einer Reihe weiterer Gremien haben sich feste Traditionen herausgebildet. So wird im Ausschuss der Ständigen Vertreter – dem wichtigen Ausschuss der Botschafter/innen der EU-Mitgliedstaaten – Deutsch/Englisch/Französisch gedolmetscht. In den Gremien der Gemeinsamen Außen- und Sicherheitspolitik wird Englisch und Französisch gesprochen – ohne Dolmetschung.

   Seit dem deutlichen Anstieg der Zahl der EU-Amtssprachen 2004 gilt für die Mehrzahl der Ratsarbeitsgruppen das sogenannte Marktmodell. Es erlaubt den Mitgliedstaaten, die Dolmetschung ihrer eigenen Amtssprache zu beantragen. Deutschland beantragt dies, wo immer möglich. [. . .]

   Deutsch genießt als eine von drei Verfahrenssprachen eine Sonderstellung in der Europäischen Kommission: Das Kollegium der Kommissare arbeitet in Deutsch, Englisch und Französisch und auf Grundlage von Dokumenten, die in diesen drei Sprachen vorgelegt werden müssen.

(German Foreign Office, www.auswaertigesamt.de/EN/Aussenpolitik/
KulturDialog/Uebersicht_node.html [accessed 29 April 2016])

- What is the distinction between the terms *Amtssprache*, *Arbeitssprache* and *Verfahrenssprache*? In principle, all 24 official languages have equal status, but how does this work out in practice?

As *Verfahrenssprachen*, English, French and, to a lesser extent, German are the languages which are used in everyday business in the European Commission (the 'civil service' of the EU). On the one hand, the use of just three languages significantly reduces the enormous bills for interpreters and translators and also makes the day-to-day running of meetings and office work manageable. On the other hand, a recent study showed that 59.7 per cent of German MPs rarely or never read EU documents which aren't in German and that 29.9 per cent feel that they always or often miss out on important content. There is thus a clear tension between assuming that the use of English in all important business is the most cost-effective and practical method of international communication and the recognition that this practically excludes important people from the discussion and hence indirectly suppresses critical engagement.

*   What is your view? Should certain languages have preferential status in the EU (and other international organisations), and what are the advantages and disadvantages? What impact, if any, do you think 'Brexit', the UK referendum decision in 2016 to leave the EU, will have on language practices within EU bodies?

3.6   Conclusion

In this chapter we considered the role of the German language in a globalised world. We established that German is competing against the dominant global lingua franca, English, in many areas, for example, in the international market of language learning and in international business communication and academic exchange and instruction amongst researchers and scholars across the globe. Although most statistics we looked at seem to indicate that English is clearly winning this competition, the numbers for German look strong: after English it is the second most widely spoken language in Europe, and worldwide more than 15 million students were learning German in 2015. Furthermore, the German language is supported by influential political and cultural bodies such as the German Foreign Office, the Goethe-Institut and a number of other *Mittlerorganisationen*.

Tasks and suggestions for research

Reflective tasks

1   Do you consider the increasing importance of English as a lingua franca in the modern world a positive or a negative development? Draw up a list of arguments for both positions.
2   What do you feel you have learned about the changing position of the German language in the world? Which factors do you think will be most significant in shaping its future status?

Research tasks

1   Find German newspaper articles online that deal with the topics 'Englisch als Unternehmenssprache' or 'Englisch als Firmensprache'. Analyse the articles and pay special attention to the commentaries written by their readers. Describe the general attitudes towards English in the workplace in German companies and compare your findings with published research on language policy in business.

2   Find out as much as you can about the German and/or Austrian government's current policies on promoting the German language abroad. What different means, direct and indirect, do they use to pursue this aim?

Project ideas

1   Imagine you were given the task of 'selling' the German language abroad: make a list of the positive factors associated with it that you would therefore want to highlight, and of the negative factors that you would have to try to counteract.
2   Choose a major German company (e.g. Siemens or Volkswagen) and find out what you can about its language policy. Then put yourself in the position of CEO of an imaginary German company with international customers and devise a language policy for your firm.

Annotated further reading

Ammon (2015) is the most comprehensive and authoritative study on the current state of the German language in the world.

Appadurai (1996) is a seminal study that analyses globalisation in the Modern Age and its impact on culture(s) from an anthropological point of view.

Auswärtige Kultur- und Bildungspolitik (published by the German Foreign Office) contains a detailed overview of the development and focus of German cultural relations and education policies.

Blommaert (2010) is an excellent introduction to the changed parameters for linguistic analysis in the age of accelerated globalisation.

Coupland (ed.) (2010) is a handbook that provides state of the art articles on aspects of linguistic research on language and communication in the globalising world.

Deutsch als Fremdsprache weltweit. Datenerhebung 2015 (published by the German Foreign Office and the Goethe-Institut) provides comprehensive statistics on the learning of German as a foreign language around the world.

Ehrenreich (2010) is an interesting case study of language policy in a German multinational business.

Elon (1990) is a very well written account of the contribution of the Jewish minority to Austrian and German society, culture, science and scholarship between 1743 and 1933.

The Goethe-Institut's website (www.goethe.de/en/index.html [accessed 10 September 2016]) offers a wealth of information on German as a foreign language worldwide.

Krumm et al. (eds.) (2010) is a handbook that provides state of the art research articles on all aspects related to the study of German as a foreign or second language.

Kruse (2013) discusses language practices in EU institutions from the German perspective.

Nekvapil and Sherman (2009) give a detailed analysis of language policy and practice in a Czech subsidiary of a German multinational company.

Vollstedt (2002) is a detailed study of language policy in international businesses.

Part 2

Aspects of German in use

4   Regional variation

4.1   Introduction

One of the most noticeable aspects of German, even to the casual observer, is how different pronunciation and vocabulary are in different regions: if you were taught formal **standard** German at school you will notice these differences as you travel around the German-speaking countries. For example, in the north, people will often say *Tach* (/tax/) for *Tag* (instead of /ta:k/) and *nich* (for *nicht*); in the west, the word *ist* may be pronounced *ischt* (/ɪʃt/); in the east, you will sometimes hear *müde* with an **unrounded vowel** (/mi:də/); and in the south, you will come across the pronunciation of *nicht* as *net* and word-initial <s> as **voiceless** /s/ (as in English 'soap'), not as a **voiced** /z/ as is common elsewhere in the German-speaking areas (in *Seife*, for example).

The existence of regional differences is common in many, perhaps in most, languages, and for German we find evidence for such differences from the oldest texts onwards. What is striking is not that such differences already existed so long ago but that they continue to survive into the present day when the German standard variety is used virtually exclusively in formal written and spoken discourse (see Chapter 5). Many academic linguists and casual observers have claimed that the degree of regional variation in the German-speaking countries is greater than in other European countries of comparable size, and this is, in part, explained by the long-lasting political fragmentation of Germany and the late **standardisation** of the language: regional pride, it is argued, is more deeply rooted in Germany, Austria and Switzerland than elsewhere, and **dialects**, as expressions of linguistic regional difference, are thus more likely to survive for this reason.

As a counter-balancing development, the use of the standard variety in public life, including the important domains of education, public administration and mainstream media, has virtually eradicated regional language use in these contexts. While regional variation is seen as a socio-cultural asset in everyday speech, it is considered a sign of lack of education in (formal) writing. The dominance of standard German is generally attributed to its 'social capital': proficiency in the standard variety is an important component of upward social mobility. Why, then, do regional varieties continue to survive and even thrive? In this chapter we will examine the use of local and regional dialects, and contrast this with their perception and their function in contemporary society.

- What regional varieties of German have you heard of already? Do you associate any linguistic or social features with any of them?
- Search on YouTube for *Asterix* in dialect, for example, in *Hessisch*. Why do you think some, but not all, characters speak in dialect? What effect does this have on the way you view the film?

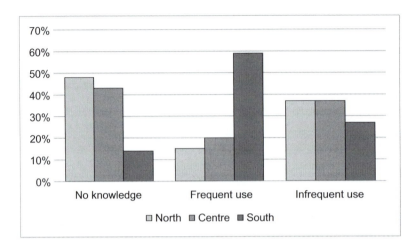

Figure 4.1 Geographical distribution of dialect speakers in Germany
Source: based on Eichinger et al. 2009: 18

4.2   Dialect use today

In an opinion poll commissioned by the Institut für Deutsche Sprache (Mannheim) in 2009, some 2000 informants from across Germany were asked about their views on language: for example, perceptions of recent language change or rating the 'pleasantness' of foreign accents in German. The use and perception of regional variation were also elicited. The survey found that 60 per cent of informants claimed to speak dialect, with a tendency for older and male informants to record higher scores than younger and female ones. While these age- and gender-related patterns may not be very surprising, as they match findings for other languages and countries, the German survey also found that there was no significant correlation between competence in dialect and level of education; in other words, highly educated people were just as likely to report dialect competence as less-educated informants.

Another striking result of the survey was the north-south contrast as regards the overall level of competence and actual frequency of dialect use. The highest scoring areas in terms of dialect competence were the Saarland, Bayern and Baden-Württemberg (all more than 80 per cent), with the lowest scores (though still more than 30 per cent) for Brandenburg, Sachsen-Anhalt, Nordrhein-Westphalen and Mecklenburg-Vorpommern. In terms of how frequently people actually used dialect, 59 per cent of southerners claimed to speak dialect frequently (*häufig*) or always (*immer*), while only 15 per cent of northerners replied in the same way (see Figure 4.1).

- The survey also found that 83 per cent of east Berliners said they spoke dialect compared with only 63 per cent from the west of the city. Can you imagine a reason for this discrepancy?

The relatively high level of dialect competence in Germany is likely to be due to the fact that many associate a positive emotional response with hearing dialect. The opinion poll revealed that 63 per cent found dialectal German *pleasant* or *very pleasant* ([*sehr*] *sympathisch*) and only 7 per cent did not like regionally marked German (see Figure 4.2).

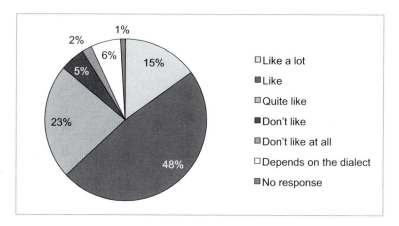

Figure 4.2 Positive evaluation of dialect speech in German
Source: based on Eichinger et al. 2009: 26

This does not mean that all dialects are equally popular: many informants readily identified dialects they really did not like, and most speakers rated those dialects highest which were identical or very similar to their own. But how linguistically different from each other are German dialects? Assessing this raises a difficult terminological problem since people have very different views as to what a dialect actually is. In the next section we will present some of the most well-known linguistic features associated with regional variation in German.

4.3   German dialects and geographical boundaries

There is evidence of an awareness of regional linguistic differences in German since at least the Middle Ages. We can see this, for example, in Berthold von Regensburg's famous thirteenth-century quotation on the difference between **Upper** (i.e. southern) **German** and **Low** (i.e. northern) **German**:

> Ir wizzet wol, daz die Niderlender und die Oberlender gar unglîch sint an der sprâche und an den siten. Die von Oberlant, dort her von Zürich, die redent vil anders danne die von Niderlande, von Sahsen, die sint ungelîch an der sprâche.
>
> (cited in Glück 2002: 25)

> (It is well-known that the Lowlanders and the Highlanders are quite dissimilar as regards languages and customs. Those from the Highlands, e.g. from Zurich, speak quite differently from those from the Lowlands, from Saxony, they are quite different linguistically.)

So the earliest references to regional diversity already identify a north-south division, as continues to be the case today. The linguistic difference between Low German and High German[1] (comprising **Central** and **Upper German**; see Figure 4.3) is still considered the most important division of German dialects, even though its primary criterion, the

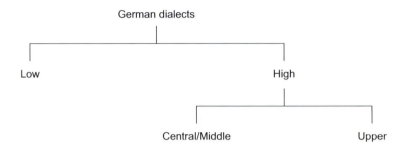

Figure 4.3 German dialects: basic divisions

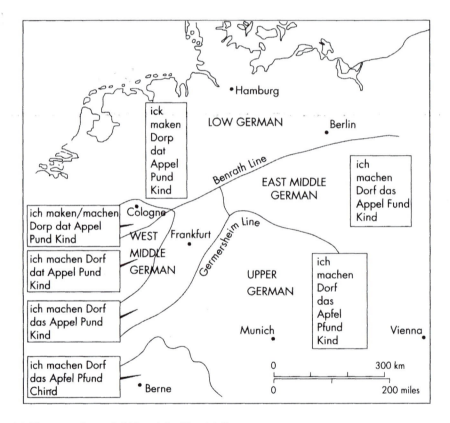

Map 4.1 The second sound shift and the Rhenish Fan
Source: Barbour and Stevenson 1990: 79, adapted from König 1978: 64

absence vs. presence of the **second sound shift (*die zweite Lautverschiebung*)**, affects only a very small part of the language, namely three consonants (*p*, *t*, *k*), which are pronounced differently across the German-speaking regions.

This phonological change began in the south-east of the German-speaking area of Europe and gradually spread north and west roughly between the fifth and eighth centuries AD (see Map 4.1). In those dialects in which the shift has taken place, the **stop** or **plosive** consonants

Table 4.1 Presence and absence of the second sound shift in Germanic varieties

Germanic language varieties without the second sound shift	/p/: English *path, leap*	/t/: English *ten, eat*	/k/: Dutch *kerk, maken*
High German varieties, in word-initial position	/pf/: *Pfad*	/ts/: *zehn* [tse:n]	/x/ or /kx/: *Kind* [xint] or [kxint][1]
High German varieties, in other positions	/f/: *laufen*	/s/: *essen*	/x/: *machen* [maxn]

[1]Southernmost Upper German only

/p, t, k/ have been replaced by **affricates** /pf, ts/ or **fricatives** /s, x/: this is summarised in Table 4.1. All but one of its stages can be found in the standard variety of German: the only exception is *k => kx* in word-initial position, which is restricted to Swiss German and some southern varieties spoken in northern Italy and Austria (see Chapter 5 on **standardisation** to help work out why this is).

- Find three more examples of *p, t, k* in words in Germanic language varieties other than High German dialects (for example, English or Dutch) and check their pronunciation. Have the sounds shifted in these examples too? (If not, use an etymological dictionary to work out why.)

The second sound shift didn't apply evenly across the High German-speaking area, and it is a bit of a mystery as to why such a widespread change took place in almost wave-like patterns (cf. Map 4.1). As the so-called *Rheinischer Fächer* (Rhenish Fan) shows, these sound changes advanced fairly uniformly until they reached the Rhineland around Cologne, where some individual changes (marked on the map by **isoglosses**) progressed further than others.

The dialects of northern Germany – called Low German, because they are spoken in the geographically low-lying areas of Germany – did not undergo any of the stages of the second sound shift, which is therefore used as a principal defining feature to classify dialects as High German or Low German (although there are many more beside these). The dividing line (actually a bundle of isoglosses for individual sounds) between Low German and Central German is commonly referred to as the Benrath Line, whereas the isogloss distinguishing Central German from Upper German dialects is called the Germersheim or Speyer Line. The isoglosses that demarcate the different pronunciations of /p, t, k/ are remarkably stable, with only very little significant shift over the centuries.

However, regional language varieties do change, especially in the absence of geographical isolation (large woods or swamps, high mountains, wide rivers) and in the presence of in-migration or trade routes (see Maps 4.2 and 4.3).

The *Rheinischer Fächer* (Map 4.2) shows that the use of the southern forms *uns, er* and *als* (as opposed to their northern counterparts *us, he* and *as*) extends into more northerly areas along the river Rhine. This is most plausibly explained by contact between northern river-dwellers and southern tradespeople, causing the northerners to change their language in order to sound more southern, presumably because the southerners – and, by association, their language – had more prestige.

A second famous example of migration affecting the dialect map of Germany relates to the Central German linguistic enclave in the formerly Low German-speaking Harz mountains

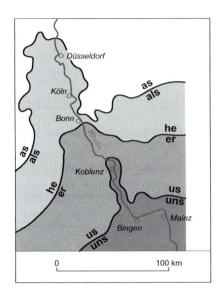

Map 4.2 The *Rheinischer Fächer* (Rhenish Fan)
Source: König et al. 2015: 140

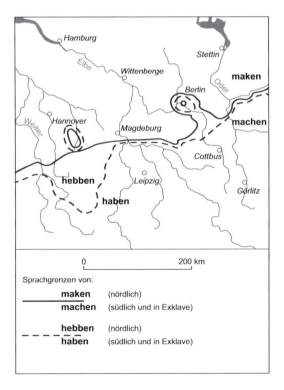

Map 4.3 Central German enclave in the Harz mountains
Source: König et al. 2015: 140

(see Map 4.3). The area boasted rich mineral resources and attracted significant migration of miners from Central German-speaking areas. Due to the resulting language contact between Low German and Central German-speakers, the local dialect changed significantly and would now be more suitably described as Central German, rather than Low German.

So geographical factors played an important part in the emergence and retention of distinct regional varieties in that they affected people's mobility, with the presence of trade routes (rivers, roads) facilitating communication between separate groups. Where speakers from distinct linguistic backgrounds communicate with each other on a regular basis, their speech forms typically lose their distinguishing features, by a process of **accommodation**: speakers adjust their speech so as to minimise those features that make them sound different from each other (assuming that the power relations between the speakers are sufficiently even). In this way, linguistic differences are levelled out. This applies both to very local speech communities and also in supra-regional communication. In contrast, where communities are prevented from interaction by geographical barriers, their linguistic distinctiveness survives for much longer: language use remains regionally restricted, and we call such varieties *Dialekt* or *Mundart* in German.[2]

4.4   Dialect and *Alltagssprache*

The history of German has seen not only linguistic changes within and across regional dialects but also the emergence of a prestige variety which began as a purely written form but which also influenced spoken language use on account of its social capital (see Chapter 5 on the process of **standardisation**). The presence of two (or more) distinct but related language varieties in each speaker community led to variable use: sometimes speakers would use more local dialect; sometimes they would aim to use the prestige variety. Such different practices would lead to a certain fluidity between the different forms, and a number of distinctly regional features became established in the regionalised standard varieties of a particular area. Even when speakers try to speak a supposedly 'accent-free' standard German, most retain a distinct regionalised pronunciation: for example, northerners will say *Tach* for *Tag*, southerners will say *Kina* for *China* and speakers of Central German will say *glabbe* for *klappen*.

What is very striking is that even though geographical factors such as mountain ranges or large forests no longer constitute actual barriers for communication, having a regionally distinctive way of speaking is still typical for most native speakers of German. Nonetheless, a number of important social changes have affected the use and perception of regional dialects over time: for example, the mass migrations from the countryside to the cities during the period of industrialisation in the nineteenth century (the so-called *Landflucht*), the frequent contact with standard German in written and spoken media, and the acknowledgement that proficiency in standard German is an important tool for upward social mobility. However, there is a sort of hierarchy of differences. On the one hand, primary dialect markers are localised features which speakers know to be peculiar to their area. Secondary dialect markers, on the other hand, are regional features which are used in a wider geographical area and which speakers are often not aware of as being different from the standard variety.

In order to offer some clarity on the different types of linguistic varieties, linguists simplify their models by suggesting that there is a continuum of varieties, with very local dialect as the one extreme and the written standard variety as the other, and regional colloquial varieties ranging in between:

Local dialect – – Regional colloquial varieties – – – Standard variety

The range between the two extremes is illustrated by Rudolf Grosse for Upper Saxon (König et al. 2015: 135). Consider these five versions of the sentence 'Es wird bald anfangen zu regnen':

1   s ward bāe uanfang mid rāin
2   s ward bāle ānfang mit rān
3   s wärd balde ānfang mit rächn
4   s werd balde anfang dse rächn
5   s wird bald anfang dsu rēchnen

- Compare the five versions and identify the linguistic differences between them. (The 'macron' on some of the vowels, as in *rān*, indicates a long vowel.) Where do you think the change is from local/regional varieties to the standard pronunciation?

The principal difference in this set of examples is in pronunciation, with only one word being changed between the local dialect and the standard German versions (*mit => zu*). In practice, the two end-points of the scale are arbitrary: both local dialects and the standard variety are subject to variation, so these terms merely serve as aids to identify a particular speech sample as leaning more towards one end-point or the other on the continuum. Even trained speakers, such as TV newsreaders, will betray their regional origins on a phonetic level, albeit ever so slightly.

The degree to which people use regional features will vary, and it is fair to say that as regards **syntax** and **morphology**, there is a general correlation between using standard forms and the level of education and geographical mobility: the more educated one is, the more one will be aware of and practised in using the standard variety. Similarly, speakers who use the most local varieties will typically conform with the stereotype of Non-mobile, Older, Rural Males (the acronym NORM was coined by Chambers and Trudgill 1980): the less contact you have with speakers of other varieties, the less your own variety is likely to change. However, we need to be careful not to associate the use of regional language directly with the particular social profile of a speaker.

The *Atlas zur deutschen Alltagssprache* (*AdA*), which is based on online questionnaires from some 20,000 informants from across the German-speaking areas, provides a fascinating account of regional variation in contemporary colloquial German. Crucially, this atlas does not aim to record the most local dialect – in contrast to much work in the traditional dialectology of the nineteenth and twentieth centuries – but rather the way language is commonly heard in a town or village: 'Bitte geben Sie bei den folgenden Fragen jeweils an, welchen Ausdruck man in Ihrer Stadt normalerweise hören würde – egal, ob es mehr Mundart oder Hochdeutsch ist' (*AdA*). By calling the target variety of the atlas *Alltagssprache*, the compilers, Stephan Elspaß and Robert Möller, sensibly avoid terminological confusion on behalf of the informants (since asking for *Dialekt* might steer them towards particular and perhaps unrepresentative answers). Their results are striking in at least three regards:

1   There is a great deal of regional variation, on all linguistic levels;
2   Regional variation is not restricted to old agricultural terms but includes new words and very common words; and
3   For most items, clear regional patterns can be made out, but overlaying the maps does not result in clear isoglosses, thus challenging the perception of the existence of discrete, linguistically identifiable dialects.

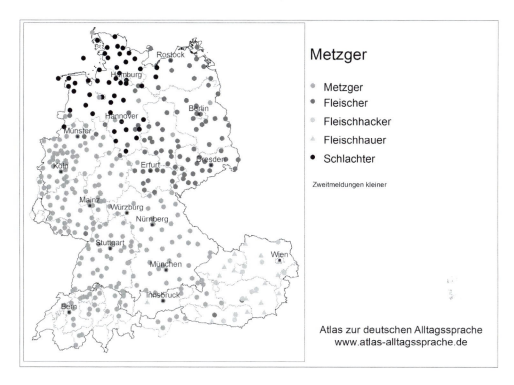

Map 4.4 Regional variants for 'butcher'
Source: www.atlas-alltagssprache.de/runde-2/f09a-b/

Consider the map for 'butcher' (Map 4.4). (To fully appreciate the detail of Maps 4.4, 4.5 and 4.6 see the original versions in colour on this book's web page: www.routledge.com/9781138858428.)

The map presents a well-defined picture with five major variants, each of which is very clearly localised. All of these **lexemes** are part of the standard variety of German: none of them is considered 'dialect' by the population, but living in one particular region will mean that you are likely to use a particular word, and *only* that particular word.

Contrast this with the map for 'stapler' (Map 4.5). Here we also have a fairly clear regional distribution of the four major variants, but the isoglosses run along political borders, with *Bostitch* the common word in Swiss German, *Klammermaschine* in most forms of Austrian German and *Klammeraffe* exclusively used in the regions of the former GDR, though *Tacker* (the word most commonly used in the rest of Germany) is also used there.

The picture is much more complicated on Map 4.6, representing words for 'safe place when playing catch'. The map shows a vast number of variants and a great mix of regional distribution. There are, however, discernible linguistic regions with regard to the variant, but the regions are much smaller and not so easily related to political borders as for the previous map.

• Why do you think the last map has so many more variants than the previous two?

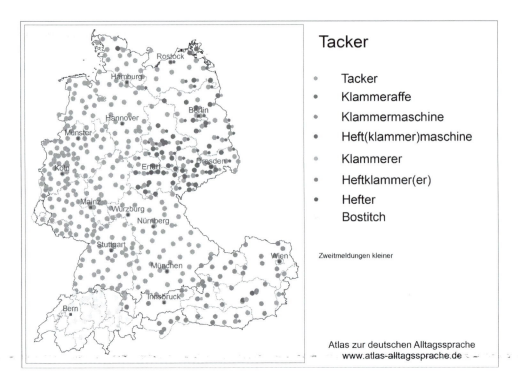

Map 4.5 Regional variants for 'stapler'
Source: www.atlas-alltagssprache.de/r8-f3g-2/

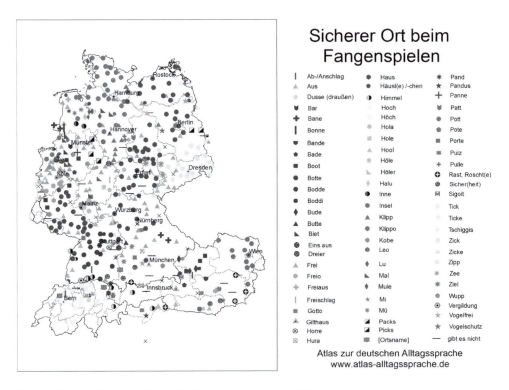

Map 4.6 Regional variants for 'safe place when playing catch'
Source: www.atlas-alltagssprache.de/sicherer-ort/

4.5   Enregisterment: marketing regional varieties

In section 4.2 we saw that people have clear emotional associations with regionally marked forms of language. Rural dialects connote a rustic life, typified by old farmers in traditional clothes, working the land in archaic ways. Similarly, urban dialects are also associated with older, manual labourers who are seen as typical for a particular city: for example, *Hamburgisch* evokes speakers who work in the docks or as fishermen. This has little to do with the reality of who speaks dialect, of course, even though the most conservative dialect speakers tend to belong to the older generations.[3] The positive association of traditional rural dialects with an old-fashioned way of life is well established in many societies and for German dates back to at least the period of Romanticism in the early nineteenth century. Many modern dialectological studies were driven by the premise that traditional dialects preserve archaic forms and thus studying modern dialects would help understand much older stages of the language's evolution (cf. Georg Wenker's famous *Sprachatlas* [www.regionalsprache.de]).

A striking development of the last 40 years or so is the positive re-evaluation of dialects. This 'dialect renaissance' began in the 1970s and is often linked to a more general desire for a less crowded life, a return to the countryside and a new interest in traditional crafts and foods. Things that are seen to be local or regional are no longer considered as backward or 'provincial' but instead as original, honest and eco-green. As regards language, dialects are clearly very much seen as local and thus form part of the regional heritage of an area. Even, or perhaps especially, in areas where the actual use of and competence in dialects significantly declined during the twentieth century, it has become very popular to use dialect words and phrases in the public domain, to symbolise and market regional distinctiveness.

The dialect renaissance, which was by no means restricted to the German-speaking areas, saw the emergence or restoration of cultural activities conducted in dialect, such as amateur drama or regular columns in newspapers, albeit usually covering only light-hearted topics. A very visible way to demonstrate regional linguistic distinctiveness is by way of public signage: for example, bilingual street signs or the use of dialect in adverts (see also Chapter 9, which deals at length with such visual manifestations of language). Reershemius (2011) studied the use of Low German on public signage in East Frisia in northern Germany. Interested in how a lesser-used linguistic variety, such as a dialect, a minority language or a regional language like Low German, is used as a resource for identity construction by individual speakers and speech communities, Reershemius found examples of Low German in prominent positions in texts advertising local products or tea rooms with a local emphasis.

- Discuss the use of language and font in the sign in Figure 4.4. Have you seen similar things in other (not necessarily German-speaking) places?

Public signs advertising guest-houses, holiday cottages, coffee shops, tea rooms, pubs, shops and events make frequent use of Low German, as in Figure 4.4: the name of the tea room, *is Teetied* (it's tea-time), is in Low German, but it is presented in quotation marks, perhaps implying 'as we used to say'.[4] What appears striking at first glance is that the use of Low German is aimed at tourists – even though they are the least likely to speak the language. So Low German is used here not primarily to offer literal communication but rather to signal to the reader that the tea room is traditional, a place where tea is served as it was in the olden days.

Figure 4.4 Advertisement for a tea room
Photo: Knud Kamphues. Source: Reershemius 2011: 40

It is likely that most readers will be able to work out what *is Teetied* means as the linguistic distance is not too far from most other German varieties. But even where the words are not clear literally, the message of the sign still conveys what was intended. In a second example, Reershemius quotes from a brochure for tourists, *Ferien an der ostfriesischen Nordseeküste*:

> In die Tasse gehört ein KLUNTJE (Kandiszucker), damit es beim Einschenken knistert.
> (Reershemius 2011: 44)

> (There must be a piece of *Kluntje* (rock candy) in the cup, so that there's a crackling sound when the tea is poured.)

Here a translation of the Low German word Kluntje is given to the reader, but the very fact that the Low German word is inserted into the standard German text shows how the writers aim to impart authenticity or insider knowledge about the East Frisian tea ceremony. Adding sugar in this special way is how the locals do it, and as a good and interested tourist, your ambition is to copy this – and with the correct procedure comes the appropriate use of the correct terminology. What is striking is that what had formerly been stigmatised as backward has now become fashionable. The use, or at least knowledge, of dialects – in these very specific contexts – has become desirable.

A key reason why these examples are so popular and widespread is because they neither endanger communication with monolingual German-speaking tourists nor challenge the established position of standard German as the only acceptable variety in formal, written and educated discourse. The use of Low German has become **enregistered**, by which we mean that the relationship between specific linguistic features (or in this case an entire language variety) and certain cultural values is sufficiently well established to be widely recognised. In this particular context, the enregisterment of Low German allows it to be used to signal or **index** a sense of 'authenticity' and local identity (see also Chapter 7).

In a similar vein, Horan (2016) studies the use and perception of a very unusual institution, the Akademie för uns kölsche Sproch (Academy for our Cologne German). The academy was founded in 1983 and offers courses in learning *Kölsch*, the history of the dialect, local history and traditions. Horan's study shows how the dialect tends to be used in public for symbolic purposes, with speakers inserting individual dialect words or phrases into their otherwise standard speech in order to 'perform' or 'enact' a local identity. Most of the participants on the language courses were locals, whose motivation for learning *Kölsch* seemed to be as a means to reinforce their local status and sense of belonging. Asked why they wanted to learn *Kölsch*, participants typically answered:

- Um die Sprache meiner Stadt zu lernen. Ich fühle mich bereits Kölsch.
- Weil ich in Köln geboren bin, aber leider nie gelernt habe, Kölsch zu sprechen.

4.6　Conclusion

In this chapter, we examined the way regional variation forms part of the sociolinguistics of modern German, linking the past with the present in interesting ways. The role of dialects as a key feature of individual and community identity formation plays an important part in the survival of linguistic regional distinctiveness. The much greater mobility of people today and the ready availability of supra-regional language forms, including the standard variety, through the media and the internet have played a part in the decrease of very local dialects. However, in their stead we find distinct varieties, which, though covering much larger areas than local dialects, are nonetheless regionally identifiable. The continuing social value of regional varieties is also attested by the significant emotional responses they evoke, as shown by the section on attitudes towards language. That dialects and regional forms are seen to be a positive thing on the whole is not just demonstrated by the fact that 60 per cent of Germans claim to speak, or to be able to speak, dialect but also by the way enregistered forms of regional language are used in public contexts to construct a sense of place, a topic we return to in more detail in Chapter 9.

Tasks and suggestions for research

Reflective task

Why does regional linguistic diversity in spoken language continue to survive when the written language is virtually uniform across the German-speaking countries? Does the degree of regional variation in German seem similar to or different from the extent of variation in other languages you are familiar with?

Research task

Focus on one particular region or area and look up five maps in the online *Atlas zur deutschen Alltagssprache*: with which other areas does your region share linguistic features? Contrast your findings with the traditional classification of German dialects, as found, for example, in the *dtv-Atlas zur deutschen Sprache* (König et al. 2015). Do your findings match or challenge this classification?

Project ideas

1   Use a library or the internet to find sources on dialects of particular German-speaking regions. Discuss how dialects are described, what aims the authors of books or websites on dialects have and what their target audience appears to be. Compare and contrast this with websites on English (or other non-German) dialects.
2   Devise a small survey to gather perceptions of varieties of German and/or English and compare your findings with published research on local and regional variation.

Notes

1 Note that, rather confusingly, *High German* or *Hochdeutsch* refers to two rather different (albeit historically related) things: dialectologists speak of *High German* as the collection of dialects that are spoken in the 'high' lands of the centre and south of Germany and in Austria and Switzerland. More commonly, however, *High German* refers to the standard variety of German rather than to dialects. See Chapter 5 for an explanation of this ambiguity – and be careful when you encounter (and use) this term.
2 Note that the English term *dialect* is usually applied to *any* distinctive variety of a language (Trudgill [2004: 2] speaks of dialects as 'social and geographical kinds of language'), whereas in the German tradition *Dialekt* is largely used only to describe *regional* varieties of a language.
3 Cf., however, the linguistic varieties of young urban speakers which, too, demonstrate clear regional origins and serve as important markers of regional or general urban identity (see Chapter 7 on language and popular culture).
4 It is worth pointing out that the original sounds as wooden as the English translation: 'A warm welcome to the *it's tea-time*'.

Annotated further reading

Atlas zur deutschen Alltagssprache (*AdA*; www.atlas-alltagssprache.de/) is an excellent resource on the visual representation of regional diversity of everyday German.
Barbour and Stevenson (1990), Chapters 3, 4 and 5, provide a standard work on the form and study of regional variation in German.
Chambers and Trudgill (1980) provide a classic introduction to dialectology and an exceptionally insightful chapter on the difference between language and dialect.
Durrell (1992), Chapter 1, gives a good introduction to general aspects of regional variation, with many useful examples.
Eichinger et al. (2009) offers a comprehensive survey of attitudes to and perceptions of linguistic varieties in the German-speaking areas.
Johnson and Braber (2008) offer a very readable introductory chapter on regional language use in German.
König (with Elspaß and Möller) (2015) is a must-have reference work for any scholar of German linguistics, containing amongst many things plenty of colourful maps on regional variation.
Russ (ed.) (1990) offers detailed descriptions of the traditional dialects of German and also includes a chapter on Frisian.

5 Standard German

5.1 Introduction

As a student of German you will often consult a *Deutsches Wörterbuch* or a *Deutsche Grammatik* when you are unsure as to the meaning or plural form of a particular word or whether a grammatical construction is 'correct' German. So you may find it puzzling that we keep saying that there is no such thing as *the* German language, as German, like all other languages, exists only as a collection of varieties (cf. our discussion in Chapter 1). How, then, can there be books on German grammar which appear to equate German with a single variety? The answer is that most books that make an authoritative claim to represent what German is only describe the **standard variety**, in German also often called the ***Schriftsprache***. Indeed, the preface of the *Dudengrammatik*, the most well-known grammar in Germany, explicitly defines the object of its study as the written and spoken standard language:

> Die Dudengrammatik beschreibt die geschriebene und gesprochene Standardsprache der Gegenwart.
>
> (Duden 2009: 5)

But on the cover page of the book, it talks more generally about the 'structure of the German language' (*Aufbau [. . .] der deutschen Sprache*), hence equating, by implication, the standard variety with the language as a whole. In this chapter we will look at the history of the standard variety of German, which began in the fifteenth century and has continued to evolve ever since, and then consider the role of the standard variety in German sociolinguistics. We will discuss the notion of a standard language variety in general and challenge some assumptions that are often made in relation to standard German in particular.[1] These assumptions are:

1   The standard variety is the original form of the language;
2   The standard variety is invariant across the German-speaking areas;
3   The standard variety has not changed and will not change; and
4   The standard variety is the correct form of the language.

- If you look up the term *standard* in an English dictionary, you will find a possibly surprising list of different meanings: it is used, for example, in relation to notions of prestige or quality; in the sense of 'normal, usual, accepted'; and with the meanings 'fixed measure, yardstick' and 'flag, emblem'. Which of the various meanings of the term seem to you to be applicable in relation to language?

The history of standard German suggests that there were three principal motivations for creating a standard variety: first, to promote the use and status of German, as opposed to other languages such as Latin and in particular French; second, to promote the use and status of one particular variety of German, in the belief that this variety was particularly elegant and pleasant sounding; and third, especially from around the mid-nineteenth century, to create a focus for a sense of national belonging (see Chapter 2). We will focus here on the historical processes and their consequences for the language and its speakers (and learners) today.

5.2   Processes of standardisation

A quick look at the history of German will immediately show that there was not always a uniform way of writing, let alone speaking, the language. Until about 1700, the place or region where a text was written could usually be determined by the linguistic variants it contained. For example, until at least the eighteenth century formal and printed texts from the south often had *nit, kommen, pey*, where texts from central and northern Germany had *nicht, gekommen, bey*.

A central question for this chapter is how we got from a stage where German existed in many more or less equally valued varieties in the past to the current state where there is one particular variety – standard German – which enjoys much greater authority and prestige than others. Researchers sometimes talk about the 'verticalisation' of varieties, meaning that before the fifteenth century regional varieties were seen as equal (that is, we might say, 'horizontally' ordered), but since that time some varieties have attained more prestige than others (that is, they have become 'vertically ordered'), with the precursors of standard German perceived as having a higher status than other **dialects** and **sociolects**.

This process of verticalisation was not a straightforward matter. The result, however, is easier to describe: there is undeniably a recognised variety of German called standard German, and this variety can be defined in both sociolinguistic and linguistic terms, albeit without clear regional and stylistic boundaries and with some significant linguistic variation. For example, using the **subjunctive** in reported speech or using the genitive after the preposition *wegen* are part of the grammar of standard German – and *only* of standard German. Using the **periphrastic possessive** (*dem Markus sein Pferd*) or using the verb *tun* as an auxiliary (*Anna tut Kuchen essen*) are part of many, indeed almost all, varieties of German *except for* the standard variety. But how was it decided which grammatical forms should be part of the standard variety and which should not?

The process of standardisation was not restricted to German, and it is a striking fact that most European languages have a standard variety – though to different degrees and with different usages. Einar Haugen investigated the similarities of standardisation histories and proposed a set of four stages to describe how a standard variety of a language typically comes about:

> selection
> **codification**
> implementation
> elaboration

The most challenging stages for the historical linguist are the first two: how were particular linguistic variants and varieties selected to 'become' the standard variety and how were such varieties linguistically fixed (or 'codified') in grammars and dictionaries?

From the late Middle Ages onwards we have evidence that particular changes in society affected communicative practices in the German-speaking areas. Societal modernisation, that is, the change from a feudal society to a centralised modern mass society, started in Germany in the fourteenth century. Geographical and social mobility, in particular in the newly emerging cities, led to a process of sociolinguistic blending, or towards homogenisation of previously distinct linguistic varieties. In terms of language use, we see these changes reflected in a much wider range of text types, a much greater use of German – as opposed to Latin – in writing and the reduction of linguistic features which are considered very local or regional: writers and printers became aware of the status of particular features and consequently either avoided or promoted them. The written and printed language of chanceries and printing presses in particularly important and powerful cities such as Augsburg or Nuremberg gained prestige, with other places accommodating their language use towards the practices in these influential centres. In addition, the language used by the chancery of Emperor Maximilian I (1493–1519) in Vienna became known as *gemeines Teutsch* and was increasingly used as a supra-regional variety. These developments resulted in the suppression of regionally or socially marked linguistic features in writing: and this marks the beginning of the standardisation of German.

The *gemeines Teutsch* of the Habsburg chancery was selected – to use Haugen's terminology – as a linguistic variety that commanded prestige across a vast part of the German-speaking area. However, standard German today does not conform to the historical writing practices of Vienna: the emergence of modern standard German was a complex process that involved more than simply the promotion of the linguistic variety of a particular institution, class or region. In fact, in the fifteenth and sixteenth centuries, the *gemeines Teutsch* competed with a number of other supra-regional varieties. The most important hailed from Thuringia and Saxony: called East Central German (ECG) by modern linguists, its contemporary term was *Sächsisch* or *Meißnisch*, and it was the variety used by Martin Luther (1483–1546), including in his astonishingly successful Bible translation (1522 [NT] and 1534). In his portrayal of his own language use, Luther did not distinguish between ECG and the *gemeines Teutsch* but said, instead, that he used the common German language as spoken in the Saxon chancery as well as by leading kings, princes, courts and imperial cities:

> Ich rede nach der Sechsischen cantzley, *quam imitantur omnes duces et reges Germaniae* [as used by all princes and kings in Germany], alle reichstette, fürsten, höfe, schreiben nach der Sechsischen cantzeleien unser churfürsten.

The importance accorded to Luther's writings since the sixteenth century bestowed considerable prestige not just on his linguistic style but also on his choice of particular words or phrases, and ECG became known to contemporaries and future generations as *Lutherdeutsch* – even though the suggestion, still frequently heard, that Luther was 'the father of standard German' is grossly exaggerated. (And if you look at Luther's writing in the original, you will immediately see that it is fairly different from modern standard written German: see, for example, http://lutherbibel.net/ for some original texts.) The division of Germany into Catholic and Protestant parts also resulted in distinct writing practices, and it was not until the late eighteenth century that the (Catholic) Habsburg Empire – by imperial decree and through school reform – adopted ECG as its official written language, which thus constituted a significant push towards linguistic uniformity (at least in writing) across the German Empire.[2]

The selection of ECG and *gemeines Teutsch* – henceforth East Upper German (EUG) because of its provenance in Austria – as prestige varieties during the sixteenth century was followed by the process of codification in the seventeenth century. Language became a symbol of culture, and a self-proclaimed *Kulturnation* such as the German people would need a national language that was refined and cultured. In codifying a language, particular variants or varieties are described in grammars and dictionaries, the collection of authoritative reference works often referred to in historical linguistics as the 'codex'. It usually records what constitutes standard language use and therefore also, by implication, which language usages are not standard (we return to this point in Chapter 11 when we discuss the importance of the codex in modern schooling).

In the seventeenth century, the first grammars of German were published amidst an intense discussion on what a 'correct' German should look like. In 1617, the Fruchtbringende Gesellschaft (Fructifying Society) was founded by aristocrats and members of the bourgeoisie concerned with promoting the status of German as a language of learned writing, poetry and prose. The 'best' German (referred to, rather confusingly from our perspective, as *Hochdeutsch* – see Chapter 4, endnote 1, on the ambiguity of this term) was seen to be the one used by the 'best authors' of the time, but it was also acknowledged that '*Spracharbeit*' would need to be undertaken on the existing linguistic diversity of German in order to create – or, indeed, re-create – a variety of German that was sufficiently clear, pure and beautiful to be used in the highest registers. Most participants in this *Spracharbeit* came from the ECG area, and it is therefore no surprise that many simply argued in favour of granting *Meißnisch* the status of exemplary German. A number of grammars and dictionaries were published in the seventeenth and eighteenth centuries, aimed at recording good use of German and, by implication, stigmatising any features of the language which were not described in these publications.

To what extent such prescriptive accounts directly affected or changed contemporary language use is difficult to say. What is certain, however, is that grammarians knew about each other's work and that there are clear continuities in the grammar-writing of German from its beginnings in the sixteenth and seventeenth century to the present day. In this sense, it is appropriate to speak of the codex of German as a single entity, even though the standard and prestige variety of German of the seventeenth century looks rather different from present-day standard German.

With the publication of grammars and dictionaries aimed at school teaching, the implementation of standard norms accelerated. From the second half of the eighteenth century onwards, children were explicitly taught that certain constructions and usages were deemed incorrect and that only the standard variety was acceptable in formal writing. In Austria, the school reform of 1774 was a particularly famous case of norm implementation: through the appointment of a Prussian educationalist, Johann Ignaz Felbiger, to implement ECG norms in schools, based on Johann Christoph Gottsched's *Sprachkunst* (1748), children in Austria were explicitly taught that good German was not Austrian German but *Meißnisch*, with consequent repercussions on the status and use of their own variety of German in writing and speech.

The text excerpt in Figure 5.1 is taken from the *Teutsches Namen- oder Lehrbüchl*, printed in 1750 in Austria. Aimed at school teachers, it presents the 'undesirable' dialect forms in the left-hand column and the 'correct' High German in the right-hand columns. It marks the Austrian forms as incorrect and thus serves as a clear example of how school books contributed to the stigmatisation of local and regional language.

- Transcribe the two columns at the bottom and reflect on the language: what differences can you make out? Is there anything that is still part of Austrian German today?

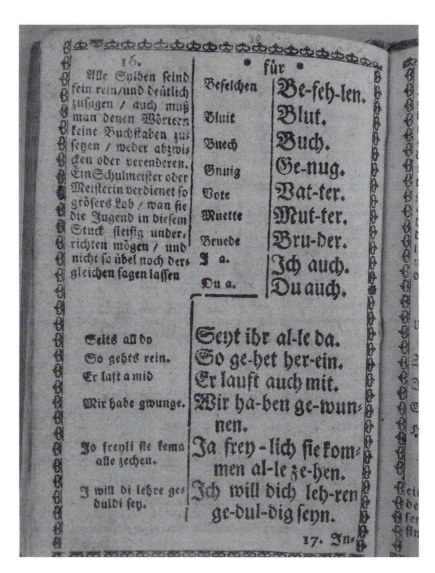

Figure 5.1 Stigmatisation of Austria's regional varieties in the *Teutsches Namen- oder Lehrbüchl* (c. 1750)

Source: Havinga 2015: 272

The implementation of standard norms in institutional contexts such as schooling has a very direct effect on the sociolinguistic balance of a society: those who master the new norms can use them as powerful tools in their upward social mobility; those who do not risk being ridiculed for their language use and face the stigma of being seen as uneducated. These dynamics still play an important part in the role of language in society today (see Chapter 11). Its complicated history outlined earlier showed that standard German does not simply originate from one particular region, century or group of speakers. As a result of this, in modern standard German, there continues to be significant variation between regions. For example, *ich bin gesessen* (rather than *ich habe gesessen*) is considered standard German in the south, while nobody in the north would think that *Wie geht dir das?* is in any way odd or marked, even though the construction is only used in the standard variety of northern Germany. Yet despite these differences, many speakers do not see standard German simply as one of many varieties of German but, in fact, as *the* 'correct' form of the language, as codified in grammars and dictionaries, and therefore always to be used in formal and written discourse.

5.3   Standard German today

The concept of a standard variety of German has therefore existed for many centuries, and when reading texts that are as much as 200 or 300 years old, we experience relatively little *linguistic* difficulty in understanding them because despite the considerable difference in *speaking* German across the regions, the standardisation process has largely eliminated any significant differences in *writing* the language. The standard variety is the agreed norm for printed and formal texts, and is used in school teaching and in formal correspondence. The only area that is officially codified by the state authorities (in all states where German is an official language) is, however, **orthography** – all other parts of the language are regulated by general agreement, not state interference.

This codification of German orthography dates back to the late nineteenth century, when the spelling rules proposed by Konrad Duden, a school head teacher, were adopted for Prussian schools, and later, in 1903–1904, throughout Germany. The official endorsement of Duden's spelling dictionary by the authorities[3] has led to its recognition as recording the 'correct' forms of German in general. If you ask people in Germany or Austria whether something is a proper word or not, you are likely to be told to 'look it up in the Duden': if the word is in the Duden, it is a word of German! This view that you can simply look up correct German also applies to all other areas of the language, and it was an economically sound move of the Duden publishing house to add to its list reference works on grammar (since 1937), meaning, pronunciation and style (*Richtiges und gutes Deutsch*). You will find a copy of the *Duden Rechtschreibwörterbuch* on the desks of most administrators, teachers, journalists and students, and even though the book is technically just a spelling dictionary, it is used and perceived as the complete collection of words that make up standard German.

The *Dudenverlag* is not, however, the only place that promises certainty in *Zweifelsfällen*, that is, where speakers are doubtful about the correctness of a particular linguistic feature. There is a long tradition of publishing guides to good speaking, elegant writing or correct forms of expression, which continues to the present day. The authors of such books are often journalists who are concerned about a perceived decline in the linguistic abilities of adults, and this topic is explored more fully in Chapter 10. (Somewhat ironically, many such books name journalists as particularly culpable for corrupting good language use!)

*   What books, authors or institutions contribute to the codex of your main language(s)? Does any one in particular have the same degree of authority as the Duden does for German-speakers?

5.4   German as a pluricentric language

As we have already seen in Chapter 1, German is used in many parts of the world, but its status and functions vary from one country to another. In many countries, for example, in South America or in the United States, there are tens of thousands of native speakers living in areas where German is the family or community language but it is not formally recognised in any way. In eight countries (Russia, Poland, Slovakia, Romania, Hungary, Czech Republic, France, Denmark) it is officially acknowledged as a minority language with varying degrees of recognition in terms of its use in public institutions. And, of course, in addition to Austria and Germany it is widely used in public domains in Switzerland, Liechtenstein, Luxembourg, eastern Belgium and northern Italy (South Tyrol/Alto Adige). The systematic use of German in these latter seven countries requires the adoption of a standardised form of the language, and they all in fact have different national standardised varieties. For this reason, German is often referred to as a **pluricentric** language.

In a school in Germany, to look up words of standard German you will be asked to own and use a *Deutsches Wörterbuch*. In Austria, however, pupils will resort to the *Österreichisches Wörterbuch* (ÖWB), a dictionary that was first published in 1951 and has since seen 38 editions. Note the respective titles of these authoritative dictionaries: *Deutsches Wörterbuch* gives the impression that the German of Germany is synonymous with the language as such (*Deutsch*), while *Österreichisches Wörterbuch* suggests there is something distinctive about Austrian (standard) German. The very existence of separate lexicographical codices for Germany and Austria seems to confirm the pluricentricity of the language.

The fact that there is an authoritative Austrian dictionary, published by the Ministry for Education and used in schools, demonstrates that Austrian German – at least its lexis – is codified. This is emphatically spelled out in the first edition:

> Auch das Österreichische Wörterbuch ist ein Wörterbuch der guten, richtigen deutschen Gemeinsprache. Es ist jedoch in erster Linie für Österreicher bestimmt und wird vor allem von Österreichern benützt werden. Deshalb enthält es auch zahlreiche allgemein verwendete Wörter der österreichischen Umgangssprache und österreichischer Mundarten, wenngleich keine Wörter in mundartlicher Schreibung. Solche Wörter sind aber ausdrücklich [. . .] gekennzeichnet, und neben ihnen stehen gemeinsprachliche Ausdrücke. Damit werden die Benützer des Wörterbuchs vor der Verwendung der Umgangssprache und der Mundart in der gehobenen Sprache ausdrücklich gewarnt und zugleich zu den guten gemeindeutschen Formen hingeleitet.
>
> (ÖWB 1951: 6)

• What do you think the editors of this dictionary wish to achieve in the way Austrians use language?

The Austrian dictionary has a firm place in the codex of Austrian German (AG), and in recent years there has been a great deal of research on the form and status of this standard variety. One of the most active and influential research centres in this field is the Forschungszentrum Österreichisches Deutsch (www.oedeutsch.at), led by Rudolf Muhr at the University of Graz. The centre's *österreichisches Aussprachewörterbuch/österreichische Aussprachedatenbank* (www-oedt.kfunigraz.ac.at/ADABA/index.html) contains the pronunciations of the respective standard varieties of Austria, Germany and Switzerland, based on the pronunciation of TV and radio presenters. The pronunciation dictionary shows that there are some noticeable, regular differences between the three national varieties, but there are also differences within the national norm of each country: a standard German-speaker from Hamburg, for example, will typically sound different from a standard speaker from Stuttgart. Furthermore, the speech practices of media presenters represent a rather limited model, as the pronunciation of standard varieties of German encompasses much more variation than this suggests.

- Identify five examples of different pronunciations of the same word in another language you are familiar with and discuss to what extent they are typical of a particular regional or social background. Is the situation similar or different to the one for German?

The concept of pluricentricity is helpful in accounting for the existence of national standard varieties of German that are very similar to each other while also containing certain individual distinctions (not only in pronunciation, in fact, but also in the vocabulary and grammar). However, it is problematic in the sense that the different national standard varieties don't enjoy equal status. There is a long-standing popular view that the 'real' or 'correct' German is the one spoken in Germany, and that within Germany, northern German is 'better' than the German spoken elsewhere. As we have seen, both in lay discourse and also in publications such as the Duden dictionary, there is a striking imbalance in that the standard variety in Germany is simply called *Deutsch*, while its counterpart in Austria is called *österreichisches Deutsch*. The perception that German German (GG) is somehow more prestigious than AG is reinforced by the fact that when foreign language films and TV series are dubbed into German, they are invariably dubbed into GG.[4] This gives the impression to the Austrian public that GG is better or more appropriate for such formal language use and to the German public that GG is really the only acceptable form. Similarly, while Austrian writers may be asked to remove **Austriacisms** from their work when publishing for the general German-speaking market, German writers will never be asked to remove **Teutonisms** (words that are only used in Germany).

The standard **language ideology** (see Chapter 2), which perpetuates the belief that only the standard variety and not any dialect or colloquial variety should be used and accepted in formal discourse, thus often extends to tacit censorship of any standard language variety that isn't part of the dominant country or speaker community. This censorship does not take place at an official level – in the form of legislation – but is prescribed and policed at more local levels, for example, in school curricula or guidelines for journalists and publishers. For instance, while in Austria the norm of the state broadcasting network, the ÖRF, is considered to be the standard variety of the country, in Germany many of those linguistic features would be considered incorrect or belittled as 'cute'.

The perception that Austrian German is somewhat inferior to German German dates back to at least the eighteenth century, as shown previously with the example of the introduction of Gottsched's language norms to Austrian schools. This imposition of a 'foreign' norm of speaking and writing in Austrian schools is likely to have been the cause of the feeling of inferiority amongst speakers of Austrian standard German, which, remarkably, persists in various ways to the present day. A telling example of this occurred at the time of Austria's accession to the EU in 1995. Emphasising that Austrian German is not the same as the German spoken in Germany, the Austrian government insisted that the official variety of German used as a working language in the EU needed to be extended by a list of 'spezifisch österreichische[r] Ausdrücke der deutschen Sprache', and consequently *Protokoll 10* of the accession treaty listed the following 23 Austriacisms, which now formally enjoy equal status in official EU documents to their German German equivalents (marked as 'D' below):

Beirid	D: Roastbeef
Eierschwammerl	D: Pfifferlinge
Erdäpfel	D: Kartoffeln
Faschiertes	D: Hackfleisch

Fisolen	D: Grüne Bohnen
Grammeln	D: Grieben
Hüferl	D: Hüfte
Karfiol	D: Blumenkohl
Kohlsprossen	D: Rosenkohl
Kren	D: Meerrettich
Lungenbraten	D: Filet
Marillen	D: Aprikosen
Melanzani	D: Aubergine
Nuß	D: Kugel
Obers	D: Sahne
Paradeiser	D: Tomaten
Powidl	D: Pflaumenmus
Ribisel	D: Johannisbeere
Rostbraten	D: Hochrippe
Schlögel	D: Keule
Topfen	D: Quark
Vogerlsalat	D: Feldsalat
Weichseln	D: Sauerkirschen

The list is not exhaustive and thus somewhat misrepresents the extent of lexical differences between Austrian standard German and other national varieties of standard German. In addition, because all of these terms refer to culinary items, the national stereotype of Austria as a *gemiadlich* (*gemütlich*, 'cosy') nation was somewhat corroborated. Emphasising, on the one hand, the important linguistic differences between GG and AG, and on the other hand coming up with only a short list of relatively unimportant words, fuelled contemporary accusations of pettiness and desperation. The inclusion of the 23 words was highly symbolic, demonstrating that Austria is an independent nation with its own national language and not (linguistically) subservient to Germany.

5.5   Conclusion

The historical process of standardisation and the topic of standard German command a particular place in the sociolinguistic landscape of the German-speaking countries. In the perception of speakers, the standard variety is often seen as epitomising the correct and uniform version of modern German, despite the fact that its history is rather diffuse and that its modern forms display a significant degree of regional and stylistic variation. This chapter related the complex history of standard German and discussed the social value of the variety, as illustrated in prescriptive comments embedded in the complaint tradition and in the role of language in the creation of national identity, using the example of Austria.

Tasks and suggestions for research

Reflective tasks

1   What are the sociolinguistic and linguistic reasons that led to the standardisation of German?

2   At the beginning of this chapter, we stated four general perceptions of the concept *standard variety*. In what ways, if at all, has your own thinking on these assumptions been influenced or changed by what you have read here?

Research task

Read up on the history of another standard variety (for example, from Deumert and Vandenbussche 2003). What are the principal similarities and differences to the history of standard German? What were the motivations, who were the principal agents and what metalinguistic sources are considered authoritative for the standard variety today?

Project idea

Looking at the concept of pluricentricity from a sociolinguistic perspective, we can see that it has implications on the symbolic, as well as the descriptive, level: if one of the functions of the standardisation process is to underwrite the existence of a 'nation' or 'people' (i.e. by establishing a 'national language variety'), what consequences does the adoption of the concept of German as a pluricentric language have for the process of nation-building? Try to answer this question by conducting interviews with people from different 'German-speaking' countries.

Notes

1 Many words and pronunciations are considered standard within a particular speech community but are still very regionalised. See the *Atlas zur deutschen Alltagssprache* or the *Atlas zur Aussprache des deutschen Gebrauchsstandards* for plenty of insightful examples.
2 The case of Switzerland was and remains rather special in this regard.
3 In the 1950s, the Culture and Education Ministers of all West German *Bundesländer* officially decreed that in cases of disputes on spelling matters the Duden rules would prevail. This decree, which remained in place until 1998, is extraordinary in that the state officially handed the monopoly (on spelling matters) to a private publishing house.
4 There are some very marked exceptions, but generally any deviation from the codified German German norm is triggered by artistic considerations (e.g. to show linguistically the different regional origin of a character in a film, as was done for example in *Angela's Ashes*).

Annotated further reading

Ammon (2015) offers an account of the uses and functions of standard German.
Ammon et al. (2004) is a dictionary of the standard varieties and variants of the German language.
Clyne (1992) introduces and explains the concept of pluricentricity in relation to languages.
Davies and Langer (2006) offer a scholarly history of non-standard German, i.e. it contains the (hi)stories of 13 morphosyntactic constructions which are deemed ungrammatical in modern standard German.
Deumert and Vandenbussche (2003) provide chapters on the standardisation histories of all Germanic languages.
Ernst (2005) offers a brief textbook account of the major milestones in the history of standard German.
Johnson and Braber (2008) provide a readable overview of the standardisation of German.
Linn and McLelland (2002) provide a number of case studies covering aspects of standardisation histories of various Germanic languages.

Macha (2006) is a discussion of different writing practices of Catholics and Protestants in the Early Modern Period.

Mattheier (2003) is a concise account of the history of standard German, using Haugen's model as a theoretical framework.

Muhr (2007) provides recordings of Austrian, Swiss and German standard pronunciations online at www.adaba.at/.

Salmons (2012) contains a useful chapter on the standardisation of German.

6 Patterns of variation and change in contemporary German

6.1 Introduction

In this chapter we will reflect on processes of language change in German: where do we find them? Why do they happen? How do they occur? Answering the question of why languages in general are never static entities, but instead subject to constant change and development, has been one of the main challenges of the discipline of linguistics since its beginnings in the nineteenth century. From a sociolinguistic point of view, languages change because speakers find new ways of using language to meet their changing needs. In this chapter we will introduce examples of change in German in the areas of the **lexicon**, **semantics**, **syntax** and **pragmatics**.

6.2 Changing linguistic practices

To begin with, let's go back in history roughly a century and consider the following job advert, published in the *Neue Zürcher Zeitung* in 1904:

> Bei einer Herrschaft in Schaffhausen
> findet eine gut empfohlene
> Kammerjungfer
> dauernde Stelle.
> Offerten beliebe man mit Zeugnis-
> abschriften und Photographie unter
> Chiffre § einzusenden an
> Rudolf Mosse, Schaffhausen.

Example 6.1 Extract from *Neue Zürcher Zeitung* 1904
Source: www.linguistik-online.de/18_04/ladstaetter.html

- Describe the type of text (**genre**) we are looking at here. What does the advert tell us about the employer? What do we learn about the relationship between employer and the prospective employee?
- Compare the job advert from 1904 with the following one from 2015, published on an internet job-advertising website:

Gesucht wird für einen 2-Personen-Privathaushalt in Düsseldorf, eine flexible, unabhängige & reisefreudige Haushälterin/Wirtschafterin (m/w) die für den 300 qm großen Haushalt zuständig sein sollte. Unterstützt werden Sie 2x wöchentlich durch eine Haushaltshilfe. Des Weiteren hat die Familie noch Feriendomizile in der Türkei und Neuseeland. Daher sollten Sie mit auf Reisen gehen. Die Familie hält sich circa 8 Wochen in der Türkei und circa 2 Monate in Neuseeland auf. Es wird sich eine Fachkraft vorgestellt, die hauswirtschaftliche Abläufe im gehobenen Niveau umsetzen kann (Sauberkeit, Garderobe- /Wäschepflege und teilweise Nahrungszubereitung). Sie sollten über entsprechende Berufserfahrung und Nachweise aus einem Privathaushalt verfügen, einen Führerschein besitzen und der englischen Sprache ein wenig mächtig sein. Bei der Wohnungsbeschaffung ist die Familie gerne behilflich. Die Position ist nach Absprache zu besetzen, spätestens zum 01.01.2016 und wird überdurchschnittlich hoch vergütet. Referenz-Nr.: 15/6656 D

Example 6.2 Advert from job website
Source: www.lesaco.de/download.htm

Examples 6.1 and 6.2 are different for a number of reasons. First and foremost, the job of a *Kammerjungfer*, 'lady's maid', does not exist anymore, even if you check job advertisements for what the website calls *den gehobenen Haushalt*, 'households of high standing'. People with sufficient money to afford domestic staff require different services today; they are looking, for example, for a *Hauswirtschafterin*, a 'housekeeper', as in Example 6.2, meaning someone who runs the household rather than someone who attends to the 'lady of the house'.

- There are numerous social, economic, cultural and technological changes underlying the move from *Kammerjungfer* to *Hauswirtschafterin*. Can you name some of them?

As a reader of German you may still encounter the word *Kammerjungfer*, for example, in novels from the nineteenth century, but rarely in modern texts. Here we have an example of lexical change: one word has become obsolete, and another has taken its place. Lexical change can also affect the semantic component of words, for example, when we look at the noun *Herrschaft* in the advert from 1904. We would use *Herrschaft* in contemporary German only in the sense of 'power' or 'rule'. In 1904 it could also mean 'persons of high standing'.

- Can you think of four examples of lexical change in other languages you know, including semantic changes? In what ways do these linguistic changes reflect changes in the social, cultural, economic and political contexts in which the words/lexical items are used?
- Our two texts differ not only in terms of the words they use – the text conventions are also different today from 1904. Compare them in terms of the way they are structured and which **styles** are used. Re-write Example 6.1 as it might appear in a newspaper today. Which parts of the advert are difficult to 'translate' in this way, and why do you think this is?

Examples 6.1 and 6.2 show that it is not only the form of the German language that has changed, but also the way speakers/writers use it. Language change doesn't 'come from nowhere'; it is the result of speakers changing how they use language (their 'linguistic practices') in a relatively systematic way. But what motivates people to speak and write their language differently?

Table 6.1 Why do speakers change the way they use their language(s)?

Socio-economic change	Changes in the social circumstances of speakers require new linguistic forms.
Language economy	Speakers find ways to express what they want to say in a more concise way.
Increasing complexity of social life	Speakers find new words and expressions to account for the increasing complexity of their lives; new concepts, objects and processes may be introduced to the daily lives of speakers which require new terminology, e.g. by borrowing from other languages speakers have access to.
Identity construction	Speakers use language in ways that reflect the way they see themselves or want to be perceived by others.
Mediatisation	New media shape the way language is used (see Chapter 8).
Public discourses on language	Political debates on issues such as gender representation can lead to changed linguistic practices.

By comparing the two job adverts we can observe an example of socio-economic motives for linguistic development; social change led to the use of a terminology that reflects evolved relationships between employer and employee in the twenty-first century. There are other reasons for people to change their linguistic practices too; see, for example, Table 6.1.

What, then, is the relationship between language change and sociolinguistic change? Language change can affect all areas of language as a system: the lexicon, its **morpho-syntax** and its **phonology**. Since sociolinguistics emerged as a discipline it has set out to explain *why* languages change. Some researchers followed the established paths of historical linguistics, where texts or speech from different times are analysed and compared. Others developed the methods of quantitative sociolinguistics, where change in progress is observed, focusing on variables such as the changing pronunciation of a certain sound.

In his seminal studies on language change William Labov distinguishes between social and internal factors influencing change. Internal factors concern language as a system, where language-specific structural constraints determine the way a language can develop. It would be unlikely, for example, for words with the 'th'-sound to be introduced into German since it is no longer part of the German sound system. Recent sociolinguistic approaches highlight the fact that all forms of linguistic change, internal ones included, are socially motivated, and therefore analyses should not only focus on discovering changes in language structure, but should also consider changes in communicative practices and their social causes. This approach requires us therefore to analyse sociolinguistic change as a prerequisite and condition for structural language change.

Nikolas Coupland suggests five dimensions for the analysis of sociolinguistic change (see Figure 6.1).

- What do you think **discursive practices**, **language ideologies**, cultural **reflexivity** and social **norms** refer to in the context of language?
- Friedrich Krotz (2009: 24) defines **mediatisation** as 'a historical, ongoing, long-term process in which more and more media emerge and are institutionalized', so that 'media in the long run increasingly become relevant for the social construction of everyday life, society, and culture as a whole'. Why do you think Coupland has put mediatisation in the centre of his model explaining sociolinguistic change?

We have discussed lexical change from various perspectives, showing, for example, how socio-economic changes drive changing linguistic practices. Another reason for lexical

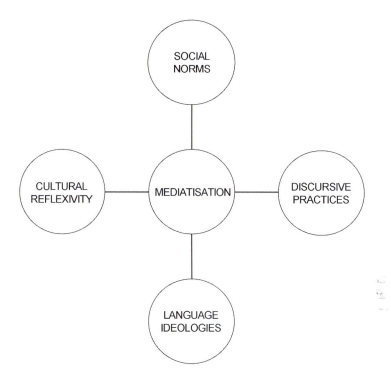

Figure 6.1 Sociolinguistic change
Source: adapted from Coupland 2014: 74

change is language contact, for example, in the case of German with the dominant globalising language English (see Chapter 3). Yet another trigger of lexical change can be regional variation (see Chapter 4). Especially in spoken forms of German, words and phrases that used to be restricted to certain areas of the German-speaking countries in the past are now used more widely, while others are almost extinct.

Consider the example of an everyday word such as *Brötchen*. The *Wortatlas der deutschen Umgangssprache*, published in 1978, shows the geographical distribution of words for 'bread roll' at that time (see the map reproduced at www.atlas-alltagssprache. de/wp-content/uploads/2012/05/Broetchen.jpg). The *Atlas zur deutschen Alltagssprache* (www.atlas-alltagssprache.de/brotchen/), an ongoing project publishing research findings on regional lexical variation online, allows us to compare this historical linguistic map with more recent language use.

• Study the 1978 map for *Brötchen* and compare it with the more recent maps for *Brötchen/Semmel*. What has changed during the intervening period? What might the reasons behind the changes be?

So far we have been discussing general principles of language change, focusing in our examples mainly on the lexicon of German. We will now broaden our view and look at recent changes in linguistic practices in other areas of German, in relation to syntactic structures.

6.3   Syntactic change?

Some areas in a language are more prone to change than others: the lexicon is easiest to influence, followed by the phonological system. Morpho-syntax, however, is an area where change does not happen easily, especially when a language such as German has a standardised written form that is reinforced by a state institution such as the education system (see Chapters 5 and 11). Interestingly, however, it is precisely a change in syntax in German that has been widely discussed in the media and debated amongst linguists over the last 15 years.

- Read the following text by the Austrian journalist Bettina Steiner. What exactly is happening, according to Steiner? Describe the issue in your own words.

> Für Sprachpuristen ist die Sache klar: Auf *weil* hat ein Nebensatz zu folgen. Überall. Ausnahmslos. Also: Ich liebe die deutsche Sprache, weil ich sie beherrsche. Nicht: Ich liebe die deutsche Sprache, weil ich beherrsche sie. Wer einen Hauptsatz anfügen will, der muss ein anderes Wörtlein zu Hilfe nehmen, das hübsche *denn*. Leider macht sich das *denn* in der mündlichen Kommunikation zunehmend rar. So rar, dass auffällt, wer es verwendet. Um es in Amazon-Sprech zu sagen: Wer das Wort *denn* verwendet, der verwendet auch den *Konjunktiv eins* und *buk, frug, stak*.
>
> Warum das Hauptsatz-*Weil*, das mündlich schon lange in Gebrauch ist, die Schriftsprache erobert hat, ist umstritten. Manche meinen, es war wieder einmal die Übermacht des Englischen, die uns eine falsche Konstruktion beschert hat. So wie wir immer öfter hören, etwas *mache Sinn*, weil wir *„makes sense"* im Ohr haben, übersetzen wir auch den englischen Kausalsatz patschert eins zu eins ins Deutsche: „Because it is easy." Weil es ist leicht.
>
> Ein Kollege meint, das Englische sei in diesem Fall unschuldig, verantwortlich seien Intellektuelle rund um die österreichische Kabarettszene. Sie hätten die ironische Verwendung des Hauptsatz-*Weils* so hartnäckig betrieben, dass sie irgendwann selbst glaubten, es sei korrekt. Kann aber auch sein, dass das in Wort und Schrift zurückweichende *denn* schlicht eine Lücke hinterlassen hat, die so gefüllt wurde. *Denn* oder *weil*, alles egal.

Example 6.3 Newspaper article on the use of *weil*
Source: *Die Presse* 21 January 2014

According to Bettina Steiner, German-speakers are in the process of abolishing the **subordinate clause** (*Nebensatz*) introduced by the **conjunction** *weil* (because). They do so by placing the **finite verb** of the subordinate clause in second rather than final position, thus apparently changing it into a **main clause** – and the reason for this change, she suggests, is the influence either of the English language or of Austrian comedians.

From a linguistic point of view we need to be more careful about arriving at such explanations. First of all, it is important to establish whether such a change (as opposed to random variation) is actually taking place. One way of doing this is to conduct a quantitative analysis or look at existing linguistic corpora. A search for clauses introduced by *weil* in the GeWiss-corpus, an electronic linguistic corpus of academic lectures in German (GeWiss – *gesprochene Wissenschaftssprache*, https://gewiss.uni-leipzig.de/index.php?id=search), shows that in 41 out of 191 occurrences the finite verb was not placed in the last position in the clause. This suggests that the construction is fairly widespread, even in a genre of high-register spoken German (academic lectures) which can plausibly be assumed to be close to the standard norms. Furthermore, the 'new' *weil*-construction does not seem to be related to a lack of education, of speakers not knowing the rules of word order in standard written German, since the corpus consists of lectures delivered by academics, all highly educated and eloquent. However, the corpus also shows that the same speakers use both constructions, the verb-end pattern (*weil*+Vend) and the verb-second pattern (*weil*+V2).

As Steiner says, some people argue that speakers may use *weil*+V2 constructions because they copy the word order from English. This explanation is not shared by academic linguists as it overstates the role of English in changing German syntax, and, more importantly, it ignores the fact that the 'new' *weil*-construction can in fact be found in German well before English was in close contact with German. The construction is therefore not new at all as there is evidence for it as early as the Middle Ages. So what *is* happening in contemporary language use? Let's analyse in which contexts and to what effect the construction is used, in other words, taking a qualitative rather than a quantitative approach.

25	Almaich	würd echt gern HEUT ins kino,	
26		weil das mein EINziger freier Abend is.	
27		weil (-) zur zeit hab ich ECHT STRESS.	

Example 6.4 Kinoabend
Source: Günthner 2008: 107

First, look at utterances (25) and (26): (26) is an example of *weil*+Vend, and it is syntactically and pragmatically subordinated to the main clause (25). It could also stand in front of the main clause: *Weil das mein einziger freier Abend ist, würd ich heut echt gern ins Kino*. The information provided in the subordinated clause (26) answers the question: WHY tonight?

If we now turn to (27) – *weil*+V2 – we can observe a short pause between *weil* and the rest of the utterance. The clause is not subordinated to the main clause (25), and it does not provide a direct reason for the content of the main clause. So it cannot be positioned before the main clause like *weil*+Vend earlier.

Susanne Günthner (2008) shows that *weil*+V2 clauses do not provide a direct reason for the content of the main clause but rather an explanation of how the speaker came to the conclusion uttered in the main clause: *weil* here has an **epistemic** function. Consider the following example:

12	Anni:	der hat sicher wieder gsoffen (-)
13		weil (-) sie läuft total deprimiert durch die gegend.

Example 6.5 Säufer
Source: Günthner 2008: 110

(13) explains why Anni assumes that 'he' – whoever he is – has been drinking again: Anni deduces this from the fact that 'she' – whoever she is – seems depressed. If Anni used a *weil*+Vend construction, the meaning of her utterance would change: *Der hat sicher gesoffen, weil sie total deprimiert durch die Gegend läuft*. Here, 'her running around depressed' would be the reason for his drinking.

In Example 6.6, *weil*+V2 in (2) explains why (1) has been uttered in the first place:

1	Bert:	und was gibts außer cinema paradiso.
2		(-) weil (-) DEN hab ich schon gesehen.

Example 6.6 Cinema Paradiso
Source: Günthner 2008: 107

Here we see that *weil* can function as a **discourse marker**. Discourse markers are elements in a language that act not at the level of the sentence but of the text. In German, they normally occur at the beginning or the end of an utterance and are pragmatic devices that speakers use in order to guide or direct their listener's attention and which allow them to supply clues for the listener as to how they should interpret utterances. You will have heard speakers of German starting an utterance with 'Also, . . . '. In German, many discourse markers have been developed from adverbs and conjunctions, which means that *weil*, for example, can be both a conjunction and a discourse marker (reinforced in Example 6.7 by being combined with *also*).

01	Nina:	ohh ja des- bei mir wars eigentlich ziemlich lustig;
02		weil also –
03		ich hatte mal ne zeitlang n auto gehabt
04		und dann ähm: hatt ich auf der autobahn ne panne,
05		und äh s ging echt nichts;
06	Iris:	mhm
07	Nina:	mehr ne ganze elektrik war kaputt und so,
08		ohh und dann äh
09		ja halt notrufsäule ne
10		dann kam halt der ADAC an

Example 6.7 Autopanne
Source: Günthner 2008: 112

In this example, *weil* introduces not the next utterance but a short narration as an explanation for (01). It connects (01) to the following text rather than just to the following utterance.

To summarise (see Table 6.2), the factual *weil* introduces a reason for something stated in the main clause: *Ich würde echt gern heute ins Kino gehen, weil das mein einziger freier Abend ist.* It answers the question: *Why* do you want to go to the cinema *tonight*? By contrast, the epistemic *weil* introduces an explanation, which is not necessarily a reason: *Der hat sicher wieder gesoffen, weil sie läuft total deprimiert durch die Gegend.* It answers the question: *How do you know* that he has started to drink again? *Weil*+V2 can, for example, indicate the reason for a speaker saying something like *Und was gibt es außer Cinema Paradiso?* He is asking the question because

Table 6.2 Types of *weil*-construction

Types of weil	Contexts of use	weil+*V2*	weil+*Vend*
factual *weil*	written and spoken	possible	possible
epistemic *weil*	to date mainly spoken	exclusively	not possible
weil related to turn-taking	to date mainly spoken	exclusively	not possible
weil as discourse marker	to date mainly spoken	exclusively	not possible

Source: based on Ziegler 2009

he has already seen this particular film. Finally, *weil* as a discourse marker motivates or justifies what the speaker is going on to say; in Example 6.7, it indicates to the listeners that the following story explains why Nina thinks that in her case things had been 'rather funny'.

This detailed analysis has shown that *weil*+V2 and *weil*+Vend clauses are functionally different constructions – they do different things. One (*weil*+V2) is found predominantly in spoken language and is not (yet) recognised as a possible syntactic structure in standard German, whereas the other (*weil*+Vend) is well established in both written and spoken language and as a feature of standard German syntax. There are studies which indicate that *weil*+V2 clauses have now made their way into written German, for example, in the review sections of newspapers. What is perceived as change by self-declared defenders of the German language (*weil*+V2) turns out to be a syntactic construction that has been around for some time but has only recently attracted the attention of observers, possibly because its use is becoming more widespread.

- Consider the reasons why the *weil*+V2 construction has become more visible recently. Similar variation (or change?) can be observed in the use of prepositions such as *wegen* (because of) and *trotz* (despite), which are often used in informal spoken contexts with the dative rather than the genitive case; can you find examples of both patterns? Are there similar examples of morpho-syntactic constructions that seem to have become more common recently in other languages that you know?

6.4 Changed linguistic practices as the result of ideological and political debates

While speakers change some of their practices at an almost subconscious level by making spontaneous decisions, other changes are deliberate and occur on the basis of political debates and arguments. Triggered by the feminist movement, gender linguistics, for example, became a much-discussed topic during the 1980s and 1990s. Demands by the movement's supporters included that linguistic practices should change in such a way that women would not feel excluded or discriminated against.

Some years ago, a high-profile debate erupted around the Austrian national anthem (*Bundeshymne*). Here is the old version (used until 2011):

---

(1) Land der Berge, Land am Strome,
    Land der Äcker, Land der Dome,
    Land der Hämmer, zukunftsreich!
    Heimat bist du großer Söhne,
    Volk, begnadet für das Schöne,
    Vielgerühmtes Österreich.
    Vielgerühmtes Österreich.
    [. . .]
(3) Mutig in die neuen Zeiten,
    Frei und gläubig sieh uns schreiten,
    Arbeitsfroh und hoffnungsreich.
    Einig laß in Brüderchören,
    Vaterland, dir Treue schwören.
    Vielgeliebtes Österreich.
    Vielgeliebtes Österreich.

Example 6.8 Austrian national anthem

- Which elements of the *Bundeshymne* do you think were contested? Can you suggest alternatives? Compare your results with the new version of the *Bundeshymne* (see, for example, https://de.wikipedia.org/wiki/Österreichische_Bundeshymne where you can also get an overview of the debates that led to the changes).

The *Bundeshymne* debate and subsequent changes to the anthem highlight the fact that many official texts and documents in German use words and phrases that exclude women. Although the discussions about the *Bundeshymne* show how emotional these debates can get, there is a fairly easy way to change a text such as *Land der Berge* – by finding other, more inclusive words and phrases.

However, German has an additional problem. Unlike English, for example, it distinguishes between three grammatical genders – feminine, masculine and neuter – and it marks gender mor-phologically, for example, *Lehrer/Lehrerin* (teacher), plural *Lehrer/Lehrerinnen* (teachers). The **generic** form tends to be the masculine – when you talk about *Die Lehrer* as a plural form you normally refer to teachers in general; it is the **unmarked** form (although it may also be used as a **marked** form to refer exclusively to male teachers – and that's the problem). *Lehrerinnen* is used only as a marked form, to refer exclusively to female teachers. This can lead to situations where women might feel excluded or the female perspective is not taken into account.

- Analyse the instructions given by the University of Graz in Austria on how to write official reports and documents in a gender-sensitive fashion: https://koordination-gender.uni-graz.at/de/services/geschlechtsneutrale-schreib-und-sprechweise/#c26251.

Another linguistic practice that has seen considerable change as a result of sociopolitical debates is the use of *du* and *Sie* as pronouns of address. As a general rule of thumb for learners of German, *du* is used within the family, amongst friends, with children and with pets (although German philosopher Arthur Schopenhauer was known to address his poodle as *Sie*). However, sociolinguists observed a proliferation in the use of *du* amongst students during the early 1970s resulting from the student uprising of 1968; Werner Besch (1996) noticed that while in 1970 only a few students used the informal *du* amongst themselves, this had been reversed by 1973 when *Sie* was only used amongst students from the more conser-vative spectrum. The revolutionaries of 1968 challenged social hierarchies and flagged this, amongst other ways, by using the more egalitarian *du*.

Du has since become the unmarked form of address amongst the younger generations and to a certain extent beyond; in certain socio-cultural spheres it is the norm to use *du*, such as on most social media platforms. In day-to-day communication it still takes negotiation and careful context analysis to get things right. It is still the older person who normally offers the *du* address as a token of familiarity to a younger acquaintance. Adults meeting for the first time still typically start off by using *Sie* in the first instance, unless they are introduced to each other by common friends.

The Duden website also urges caution:

> Oft ist es gar nicht so einfach, zu entscheiden, ob man beim „Sie" bleiben soll oder zum „Du" übergehen kann. Sicherlich gibt es einige Bereiche oder Branchen, in denen das Duzen an der Tagesordnung ist. Grundsätzlich ist im Geschäftsleben oder bei neuen Kontakten aber zunächst das „Sie" die korrekte Ansprache und gerade im beruflichen Umfeld wird dadurch eine notwendige und durchaus nützliche Distanz

gewahrt; es ist durchaus möglich, dass sich Menschen bedrängt oder nicht respek-
tiert fühlen, wenn sie ungefragt geduzt werden. Kommt man als neuer Kollege in
eine Abteilung, in der es üblich ist, sich zu duzen, sollte man dennoch nicht gleich
mitduzen, sondern zunächst warten, bis das „Du" angeboten wird. Im Berufsleben
bestimmt sich der Rang nach der betrieblichen Hierarchie, d. h., das „Du" wird von
oben nach unten angeboten, der Chef bietet es dem Mitarbeiter an, die ältere Kol-
legin der jüngeren. Doch selbst wenn man selbst in der ranghöheren Position ist, ist
es ratsam, grundsätzlich zurückhaltend zu sein, solange man sein Gegenüber nicht
richtig einschätzen kann. Längst nicht jeder möchte mit allen möglichen Leuten
per „Du" sein, auch (und vielleicht besonders) nicht mit dem Vorgesetzten. Von
wirklich schlechten Manieren zeugt es allerdings, wenn ein Ranghöherer Rangnied-
rigere ungefragt duzt oder wenn Angehörige bestimmter Berufsgruppen grundsätzlich geduzt werden.

Example 6.9 Duden guidelines on the use of *du* and *Sie*
Source: www.duden.de/sprachwissen/sprachratgeber/duzen-oder-siezen

- Devise seven communicative situations in German where it is crucial to get the form of address right. Act out these situations and analyse the results and discussions that follow.

6.5 Conclusion

In this chapter we looked at three areas of the German language where changes can be observed: at the lexical-semantic, morpho-syntactic and pragmatic levels. The analysis of the job advert from 1904 showed that some words are hardly used any more, while oth-ers change their meaning to a certain extent and new words are introduced, either newly created or borrowed from other languages. Changes in the lexicon happen easily and tend to reflect socio-economic and cultural circumstances. Changes in the morpho-syntactic structure of a language are rarer, and the reasons for them tend to be more subtle than they appear. Contrary to public perception, the increase of *weil*+V2 constructions is very unlikely to result from borrowing from English. *Weil*+V2 has been used in spoken lan-guage for a long time, and the qualitative analysis of *weil*+V2 and *weil*+Vend has revealed that we have two constructions that play different roles in communication. Public opinion on how language reflects social reality can also change the way we use language, as we have seen in the debate on the Austrian national anthem. As a result of feminist criticism many institutions in the German-speaking countries have adopted linguistic practices that ensure that men and women are equally referred to. And finally, changing patterns of address may offer a good indication of how social relationships change under particular historical conditions.

Tasks and suggestions for research

Reflective task

What would you now see as the relationship between language variation and language change? What does it mean to say that language change 'doesn't come from nowhere'?

Research tasks

1 Every year, the *Gesellschaft für deutsche Sprache* (*GfdS*) declares what they call the 'Wort des Jahres', the 'Jugendwort des Jahres' and the 'Unwort des Jahres'. Go to their website and find out how the *GfdS* makes their annual decisions. What kinds of discussion can this popular initiative potentially trigger? What does it tell us about public perceptions of linguistic innovation and language change?

2 *Weil* is not the only conjunction that can be found introducing a clause with +Vend (see, for example, Auer and Günthner 2003). Use the GeWiss-corpus (we suggest that you check the sub-corpus DEU-EV, which consists of academic lectures in German) and find examples for *obwohl*: how many instances of clauses beginning with *obwohl* do you find? How many of them are *obwohl*+Vend/*obwohl*+V2 constructions? Are there functional differences?

Project idea

In 2015, the online version of the German weekly newspaper *Die Zeit* asked its users whether they should address each other as *du* or *Sie* when writing commentaries (www.zeit.de/community/2015-05/duzen-siezen-leserkommentare). Analyse the debate and summarise the results. Then conduct your own online survey via social media to gather views of other German-speakers. How might the debate and your research findings influence your own linguistic practices, for example, as an exchange student in a German-speaking country?

Annotated further reading

Androutsopoulos (ed.) (2014) is a collection of contemporary research articles on the question of how the media instigate and shape sociolinguistic change.

Besch (1996) is a readable and informative introduction to the topic of address in German, albeit now rather out of date.

Coupland (2014) is a theoretical reflection on sociolinguistic change and the role the media can potentially play in this process.

Denkler et al. (eds.) (2008) offers a collection of linguistic analyses of current developments in German, which focuses on linguistic change rather than language decay.

Freywald (2010) reflects on historical aspects of word order in subordinate clauses in German.

Günthner, Hüpper and Spieß (eds.) (2012) offer a collection of articles that sums up the current state of what is called gender linguistics in relation to German.

Labov (1994, 2001, 2006) provides a wide-ranging overview of research on sociolinguistic variation and change by one of the pioneers in the field.

Pastor (1995) provides an interesting overview of the history of pronominal address in German.

Pusch (1984) is an entertainingly written text that triggered many of the debates around feminist critiques of linguistic practices in German in the 1980s. A classic.

Praxis Deutsch 215 Sprachwandel (2009) is a special issue of one of the most established journals on the teaching of German language and literature, dedicated to language change. It provides a linguistic introduction and discusses various examples of recent language change in German.

7 New styles of spoken German

7.1 Introduction

In this chapter we deal with an aspect of contemporary language change in the German-speaking countries that should be seen in the wider context of an increasingly globalised and media-influenced world. The three main components of this change are the use of English in many domains of communication (see Chapter 3), an increased visibility of multilingualism in society (see Chapter 9) and the emergence of new forms of speech originating in urban communities, principally as a result of greatly increased migration over the last 25 years. We will focus here on the third component and look at two forces that drive its development: communities of practice amongst young people and the media.

- Can you think of words or phrases you and your peers used when you were teenagers that would have been incomprehensible to your parents? When and where did you use them? Do you still use them?

In the mid-1990s two books were published in Germany that alerted the interested public to a new emerging subculture in urban centres such as Berlin and Frankfurt or the cities in the Ruhr area. First, in 1995 Feridun Zaimoglu published his collection of semi-fictitious interviews with young men from Turkish backgrounds under the title *Kanak Sprak*.

- Where does the word *Kanak* come from? What exactly does it mean? Why would Zaimoğlu and his participants use this term to describe the way they speak?

In Zaimoglu's book, men from Turkish backgrounds living in Germany tell their stories, angrily reclaiming the way they speak German – disregarding many standard rules – as an expression of their identity. The book was highly acclaimed by critics and made Zaimoglu a household name by way of reviews, interviews and appearances on TV talk shows.

- Read the following extract from *Kanak Sprak*. How does it differ from what is normally perceived as standard German?

Ich sag dir, bruder. In diesem land läuft's zum teil stinkig, für'n alemannen is es schon'n aufwand, wenn er dir zum gruße die flosse reicht, und wenn die dich zum frühstück einladen, sagen die dir, du sollst bitteschön brötchen mitbringen und vielleicht auch noch kaffeesahne. Da bist du also nur zum drittel oder viertel willkommen, wenn du mit leeren händen antanzt. Und überhaupt: 'n kanake als freund rangiert ganz unten auf der multikultiliste, besser is'n jamaikanigger mit ner zottelperücke, besser noch'n schmalzlatino, und die ganz heiße oberfesche krone is denn 'n yankee-nigger, auf den das einheimische mösenmonopol abfährt.

(Zaimoglu 1995: 25)

A year later, in 1996, the ethnographer Hermann Tertilt published his study *Turkish Power Boys: Ethnographie einer Jugendbande*, based on participant observation conducted in inner-city Frankfurt. The young men he describes in this book are also mainly from German-Turkish backgrounds. They, too, use language differently from what would be perceived as the typical spoken **vernaculars** of Frankfurt. Neither Zaimoglu nor Tertilt is a linguist, and neither of them claims to have reproduced the exact way their informants spoke German. Both, however, contributed to the trend towards the end of the 1990s that alerted the German public to the concept of groups – mainly young men with Turkish or other migration backgrounds in the urban centres of the country – who had developed their own styles of speaking, variously referred to as *Türkendeutsch*, *Türkenslang*, *Kiezdeutsch*, *Migranten-Slang*, *Ghetto-Deutsch* or *Lan-Sprache*, to list but some of the labels in popular use, many of which were pejorative or derogatory. Earlier studies, in the late 1960s and 1970s, had identified similar phenomena, but at that time they were seen as a form of linguistic deficit amongst first generation migrants and referred to (both by linguists and in public discourse) as *Gastarbeiterdeutsch*. Now it had to be acknowledged that informal, hybrid vernaculars were emerging, alongside knowledge of standard and non-standard varieties of German as well as other languages, as part of the **repertoires** of second and third generation speakers.

7.2   New urban vernaculars

Reactions to these vernaculars were mixed, depending on whether they came from linguists, language purists, media commentators or parts of the entertainment industry. Many linguists were excited by the phenomenon and the prospect of new forms of German emerging, especially since similar developments were observed in other countries, such as Norway, Denmark, the Netherlands, Sweden and the UK. In response, a number of research projects were initiated in order to study the distinct linguistic features and the communicative domains and contexts in which these new ways of speaking were used.

There has been an ongoing debate ever since amongst linguists on whether these forms of speaking should be seen as a **style**, applied in certain communicative contexts for specific purposes, or a **variety**, which would add a new, structurally distinctive form to the many existing regional and social varieties that constitute 'German'. One of the terms used by linguists for such phenomena is **ethnolect**, based on the work of Michael Clyne, who defines ethnolect as the specific way an ethnic group uses a particular language. The term itself, however, is problematic since it merges the notion of ethnicity with that of the first or dominant language a person or group of people speaks: does a child growing up with French as her first language in Germany, for example, speak an ethnolect? Moreover, since features of more than one language may be combined with German (for example, Arabic and Turkish), it might be more appropriate to talk of **multiethnolects**. We will adopt here the now more widely used term **new urban vernaculars** unless we refer to the work of researchers who explicitly use (multi)ethnolect.

The following box lists the most salient features linguists have observed amongst speakers of the new urban vernaculars in Germany, not all of them used systematically and consistently all the time.

1 Coronolization of /ç/ to /ʃ/, e.g. saying 'isch' for 'ich'
2 **Reduction** of initial sound clusters, e.g. /ts/ to /s/, e.g. saying 'swei' for 'zwei'
3 Final /r/ not **vocalised**, e.g. pronouncing *oder* as 'odER' rather than as 'oda'
4 Reduction of long vowels, e.g. saying 'Straße' with a short rather than a long /a/
5 No reduction of unstressed syllables, e.g. saying 'kaufEN' for 'kaufn'
6 No case markers on pronouns and articles, e.g. saying 'sie hat 'nen Fleck auf ihre Hose' for 'auf ihrer Hose'
7 Non-standard word order, e.g. saying 'Danach ich muss zu mein Vater'
8 Omission of pronouns, e.g. saying 'wann hast du fotografiert?' for 'wann hast du sie fotografiert?'
9 Omission of prepositions and articles in directions, e.g. saying 'isch geh Schule' for 'ich gehe zur Schule'
10 Random use of grammatical gender, e.g. saying 'meine Fuß' for 'mein Fuß'
11 Discourse markers such as '(h)ey Alter!', 'lan' (Turkish: man), 'isch schwör', 'yalla' (Arabic: come on)
12 Evaluative adjectives losing some of their semantic value and being applied in new contexts, e.g. 'krass' originally meant 'glaring' or 'jarring' but is used here mainly to mean 'great' or 'interesting'
13 Generalisation of verbs such as 'gehen' and 'machen', e.g. saying 'isch mach disch krankenhausreif' for 'ich schlag dich krankenhausreif'
14 Constructions such as 'Musstu' (from 'dann musst du') or 'Lassma' (from 'lass uns mal') that serve here in order to prompt actions, e.g. 'lassma Schwimmbad' (let's go to swimming pool)
15 Offensive and/or obscene swear words, e.g. 'Spast', 'Fotze', etc.

Salient linguistic features of new urban vernaculars in German

Source: based on Androutsopoulos 2001; Keim and Knöbl 2007; Auer 2013; Wiese 2013

- Read the following extract from a conversation between five teenagers from the Berlin district of Kreuzberg. You may find it unusual to read a transcript of spoken language at first: it helps to read it aloud. Which of the features in the previous box can you identify in this conversation? Which other features here seem to you to be characteristic of informal spoken language in general?

Elif:	Isch kann misch gut bewegen, wa? Ischwöre. Egal, was für ein Hiphopmusik isch höre, ey, mein Körper drinne tanzt voll, Lan. [. . .]
Aymur:	Was steht da auf ihre Hose? [= im Tanzvideo, das im Hintergrund läuft]
Sarah:	Bestimmt ihr Name oder so.
Aymur:	"Melinda" oder so.
Deniz:	Melissa. Mann, die is ein Püppchen, Lan.
Juri:	Ihre Schwester is voll ekelhaft, Alter. Ischwöre.
Sarah:	Ey, weißte, Mann. Lara is ihre Schwester, wa. Die ähneln sisch bisschen.
Elif:	Wer?

Juri:	Sie und Lara.
Elif:	Wer is Lara?
Juri:	Die mit den Knutschfleck immer hier. Du kennst!
Elif:	Mann, die hat tausend! Jeden Tag nen neuen Freund, Mann.
Aymur:	Ja, und die hat immer hier Knutschfleck.

Example 7.1 Gossiping
Source: Wiese 2012: 11–12

In addition to an array of linguistic features typical of the new urban vernaculars, the short exchange in Example 7.1 shows two interesting things: there are not only boys talking, and the names suggest that not all of them are from a Turkish family background. Juri, for example, is a name common in Russian and Ukrainian. So the teenagers here bring more than one language and/or ethnic background into the equation.

Soon, the heightened awareness of the emerging urban vernaculars led to discussions and debates, for example, in print and broadcast mass media such as newspapers, magazines, TV and radio. This newly discovered way of speaking became **indexicalised**, which means that these vernaculars, or isolated features of them, were connected with (or 'indexed') social meanings and values. An example of this can be seen in an article published by the German weekly political magazine *Der Spiegel* in 2006, which focused on a 'failing' school in inner-city Berlin, where more than 80 per cent of students had what is called a *Migrationshintergrund* (migration background), which means that their families have moved to Germany since the 1960s. Here is a short extract:

Aufklärung? Bildung? Lernen, für Zensuren, vielleicht sogar für's Leben?
Was soll der Scheiß?
So reden die Bewohner dieser Welt. *Ey, Mann, ey, Nutte. Killer. Krass*. Es gibt viele "sch"- und "ch"-Laute in dieser Sprache, kaum noch ganze Sätze. *Dreckische Deutsche*, so reden sie.

Example 7.2 Extract from article in *Der Spiegel*
Source: *Der Spiegel* 14/2006, p. 24

• Which features of the new urban vernaculars are referred to in this short extract from the article? Who are the people the magazine characterises by this way of speaking?

Example 7.2 shows how linguistic features of the new urban vernaculars were indexicalised in relation to a subculture of perceived social deprivation in migrant communities situated in urban centres. But while parts of the population were horrified at the scenarios depicted by the press, others were fascinated; speakers of new urban vernaculars had the reputation of being tough, streetwise, unashamedly politically incorrect and masculine. This **covert prestige** was and still is appealing, for example, to rebellious teenagers and to hip hop artists.

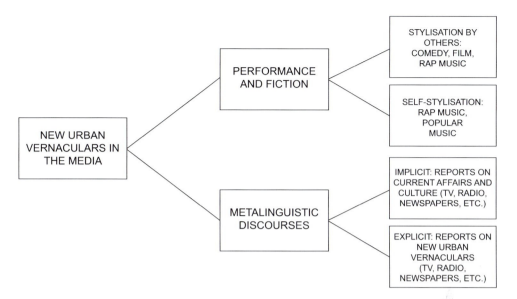

Figure 7.1 Representation of new urban vernaculars in the media
Source: based on Androutsopoulos 2007: 128

Comedians started to draw on the newly developing stereotypes by incorporating elements of urban vernaculars, or inner-city characters speaking them, into their performances, which turned out to be widely popular, if controversial.

• Watch the clip *Erkan und Stefan bei der Feuerwehr* on YouTube (www.youtube.com/watch?v=Vlo9YFLo2Nw). Which stereotypes are drawn upon, and how are they connected with linguistic features? How do you think different audiences might react to this sketch?

Figure 7.1 represents the role the media played in the emergence of new urban vernaculars. On the one hand, they were presented to and received by the wider public through reports in the media indexicalising them in relation to social problems, lack of education and a minority supposedly unwilling to integrate into German society. As such they were part of **metalinguistic discourses**, which is the way people talk about language and its use. On the other hand, new urban vernaculars were used by artists and performers in hip hop music, comedy shows, TV series and movies, creating a sometimes rather stereotypical image of urban vernacular speakers.

7.3   Becoming mainstream

As we have seen in the first part of this chapter, features of new urban vernaculars have been applied in stylised form in a variety of performances, distributed to wider audiences via TV, film or YouTube, and have become imbued with social meaning. Catalogues of indexicalised linguistic features have the potential to be **enregistered**, which means that they can be perceived collectively as constituting a new style or variety of a language, rather than simply as spontaneous or idiosyncratic speech. This process of **indexicalisation** and **enregisterment** is driven by complex, intertwined discourses between speakers, the wider public, linguists and the media, as you could see previously in Figure 7.1. The next step is to understand how a new style or manner of speaking, such as the new urban vernaculars in German, can become part of spoken German in a more general way.

Figure 7.2 shows how Auer (2003, 2013) has distinguished three phases of development in relation to new urban vernaculars – which he calls ethnolects – and their role in language variation and change in the context of German. The first stage is a *primary ethnolect*, spoken mainly (but not exclusively) by young males with a migration family background. In the second stage, primary ethnolect has been turned – indexicalised – by the media into a *secondary ethnolect*, by focusing on selected features and stereotypes and by making it known to a wider public, for example, in comedy programmes such as Stefan and Erkan. This popularised version is then picked up in the third stage by teenagers from all backgrounds, who use features of new urban vernaculars either playfully or in order to gain street credit (*tertiary ethnolect*).

So what happens when elements of the new urban vernaculars – *tertiary ethnolect* in Auer's terminology – become mainstream? In 2013, the film *Fack ju Göhte* entered German cinemas and became an overnight success. This comedy tells the story of a school in an unspecified urban setting, not unlike the notorious Berlin school mentioned in Example 7.2. The main protagonist is a criminal with unspecified migration background named Zeki Müller, who is trying to retrieve the loot from his last robbery, after having been released from prison. Unfortunately, his amateur partner in crime buried the money on a construction site, by now the new sports hall of a comprehensive school, the Goethe Gesamtschule. In order to gain access to the grounds, Zeki manages to get a job as a temporary supply teacher and starts digging for his treasure at night, though he soon finds he is surprisingly successful at his cover job. You can find trailers for the film on YouTube.

• Read the following transcript of a scene in the film (Example 7.3) aloud. Write a list with (a) features typical of new urban vernaculars (based on the box in section 7.2) and (b) features related to informal spoken language in general. Compare your results with those from Example 7.1.

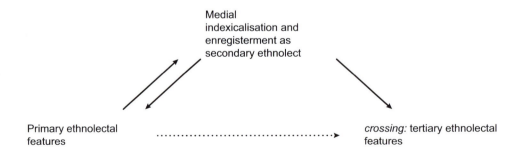

Figure 7.2 Development of primary, secondary and tertiary ethnolects
Source: based on Auer 2013: 12

CHA = Chantal (pupil)
HAU = HAU . . . (pupil from other school)
ZEK = Zeki Müller (supply teacher, main character)
ZEY = Zeynep (pupil)
(2.0) = 2-second pause / silence

Context: Zeki works as a supply teacher in a comprehensive school in a German city where many students struggle to achieve high grades. He is talking to his pupils Chantal and Zeynep about test results when they notice a fight between a group of boys from their own school ('nerds') with students from somewhere else ('Hauptschule').

08   ZEK: (5.0) ((breathes out smoke))
            in diesem test den ihr neulich gemacht habt ne?
            In this test you did a while ago

09   CHA: hä?
            What?

10   ZEK: ((smokes)) (2.0) du warst die beste
            You were the best

11   kann sogar sein dass du ne klasse überspringen
            wirst
            You might even have to skip a year

12   CHA: (3.0) aber isch hab doch voll die schleschten
            NOTen herr müller?
            But I've totally got the worst grades Mr Müller

13   ZEK: (2.0) ja: weil du unterFORdert bist-
            Yes because you're not sufficiently challenged

14   ist oft so bei hochbegabten-
            It's often like that with gifted students

15   ab jetzt wirst du speziell gefördert-
            From now on you'll be specially supported

16   kann sein dass du schon mit (2.5) SIEBzehn
            dein abi haben wirst,
            You might even get your A-levels at seventeen

17   ZEY: [a:h]

18   CHA: [wu:h_a:h]

19   oh mein gott
            Oh my god

20   ZEK: allerdings musst du aufhören dich von den
            andern so RUNterziehen zu lassen-
            *Although you have to stop letting yourself be
            pulled back by the others*

((Chantal nods several times))

21   und n_bisschen mehr einsatz zeigen-
            and show a bit more engagement

22   ZEY: ey meint der MIsch oda was?
            Oi does he mean me or what

23   CHA: ne::in,
            Nooo

24   herr müller wirklisch sie verarschen misch
            nisch, oda?
            Mr Müller you're not taking the piss are you

25   guck_ma isch zitter schon voll,
            Look, I'm really shaking

26   ZEK: schantal ich bin SELber aufgeregt-
            Chantal I'm excited myself

27   so jemand wie du das passiert ei_m nur alle
            zehn jahre,
            *Someone like you only comes along once every
            ten years*

((noises in the background))

28   CHA: oh mein gott,
            Oh my god

29   muss ich DOch nisch kassiererin werden,
            *So I don't have to work at the checkout after
            all*

((commotion by the bins))

30 ZEK: wer sind denn die da unten
           Who's that lot over there

31 ZEY: die behinderten werden von der hauptschule
           abgezogen
           The retards are being mugged by the other school

((other school's pupils' threats in the background))

32 ZEK: die sehen nich behinderter aus als ihr
           They don't look more retarded than you

33 CHA: wohl
           Yes they do

34 ZEY: ja mann wie nerds (1.0)
           Yeah man like nerds

35   jugend forscht un so
           Like, 'young scientists' and that

((commotion; Chantal, Zeynep and Müller watch))

36 ZEK: ja helft den=n mal
           Well, go and help them then

37 CHA: waru:m?
           Why

38 ZEK: weil du selber bald n nerd sein wirst
           *Because you're going to be a nerd yourself
           soon*

39   weil das die EINzigen männer sind die dich noch
           gut finden
           *Because they're the only men who will still
           like you*

40   wenn du erstma CHEmie studierst
           when you start studying chemistry

41   leberwurstflecken auf_m kittel und fettige haare
           hast
           and have stains on your labcoat and greasy hair

42   CHA: isch schwöre herr müller sie machen misch so
            fertisch
            (3.0) ((thinks))
            I swear Mr Müller you're doing my head in

43   ok=lass sie boxen
            ok let's beat them up

44   ZEY: oah=schantal eigentlich gar kein bock auf
            schlägerei=ne
            Ah Chantal really not in the mood for a fight

((Chantal and Zeynep get involved))

45   CHA: lass sie in ruhe
            Leave them alone

46   HAU: glaubst du bist besser weil du gymi gehst
            Think you're better coz you go to a grammar

47   CHA: die gehen auf meine schule also lass sie in
            ruhe=[sonst]
            They go to my school so leave them alone or

48   HAU: [<<screaming>> ey]
            Hey

((screams and commotion between pupil from other school
and Chantal))

49   ZEK: ey (1.0) die hat n messer
            Oi she's got a knife

((commotion stops))

50   HAU: <<laughing>> ha_hast du angst
            Ha are you scared

((Chantal and Zeynep overpower pupil from other school))

51   HAU: lass mich los alter
            Let me go mate

52   verpiss dich mann (1.0) schlampe alter (1.0)
            piss off man, slut

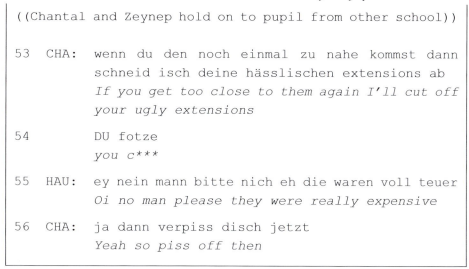

```
((Chantal and Zeynep hold on to pupil from other school))

53  CHA:   wenn du den noch einmal zu nahe kommst dann
            schneid isch deine hässlischen extensions ab
            If you get too close to them again I'll cut off
            your ugly extensions

54          DU fotze
            you c***

55  HAU:   ey nein mann bitte nich eh die waren voll teuer
            Oi no man please they were really expensive

56  CHA:   ja dann verpiss disch jetzt
            Yeah so piss off then
```

Example 7.3 Extract from the film *Fack ju Göhte*
Source: Transcription from Reershemius and Ziegler 2015

- Which characters in the film use new urban vernacular features in their speech, and which do not?
- Which distinct social groups seem to be identified in the film according to the way they speak?
- A film is a piece of art, based on a script. What is the relationship between the language used in a film and the vernacular language actually spoken in everyday life?

In the extract from the film only the teenagers Chantal and Zeynep use some new urban vernacular features: mainly coronalisation of the sound /ç/ to /ʃ/ (for example, *isch* instead of *ich*) throughout the transcript; in one short exchange the omission of pronouns, prepositions, articles or verbs (Chantal: ok=lass sie boxen. Zeynep: oah=schantal eigentlich gar kein bock auf schlägerei=ne); and once the stereotypical discourse marker *isch schwör*. While the speech in this extract may seem to be an 'authentic' representation of the new urban vernacular, it is reduced to a small number of features.

Furthermore, speakers who use these features do not all have an obvious migration background: Zeynep does; Chantal does not. The teacher speaks without any trace of new urban vernacular forms, although his name indicates that he is from a mixed Turkish-German background: Zeki is a popular Turkish first name, whereas Müller is an almost prototypical German surname. So the use of new urban vernacular forms as portrayed in the film is clearly de-ethnicized; rather than being an indicator of ethnic background, it has become a marker of age and to a certain extent social class, as more middle-class teenagers in the film do not speak like this. This way of speaking illustrates what Peter Auer calls tertiary ethnolect (Figure 7.2): a popularised version of new urban vernacular speech, based on a limited number of indexicalised features, is picked up by teenagers from all backgounds, who use them either playfully or in order to gain street credit.

7.4   Metalinguistic debates on new urban vernaculars

Metalinguistic debates on these speech styles or varieties are widespread in the German media. Many people feel that the German language is threatened by the way some teenagers adopt features of new urban vernaculars in their speech.

- Read the following newspaper article published in the *Berliner Kurier* in 2012. Who are the people engaged in the debate on '*Kiezdeutsch*', as new urban vernaculars are called in this article? What points are they making? Who are the 'language experts' the article refers to? What is your own opinion on these issues?

DANACH ICH GEH' SCHULE

Sprach-Experten warnen vor dem „Kiezdeutsch"

Von Ronald Gorny

Wirbel um das zunehmende Kiezdeutsch unserer Jugendlichen. Experten laufen Sturm gegen die Verschandelung unserer Sprache.

„Ich bin Kotti. Lassma hier aussteigen." Sprachforscherin Heike Wiese (45) spricht in ihrem Buch „Kiezdeutsch" von einem „neuen und kreativen Dialekt" und einer „Bereicherung für unsere Sprache" (KURIER berichtete). Der Verein Deutsche Sprache sieht dies völlig anders. Geschäftsführer Holger Klatte: „Kiezsprache ist ein Warnzeichen dafür, dass in bestimmten Regionen und Ballungsräumen wie Berlin die Sprachentwicklung vernachlässigt worden ist. Zuwanderer sowie Kinder und Jugendliche aus sozial schwachen Schichten sind nicht ausreichend gefördert worden."

Klatte fordert daher mehr Anstrengungen aufseiten der Politik: „Wir haben nichts gegen das Erlernen der Muttersprache bei Migranten-Kindern. Aber diese müssen bereits in der Kita auch die deutsche Sprache beherrschen. Wir brauchen dort Fachleute, die sich mit Sprachvermittlung auskennen, auch wenn dies mehr Geld kostet."

Auch die Vorsitzende des Landes-Schülerausschusses, Beatrice Knörich, kann sich mit dem Stummeldeutsch in unserer Stadt nicht anfreunden: „Das klingt voll daneben. Ich finde es äußerst bedenklich, dass auch deutsche Jugendliche mittlerweile so sprechen."

Example 7.4 Newspaper article on *Kiezdeutsch*

Source: *Berliner Kurier*, 15.2.2012, www.berliner-kurier.de/kiez-stadt/sprach-experten-warnen-vor-dem-kiezdeutsch-,7169128,11640984.html

Metalinguistic debates take place constantly in various different contexts and in relation to many languages, varieties, dialects and styles (see Chapter 10), and American linguist Barbara Johnstone claims that metalinguistic discourses can be instrumental in the emergence of new forms of language. Her example is the development of 'Pittsburghese': a limited set of pronunciations, phrases and words that have become connected by **mediatisation** (see Chapter 6) to the way people from Pittsburgh (Pennsylvania) speak. Mediatisation means here that these linguistic features have frequently been associated by the media with a particular place, Pittsburgh, thus establishing the notion of a distinct form of speaking.

- Who participates in metalinguistic debates on language issues? Can you think of similar debates in relation to other language(s)? Have you encountered similar phenomena to Pittsburghese?

7.5   Conclusion

In this chapter we looked at new ways of speaking German that are emerging through a complex interplay of contact-induced youth styles and the media. This started as a specific way of using language amongst teenagers – many of whom came from families who had migrated to Germany since the 1970s – in the urban environments of cities such as Berlin or Frankfurt. It was picked up by the media, thus turning these ways of speaking into the object of comedy, on the one hand, and public debate, on the other. Studies show that elements of these contact-induced youth styles have now spread beyond their original groups of speakers and form part of the repertoires of young German-speakers.

Tasks and suggestions for research

Reflective task

As a student of German you are no doubt constantly reminded – for example, by your teachers – to use standard forms when you speak or write in German. In this chapter you have seen how non-standard forms of German play an important part in developing new styles of speaking and using language creatively. What implications do you think this might have for you as a language learner?

Research tasks

1   The new styles of speaking in German discussed in this chapter have provoked conflicting responses from the general public and in the media – some enthusiastic, others hostile. Gather a representative range of comments (you could start with the internet portal kiezdeutsch.de) and summarise the different kinds of reactions expressed.
2   Contact-induced youth styles have also developed in non-German contexts – for example, in multilingual urban settings in the UK, the Netherlands and Sweden. Conduct a literature review and compare your results with this chapter.

Project idea

Record an informal discussion between your friends and transcribe five to ten minutes of the conversation, using the transcription conventions illustrated in Example 7.3 (or another set of conventions, if you find one that you feel is better suited for the purpose of your project). Then analyse the transcript in terms of the use of what you would consider standard and non-standard features of English (or whatever language the conversation is conducted in). Can you identify any common patterns of language use amongst the participants in this respect? Is there any evidence of what you might call new urban vernacular usage?

Annotated further reading

Androutsopoulos (ed.) (2014) is a collection of articles on the role of the media in processes of socio-linguistic change, including a chapter on 'Multicultural London English'.

Androutsopoulos and Lauer (2014) summarise and evaluate the metalinguistic debates around the new urban vernaculars in Germany.

Auer (2013) sums up the most recent debates and theories on new urban vernaculars in German, focusing on the question of whether they can be categorised as styles, varieties or dialects.

Auer and Dirim (2003) offer an interesting perspective on Turkish-German language contact, focusing on speakers who grew up with German as their first language but use (elements of) Turkish in their daily communicative practices.

Deppermann (2007a) analyses what Auer (2003) calls *tertiary ethnolect* – features of new urban vernaculars used by teenagers of all linguistic and social backgrounds as part of a general youth style.

Freywald et al. (2013) gives an overview of research into contact-induced youth styles in three northern European countries.

Keim (2012), focusing on Turkish-speakers in Germany, describes and analyses the sociolinguistic context and the linguistic practices of this community. One chapter deals with what we are calling new urban vernaculars.

Kotthoff (2004) analyses how selected features of new urban vernaculars are adapted by comedians to create stage personalities, thus contributing to the indexicalisation of a small number of linguistic forms and phrases.

Pfaff (2005) shows that the language depicted in Zaimoglu's book *Kanak Sprak* is first and foremost a piece of literary fiction.

Wiese (2012) is a very readable introduction to new urban vernaculars – '*Kiezdeutsch*', in Wiese's terminology – in Germany, based on the author's research projects. Wiese's work led to many controversies in the media and amongst linguists because she classifies *Kiezdeutsch* as a new German dialect, a notion contested by many fellow linguists that also infuriates many German-speakers. The internet portal Kiezdeutsch.de, initiated by Wiese, also provides interesting linguistic data and examples of metalinguistic discussions on the new urban vernaculars (www.kiezdeutsch.de/aufeinenblick.html).

8   Mediated language

8.1   Introduction

Ever since the emergence of writing, the use of media of one kind or another has shaped the way humans communicate. Most importantly, perhaps, it has 'translocated' communication. When, for example, in Ancient Egypt a writer carved hieroglyphs into stone, the reader of this text could be in another place or even in another time. In other words, communication became possible beyond the immediate here and now of spoken interaction. The development of media has always been connected to technological innovation such as, for example, the printing press in the fifteenth century, allowing for greater access to books and pamphlets. During the nineteenth century, the rotation press made the mass distribution of newspapers possible, followed by the telegraph, telephone, radio and television. We refer to newspapers, radio and later television as mass media due to their extended reach, in terms of both geographical coverage and number of users.

Currently, we find ourselves in the middle of yet another media revolution. When the use of mobile phones and email communication became more widespread in the richer countries of the world during the early 1990s, hardly anybody could have foreseen the dramatic changes communication would undergo globally within a very short time. In 2015, an estimated 3.4 billion people used the internet (www.internetworldstats.com/stats.htm), meaning communication occurred through the use of networked digital devices such as computers or smartphones. Their use now extends beyond one-to-one or one-to-many communication to a vast number of purposes: users watch films, listen to music, follow television and radio programmes, pay their bills, buy and sell commodities, monitor their health, get directions, check the weather forecast and so on. In the UK, the average Briton aged 16 and older spent ten hours each week actively using the internet in 2005. By 2015 this time had doubled to 20 hours and 30 minutes (http://consumers.ofcom.org.uk/news/time-spent-online-doubles/).

In this chapter we will look at the impact of these new forms of **computer-mediated communication** (CMC) – the term most frequently used in sociolinguistics to describe and analyse forms of interaction via networked digital devices such as computers – on contemporary patterns of language use.

8.2   The growth of the internet and its impact on language use

To put this topic in context, let's first look at some statistics on German and CMC and compare them with global developments. In 2015, 88 per cent of the population of Germany were internet users (in Austria, the figure was 83 per cent and in Switzerland 87 per cent).

- Go to the website Internet World Stats (www.internetworldstats.com/europa2.htm#ch) and compare the statistics for internet users in German-speaking countries with the figures for the United States, Brazil, Peru, Burundi, Nigeria, India and Nepal (or indeed, any other country). Your results will indicate that the percentage of internet users per country can differ quite dramatically: what could be the reasons for these differences?
- Access to, and use of, digital media is not equally distributed across the world. The German-speaking countries, however, rank amongst those with the highest levels of access. Compare the results for the German-speaking countries with the information provided in Figures 8.1 and 8.2.

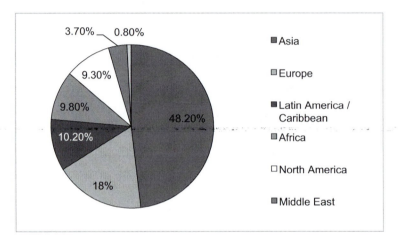

Figure 8.1 Internet users in the world by regions (November 2015)

Source: based on Internet World Stats

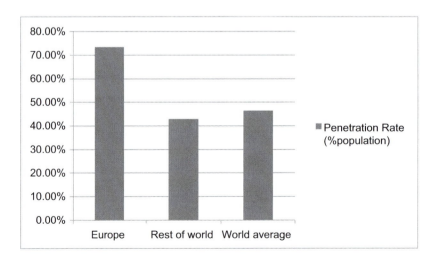

Figure 8.2 Internet penetration in Europe (November 2015)

Source: based on Internet World Stats

The statistics show that in Europe far more people are internet users compared with the world average, and users in the German-speaking countries are well above even the European average. But what about the other side of the coin: which languages are most widely used on the internet?

- Compare the figures for internet users with those in Figure 8.3, which indicates the percentage of websites according to languages they are written in (of course, many websites are multilingual, in the sense that they feature more than one language, but the statistics here assume a main or 'matrix' language for each site).

Figure 8.3 shows that the largest proportion of internet content is written in English. This is obviously not surprising as English has been the dominant language of the internet since its development within an English-speaking environment. The internet is a media platform of global reach, and the global and globalising language of the present is, of course, English (see Chapter 3). Interestingly from our point of view, though, German is in third place, even though there are fewer speakers of German globally than of other languages with lower percentages than it in this list. German is therefore disproportionately represented on the internet compared to other major languages.

In its first decades, the internet was first and foremost a platform created by a technology-savvy minority for a vast number of users who were mainly acting as consumers. This changed when technologies became more widely available, which widened commentary functions on websites and allowed users to become creators of web content themselves by posting text, film, pictures or music. The watershed for these developments, often referred to as 'Web 2.0', a term coined in 2005, is regarded as the moment when social media became widespread. For the UK, the communications regulator Ofcom states that the use of social media has tripled since 2007; in 2015, 72 per cent of internet users aged 16 and older had a

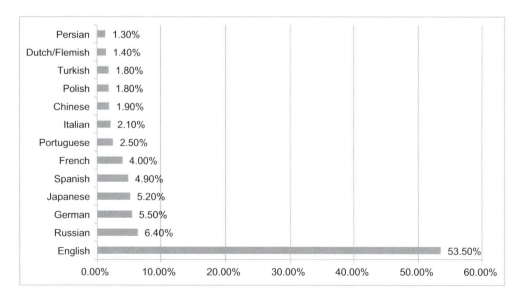

Figure 8.3 Websites worldwide according to their main languages

Source: https://w3techs.com/technologies/overview/content_language/all

social media profile compared with just 22 per cent in 2007. The biggest growth, however, has been seen amongst 35–44 year olds: 80 per cent of internet users in this age group were active in social media in 2015 compared with 12 per cent in 2007. A big surge could also be observed amongst older internet users turning to social media: in 2014 nearly half (49 per cent) of 55–64 year olds had a social media profile, compared with 33 per cent the year before (see http://consumers.ofcom.org.uk/news/time-spent-online-doubles/).

- Find comparable data for the German-speaking countries. Are the trends similar to those in the UK?

One of the most significant effects of this growth in active participation by web users has been in changes in the way people use language and communicate in general online. For example, many forms of 'digital writing' – texts/messages, comments, exchanges on discussion forums, social media posts and so on – are carried out spontaneously and sent to recipients or made publicly available without further reflection or editing. In such contexts, the most important considerations are immediacy of content, succinctness of expression and a lively, engaging style. One obvious consequence of this is a greater tolerance of unconventional grammatical and orthographical practices, such as the use of incomplete sentences, abbreviated word forms and a consistent use of lower case. What, then, are the more general implications of changes in our linguistic practices when we express ourselves and communicate online? In the next section, we'll consider in more detail what 'digital writing' entails.

- Collect all the digital writing you do/receive in one day. Compile all of it into one electronic document and apply your spell-checking tool. Analyse the results: how does your material compare with (let's say) writing in an average newspaper or magazine in terms of grammar and orthography? Why do you and your correspondents write differently from the authors of these other texts?

8.3   Digital writing

Computer-mediated communication has clearly changed the way we interact with each other. But does it change the way we use language? Does it change our languages? As in previous chapters we will approach these questions by applying a speaker- (or in this case user-) focused approach, and we will look at the individual **repertoires** of **linguistic resources** that users bring to computer-mediated communication.

The notion of linguistic repertoires is a central term in sociolinguistics, introduced by John J. Gumperz, who defined it as 'the totality of distinct language varieties, dialects and styles employed in a community' (Gumperz 1982: 155). The concept has recently been revised in order to develop approaches to the study of language and communication that are usage-based and focus on the linguistic practices of speakers as agents. In other words, language is studied here not as a system in structural terms but as a means of expression and communication in specific situations and circumstances for particular speakers and listeners. The term *repertoire* is commonly used now to point to 'the total complex of communicative resources that we find among the subjects we study' (Blommaert and Backus 2011: 3). These 'subjects' are people, whose biographies determine what exactly their individual linguistic repertoires contain; for example, different varieties, genres, styles, words, sounds and grammars of one or more languages. In the case of multilingual repertoires it is often the case that the components drawn from some constituent languages will be more developed than those from others and that these repertoires are in a constant process of evolution and change.

As we pointed out in the previous section, with the advent of social media we have entered a stage where the average internet users are not only consumers of content but creators of content themselves. In doing so, users bring their whole repertoire of linguistic resources to the task, and since the newly developing platforms for communication on the internet are not 'owned' or 'policed' by authoritative institutions such as the education system, editors or critics – normally gatekeepers for the adherence to linguistic norms and standards – almost 'anything goes' in this far less constrained context. Furthermore, internet content is now multi-medial and alongside text may consist of pictures, music, film clips or audio-recordings. The vast majority of user activity, however, is currently still conducted on the basis of writing.

In sociolinguistic terms, digital writing can occur on a continuum, where we adhere to the standard norms of writing and **orthography** at one extreme and completely ignore them at the other. Some forms of digital writing are shaped by institutional conventions, while others are open to inventiveness and creativity. We can observe an increase in what linguists refer to as '**vernacular literacy**', writing close to the way people speak or are perceived to speak. This is not a new phenomenon: forms of vernacular literacy existed in the past, for example, in letter-writing, when people used features of spoken language in order to **index** closeness and engage in language play or simply because they were not aware of existing standard conventions. In fact, for most of the dominant standard languages of the present such as English, French, German, Russian, Spanish and so on, amongst the first written texts were examples of this.

The internet, particularly social media, provides ample platforms for innovative forms of vernacular literacy. Amongst other things, this also leads to languages that were formerly predominantly spoken to acquire written forms, as emerging studies on Romani, Low German, Najdi Arabic and many more examples show; users simply write in the language they normally speak and create an agreed form of writing with other users in the process itself. This raises the question whether the internet can play a part in the efforts to maintain and preserve minority languages, many of which are predominantly spoken and not written, by creating new domains of language use.

- Think of ways and means by which computer-mediated communication can help to maintain and support minority languages.

Another question is whether digital writing practices can bring about language change (see also Chapter 6). Most of the linguistic phenomena we observe online also exist offline, but they are used, regrouped, reworked and adapted in different orders of frequency and contexts online. Look, for example, at the Oxford Dictionaries' 'word of the year' for 2015: it is an emoji (or emoticon), the laughing smiley face with tears. Pictographs such as, for example, hearts, crosses and smiley faces have been in use for a long time, mainly as part of informal, vernacular writing or graffiti. With digital writing they have become a communication tool used by millions on a daily basis.

Another phenomenon of online language is the use of **acronyms**. Acronyms are certainly not a new linguistic practice either: they are notoriously common, for example, in institutional or administrative texts. As part of digital writing, however, they are used at new levels of frequency and creativity. In German online communication, many of the acronyms used are taken from English, such as LOL, OMG, etc. There is, however, also a set of language-specific acronyms that has developed for online communication. The following is an (incomplete) list of German online acronyms currently in use for the letters A to D (see www.hschoepke.de/internet/slang/a_4.htm):

> abF – allerbeste/r Freund/in
> AdAadS – Aus den Augen, aus dem Sinn
> anW – auf nimmer Wiedersehen
> AS – Ansichtssache
> bbb – bis bald, Baby
> bd – bis dann
> BF – Blödfrau
> bG – Breites Grinsen
> bl – bitte lächeln
> BM – Blödmann
> bs – bis später
> bwai – bis wann auch immer
> bwd – bin wieder da
> daM – denk an Murphy
> DAU – dümmster anzunehmender User (Luser)
> dbddhkp – doof bleibt doof, da helfen keine Pillen
> dbel – du bist ein Lügner
> dg – dumm gelaufen
> DK – Dummkopf
> dn – du nervst
> dvHl – das verdammte Handbuch lesen

In addition to acronyms, Rebus writing – the combination of pictures, symbols and letters – has become an established feature of digital writing, particularly in social media; 'b4' for *before* and 'gr8' for *great* are familiar examples in the English context.

• Find (or invent) examples of Rebus writing in German.

Another feature frequently used online in the German-speaking context is the non-finite, uninflected form of the verb, also known as the '*Erikativ*', an allusion to the first translator into German (and editor) of Mickey Mouse cartoons, Erika Fuchs, who introduced the form to wider audiences (see Figure 8.4).

• The following comment on the use of the *Erikativ* in digital writing was published in the *Wiener Zeitung* in 2007 but has not lost any of its relevance. Read the article and decide whether you consider the frequent use of the *Erikativ* a creative use of language or as the beginning of the end of the inflected verb.

Ächz, grummel, schluck war schon in den Sechzigerjahren der Schrecken aller Deutschlehrer. Heute haben die 'Erikative' aus einem anderen Grund Hochkonjunktur. Wer ein E-Mail oder ein SMS schreibt, will Zeit und Platz sparen, er lässt alles weg, was zur Verständigung nicht unbedingt notwendig ist. Das Prinzip wird jetzt nicht mehr ausschließlich dazu verwendet, um Lautäußerungen und Geräusche wiederzugeben.

So gut wie jedes Zeitwort kann auf seinen Wortstamm reduziert werden, sofern es im weitesten Sinn dazu dient, Gefühle auszudrücken. Aus "Ich freue mich!" wird ***freu***, aus "Es ist zum Heulen!" wird ***heul***, aus "Ich umarme dich!" wird ***knuddel***. In der Wissenschaft streitet man darüber, was von dieser Entwicklung zu halten ist. Die einen sehen darin eine neue Dimension der Verständigung. Es handle sich um einen Versuch, all das schriftlich auszudrücken, was in der mündlichen Kommunikation nur durch Mimik, Gestik oder durch Körperhaltungen vermittelt wird. Die anderen befürchten eine sprachliche Verarmung. Es werde nicht mehr lange dauern, bis die Jugend den Gebrauch der Verb-Endungen verlernt hat.

(*Wiener Zeitung*, 10 April 2007)

The examples in this section have shown that the principles of digital writing, such as non-standard spelling, use of emoticons and abbreviations and Rebus writing, are global linguistic techniques used by millions across the world. However, they become a local practice when applied in the context of a particular language and embedded in specific cultural

Figure 8.4 Example of the use of the '*Erikativ*' in cartoons
Source: Rosa 2008: 67

environments. Another specific linguistic practice that is emerging in German-speaking online contexts is the use of regional varieties and dialects. Consider the following two examples, both taken from Facebook. Example 8.1 shows teenage users, whereas the contributors to Example 8.2 are in late middle age.

• Analyse the ways the participants in both exchanges employ different languages (and specific varieties of languages) in their communication. Why do you think they do this?

(Users A, B and C: male, 18 to 19 years old, from Switzerland)

A: Suecht öppert en Job? Churzfristig, ned lang. Bi mir melde :)
B: jajajaja ab wenn?
C: this nigga here. xD

A: Is anybody looking for a job? Short-term, nothing long. Get in contact with me. :)
B: yesyesyesyes from when?
C: this nigga here. xD

Example 8.1 Facebook thread 1

Example 8.2 is a dialogue from the Facebook group *Lustige plattdeutsche Wörter* (Funny words in Low German).

(A: female, in her 50s; B: male, more than 60; C: female, age unknown)

A: Kenn jie noch stiekelstarn?
B: Jo dat kenn ik! 'Stichlinge' (kleiner Fisch), die haben wir früher immer im Graben gefangen!
A: ich ok!!
C: As kind heb de ok in Schlot fangen un bi mien Goldfischen inschmetten. Anner Dag wern mien Goldfischen dod!!!
D: ick heeb de mit senke fangen
E: Jau, D, eenmol 400 Stück an een Daag, bi mi achter'd Huus!

A: Do you remember 'stiekelstarn'?
B: Yes, I do. 'Sticklebacks' (small fish), we used to catch them in ditches.
A: Me too!
C: As a child I also caught them in a ditch and then threw them in with my goldfish. The next day my goldfish were dead!!!
D: I caught them with a bait net.
E: Yes, D, 400 in one day once, at my place, behind the house!

Example 8.2 Facebook thread 2

Although the Facebook group in Example 8.2 is dedicated to Low German, users A, B and C use both Low German and standard German in this short exchange. They translate from Low

German to standard German ('stiekelstarn' => 'Stichlinge'), switch from one variety to the other within an utterance ('ich ok': standard German ich and LG ok) and borrow from standard German in an LG utterance (senke, from standard German *Köderfischsenke*, 'bait net').

This brings us back to the issue of repertoires: individual users have complex repertoires that include regional varieties such as Swiss German or Low German in the previous examples. They also have access to certain elements and phrases from other languages in very specific contexts, for example, English phrases from rap music, as user C in Example 8.1 demonstrates. All users in these two examples therefore have access to multilingual repertoires.

• Write your own linguistic biography: What language(s) did you grow up with? Do you have access – active or passive – to a regional variety or accent? Which language(s) did you learn at school or outside school? Which language(s) do you use in digital writing on social media? How and why, exactly?

Research into linguistic biographies has shown that the majority of speakers even in predominantly 'monolingual' societies have access to a multilingual repertoire, although they may only draw on some languages and varieties sporadically. The various practices in which speakers use their multilingual repertoires have been gathered by recent research under the heading '**translanguaging**'. Linguists now typically analyse multi- or bilingualism as extended repertoires rather than the co-occurrence of two or more language systems in the mind of the same speaker, and the term *translanguaging* is used to capture the dynamic ways in which speakers exploit (features of) different languages and varieties to achieve particular communicative effects. Speakers apply their whole linguistic repertoire according to the communicative requirements of specific social settings and situations and invent new words or ways to put things; borrow words or phrases from other languages, varieties and styles; switch in and out of two or more languages, varieties and styles; or translate from one into another. Many of these practices are similar to those we discussed in the context of **new urban vernaculars** in Chapter 7, and as Examples 8.1 and 8.2 previously showed translanguaging flourishes in less restricted contexts such as social media platforms. People draw creatively on their repertoires in such contexts for various purposes, such as language play, humour, signalling in or out group communication – or 'because they can' :-).

8.4   Conclusion

In this chapter we looked at some ways in which computer-mediated communication shapes and changes how people interact when using language digitally. At a macro level we observed that the percentage of CMC users in the German-speaking countries is particularly high compared with many other countries. This applies also to web content in German and is an indicator of wealth, economic power and the level of literacy in the German-speaking countries. Linguistic practices online are still predominantly based on writing. We discussed features of digital writing and its impact – current and potential – on communication in general and on German in particular. Thus far, the less restrictive nature of many internet platforms, especially those subsumed under the heading 'social media', allows users to apply features of their linguistic repertoires to writing that were formerly mainly confined to spoken language. It also encourages the linguistic practices we summarised under the term *translanguaging* and which allow for innovative and creative ways to use language.

Tasks and suggestions for research

Reflective task

In what ways has this chapter made you reflect on your own digital writing practices? As a student of German, can you think of creative ways you could exploit your knowledge of German alongside English (and other languages or varieties in your repertoire) in different forms of self-expression or communication online?

Research tasks

1   Look at the data provided by the *ARD-ZDF Online Studie* conducted in 2016 (www. ard-zdf-onlinestudie.de/index.php?id=541). Analyse how the profiles and activities of internet users have changed over the last 15 years, paying special attention to different age groups.
2   Find a German language internet discussion forum aimed primarily at participants outside the German-speaking countries. What topics are addressed? Is the discussion entirely in German – if not, which other languages are used and in what ways?
3   Go to the Wikipedia website and find out what the project's overall aims and philosophies are. Choose one of the minority languages from the German-speaking countries, such as North Frisian or Sorbian, and look at its Wikipedia profile: How many Wikipedia sites have been published in this language? Find out who authored them. To what extent do you think the Wikipedia project can support efforts to maintain and preserve minority languages?

Project idea

Draw up a list of minority languages spoken within Austria, Germany and Switzerland. Choose one of these languages and do research online in order to establish its web-profile. For example, how many websites written in the minority language can you find? How many websites feature the language as a topic? What are the websites related to the language of your choice trying to do (for example, sell, raise awareness, entertain, etc.)? To what extent, and in what ways, is the language used in social media?

Annotated further reading

Androutsopoulos (2014) provides a state of the art collection of research articles on the question of whether and how media – new media in particular – form and change language and communication. The editor's introduction is particularly interesting.

Androutsopoulos and Juffermans (eds.) (2014) offer a special issue of the journal *Discourse Context and Media* which illustrates how sociolinguists are theorizing current linguistic practices in the area of computer-mediated communication across the globe.

Deumert (2014) is a very readable overview of the implications of computer-mediated communication on the individual and societies. The book makes a point of looking at global developments, with a strong focus on Africa.

Fuchs (2014) is a textbook that discusses social media from a critical theory point of view. It asks relevant questions about the way social media form contemporary digital culture and their impact on society.

García and Li Wei (2014) provide a short, very readable and well-illustrated account of translanguaging as a new way of understanding multilingual practices.

Georgapoulou and Spilioti (eds.) (2016) provide a handbook offering state of the art research articles on various topics within the field of computer-mediated communication. Particularly interesting is the chapter by Josh Iorio on vernacular literacy.

Journal of Computer Mediated Communication is one of the journals to start with when doing research in the area of digital communication.

Reershemius (2016) is a study of digital bilingual writing practices in a non-standard language (Low German) in social media.

9   Linguistic landscapes

9.1   Introduction

In your travels, or perhaps in the place where you live, you may have noticed signs written in more than one language that bear similarities to one or both of the examples in Figures 9.1 and 9.2.

- Which languages are used, and where do you think the signs are located?
- Discuss the function of the signs and the role of respective language choice on them.

Figure 9.1 Trilingual informational sign in Biel/Bienne, Switzerland
Photo: Kristine Horner

Figure 9.2 Bilingual street sign in Strasbourg, Alsace, France
Photo: Kristine Horner

In our daily lives, we encounter myriad such 'material manifestations' of language – that is, language in a visual, tangible form – often without paying them much attention. Some have been placed in specific locations with a particular purpose and are directed at a restricted readership; others are randomly distributed and serve no discernible function. Yet, taken together, all such visual linguistic representations constitute a complex component of our physical environment and deserve analysis as much as the spoken word does. This chapter focuses on some of the ways that language forms part of the landscape in German-speaking countries, as well as in other places where German is currently used or was previously spoken, with a particular emphasis on the (sometimes competing) presence of other languages alongside German.

9.2   Material manifestations of language use on signs

Research on 'linguistic landscapes', a term that embraces all conceivable kinds of linguistic signs – from advertising hoardings through street names to graffiti – has developed over the last 20 years into a highly interesting and rapidly growing subfield of sociolinguistics. Some of this research has explored the symbolic and instrumental functions of language on signs. For example, you may note that the use of German, French and Italian on the sign in Figure 9.1 serves an instrumental function because the trilingual sign in the Swiss town of Biel/Bienne is meant to enable all Swiss citizens to understand the message. On the sign in Figure 9.2, the use of French on the street sign, as well as on the informational sign under the arrow, also serves an instrumental purpose. However, the additional appearance of the street name in Alsatian, a Germanic language variety, may be regarded as serving a more symbolic function: this form of bilingualism is **indexical** of Alsatian regional identity and is characteristic of street signs in the central tourist area of Strasbourg, which is one of the three EU capital cities and is often portrayed as an important bridge between France and Germany.

These examples show us that the public space serves as a tool in the hands of different groups for the transmission of messages pertaining to the place or value of different languages in geographical and political entities and also for influencing the ways that language policy plays out in everyday practice. In this light, the public space is an interesting site to study as a way of gaining an understanding of the relationship between language, identity and power relations. A further area that has been investigated by linguistic landscape researchers has been the role of 'top-down' and 'bottom-up' signs. The former category refers to official signs issued by institutional actors, and the latter are those put up by independent social actors as individuals or on behalf of non-institutionalised groups.

Figure 9.3 (see p. 105), showing a sign located in Colmar in the Alsace region of France, is an example of institutionalised top-down signage with French as the dominant language as well as the appearance of the Germanic place name *Unterlinden* due to the history of the region. However, there is an additional sign in the form of a partially ripped off sticker on behalf of the non-institutionalised group *Elsass Frei*, which is written in German and has been illicitly stuck onto an official traffic sign. The *Elsass Frei* sticker may be regarded as a bottom-up sign, which someone else has noticeably (and unsuccessfully) attempted to remove from its unauthorised location. Looking at Figure 9.4 (see p. 106), you will see another pair of signs located on a street corner in the Prenzlauer Berg district of Berlin, with the top sign appearing to be institutionally produced and the bottom one sprayed on with a stencil by an individual actor or non-institutionalised group.

- How would you describe the relationship between the stencilled sign and the bilingual sign in Arabic and German above it, which are portrayed in Figure 9.4? What does the stencilled sign in Arabic mean? Who might have added it?

Looking at Figures 9.3 and 9.4, you may feel that it would be useful to obtain more contextual information about how and why the signs appear as they do in order to understand better what kinds of linguistic and social actions they represent. Indeed, we might well ask how valid the dichotomy posed by labelling signs as either top-down or bottom-up is, when analysing visual multilingualism such as in the images in Figures 9.5 and 9.6 (see p. 107), located respectively in Basel, Switzerland and in Berlin. For multiple reasons, it is not really possible to determine which of these analytical categories is applicable in each case.

In Figure 9.5, you will spot the use of English, which has become quite widespread in advertisements in German-speaking countries and links to the processes of globalisation (see Chapter 3). At the same time, it is worth noting that the use of the word *Brötli*, together with the silhouette of the *Basel Minster*, the Gothic cathedral in Basel, **indexes** the locality of the café and links to notions of authenticity and 'Swissness'. In Figure 9.6, it appears that

Figure 9.3 Directional signs in Colmar, Alsace, France
Photo: Kristine Horner

the advertisers (as well as making a pun on *Farfalle*, a kind of pasta, and *verfallen sein*, to be addicted to) have localised their product marketing by using a non-standard linguistic feature (*isch* for *ich*) associated with the **new urban vernaculars** discussed in Chapter 7.

• This kind of linguistic 'fetishisation' (Kelly-Holmes 2014) is not uncommon in advertising – can you think of any examples you have come across yourself?

Visual multilingualism forms part of our everyday life in a variety of ways, with some instances of this being quite obvious and others perhaps more subtle. How can we describe

Figure 9.4 Signs on a street corner in Prenzlauer Berg, Berlin
Photo: Patrick Stevenson

and analyse this phenomenon more systematically? Scollon and Scollon (2003) suggest that 'emplacement', or the understanding of the ways in which the meaning of signs depends on where and how they are placed in the material world, is a productive way to conduct a 'multimodal' discourse analysis (in other words, including both verbal and visual texts). They distinguish between three main kinds of emplacement: situated, decontextualised and transgressive signs. The first two categories are not clear-cut and rather exist on a continuum from signs which take on their meaning from being placed in a particular location, to signs such as logos and brand names, which carry more or less the same meaning wherever they are placed. The third category refers to unauthorised signs, such as graffiti, which break or 'transgress' existing rules on what is permitted in the public space.

- Which of the signs in Figures 9.1–9.6 would you describe as situated, decontextualised or transgressive? Does more than one kind of emplacement apply?

Figure 9.5 Advertisement for a local café in Basel, Switzerland
Photo: Kristine Horner

Figure 9.6 Billboard advertisement for fast food delivery service in Berlin
Photo: Patrick Stevenson

9.3   Language and place

Following from the discussion of emplacement, or the relationships between signs and the material world, we now explore how language display is utilised to **index** locality and to create senses of place. To start, let's have a look at Figures 9.7 and 9.8.

• What products are advertised here, and what linguistic varieties are used?

While certain advertising strategies draw on the use of global Englishes or the fetishisation of foreign languages, others draw on the use of regional language varieties as a means of anchoring products to a particular place or even as a means of branding the place. In Figure 9.7, products being pitched to tourists are promoted by the image of the anthropomorphised *Kölner Dom* together with directions *Hee em Büdche* (here in the little shop) written in Kölsch, which is accompanied by an arrow to ensure that tourists find their way to the shop. In addition to other souvenirs, products such as t-shirts, baby bibs and mugs adorned with Kölsch words and phrases are sold in these shops. The use of regional language varieties on local products and souvenirs is a phenomenon that is by no means unique to Cologne or even to Germany, and it is often considered to be linked to 'glocalisation' (the adaptation of global or international products or brands to a local cultural context). We can observe a similar strategy in Figure 9.8 (see p. 109) with the advertisement for the tourist destination of Hiddensee, an island in the Baltic Sea off the north-eastern coast of Germany. The symbolic use of Low German here is very similar to the way in which this regional language is used in the tourist industry of East Frisia in the north-western part of Germany (see Chapter 4).

These examples illustrate how language is bound up with the process of commodification, which Hoelscher (1998: 22) defines as 'the process by which objects and activities come to be valued primarily in terms of their value on the marketplace and for their ability to signify an image'. He goes on to argue that this can be extended to places and their associated

Figure 9.7 Advertisement for tourist shop in Cologne
Photo: Katherine Clark

Figure 9.8 Advertisement for travel to Hiddensee, Germany
Photo: Patrick Stevenson

properties, which means that places 'may be turned into commodities in their own right'. In his study of Swiss heritage in New Glarus, Wisconsin (US), Hoelscher (1998) shows how social and economic changes, together with incentives on the part of certain individuals, gradually transformed the southern Wisconsin town into a tourist destination.

- Look closely at Figures 9.9 and 9.10 (see p. 110). What similarities and differences do you notice when looking at these images from New Glarus, Wisconsin and Remsen, Iowa (US)?

The link between language and heritage (understood here as the use of the past to achieve economic or cultural goals in the present) is evoked by the use of German in Figures 9.9 and 9.10. In Figure 9.9, a photo of the outer wall of the New Glarus Brewery in Wisconsin, the German language indexes Swiss heritage (Glarus being a German-speaking town and canton in Switzerland), which in turn bolsters the economic goal of promoting and selling the local product. Figure 9.10, on the other hand, is an announcement for a local festival, which may generate some local revenue, but the event may potentially fulfil more of an identity function as it is a means of bringing together members of the local community. These examples show that the relationship between language and heritage is multifaceted and that detailed local research is often necessary to understand the complexities that are involved. We need to ask, for example, how such signs came to be in a particular place, what they mean to local people and what alternatives might have been available.

Figure 9.9 Mural on exterior wall of the old New Glarus Brewery building in Wisconsin, US
Photo: Lucian Rothe

Figure 9.10 Advertisement for local heritage festival in Remsen, Iowa, US
Photo: Kristine Horner

Figure 9.11 Street sign and directional signs in Colmar, Alsace, France
Photo: Kristine Horner

One way of exploring such questions is through the analytical framework of **place semi-otics** (Scollon and Scollon 2003). This involves taking a highly contextualised approach to the meanings of linguistic landscapes for the people involved, by not only analysing the individual signs, but also exploring their context of production (the history of how the signs came to be in a certain place) and relating them to wider social processes. We have already discussed one component of this, emplacement; the other aspects are 'code preference' and 'inscription'. Let's consider these with the help of two examples from Alsace, France.

Figure 9.11, set in Colmar, provides us with an illustrative example of code preference: we see that French is the preferred code and that Alsatian appears below the French as the former street name (*rue des marchands* in French/*Schadelgàss* in Alsatian) as well as in brackets to indicate the name of the former customs house (*douane* in French/*Koïfhus* in Alsatian). In her analysis of the linguistic landscape of the centre of Strasbourg, Burdick (2012) explains that it is a location where two dominant languages, French and German,

Figure 9.12 Café in the tourist centre of Strasbourg, Alsace, France
Photo: Kristine Horner

intersect. She also notes how Alsatian, which has been deemed by many to be in decline, is being used as a means of promoting Alsatian places to international and domestic tourists: the word *Winstub* (standard German *Weinstube*, wine bar) is the most frequently occurring Alsatian word in the public space, as illustrated in Figure 9.12, with other occurrences of Alsatian much less common. It is also interesting to look at the inscription system here, that is, the way that signs and their (verbal and/or visual) texts are presented, with a focus on fonts as well as the materials on which the texts are written.

* What strikes you about the inscription systems on the signs in Figures 9.11 and 9.12?
* Do you notice any similarities to the inscription systems used on the signs in Figures 9.9 and 9.10? What functions does the use of various inscription systems seem to fulfil?

9.4 Multilingual borderlands

The final section of this chapter focuses on linguistic landscapes situated along Austria's southern borderlands with Italy and Slovenia. The sociolinguistics of Austria, as well as

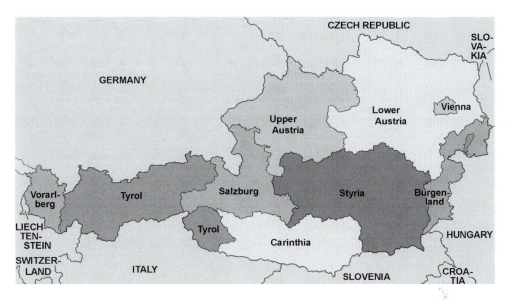

Map 9.1 Austria and surrounding countries

Source: By TUBS [CC BY-SA 3.0 (http://creativecommons.org/licenses/by-sa/3.0) or GFDL (www.gnu.org/copyleft/fdl.html)], via Wikimedia Commons

most of its bordering areas, has been shaped by the legacy of the former Austro-Hungarian Empire (1867–1918), which was highly multilingual. Following its collapse after the First World War and the ensuing turmoil linked to the Second World War, there were multiple alterations to the political borders in this European space. These shifting political borders did not necessarily coincide with linguistic borders and thus led to the creation of linguistic minorities (see Chapter 2).

Following the Treaty of Saint-Germain in the aftermath of the First World War, the southern half of the Austrian province Tyrol was ceded to Italy and subjected to a rigorous Italianisation process that involved the changing of place names from German to the corresponding Italian ones. For a brief period between 1943 and 1945, the region was occupied by Germany until it once again became part of Italy in 1946. At that time, the new Italian constitution stipulated that South Tyrol (Alto Adige in Italian) would be granted a substantial degree of autonomy. German and Italian were both granted official status, and German language education, which had been prohibited during the Italianisation period, was reinstated, as were German place names on public signage. Further negotiations took place in the early 1970s, which led to the Italian province having a greater degree of autonomy and limited the influence of Austria in the internal affairs of South Tyrol.

This historical context is essential for an understanding of the contemporary linguistic landscape of South Tyrol, which is marked by bilingual signage in German and Italian: see, for example, on the following page, the official signage in the train station (Figure 9.13) and on street signs (Figure 9.14) in the city of Merano/Meran, which is the second largest city in South Tyrol after Bolzano/Bozen.

- Why do you think that the code preference, or the sequence of languages on the signs, is different in Figures 9.13 and 9.14, even though they are located in the same city?

Figure 9.13 Informational sign at the train station in Merano/Meran, South Tyrol, Italy

Photo: Kristine Horner

Figure 9.14 Sign denoting tourist sites in Merano/Meran, South Tyrol, Italy

Photo: Kristine Horner

Figure 9.15 Sign for bike rentals at the train station in Merano/Meran, South Tyrol, Italy
Photo: Kristine Horner

Despite various negotiations and agreements, as well as the fact that South Tyrol is often held up as a model of bilingualism in Europe, some disputes on language matters periodically surface, including those about language use on public signage.

At the Merano/Meran train station, for example, the sign for bicycle rentals in Figure 9.15 was a monolingual German sign until someone drew in the addition of *Bici* (bicycles) to include Italian. Figure 9.16 (see p. 116) depicts a sign in Dorf Tirol, which is located just above Merano/Meran and can be reached by chair lift. The village is popular for its many walking trails, which are designated by a number of relatively recent monolingual German signs, although the more informational signs are usually in German and Italian. The use of language on signs for walking trails has been disputed recently, an indication of how language choice continues to express and represent political tensions in the region.

- Watch this *Deutsche Welle* video clip: 'Austria/Italy: War of the Words in South Tyrol' (www.youtube.com/watch?v=D9AIiGNXpjQ). Why do you think that place names, and the signage that marks them, bear such symbolic power?

Moving geographically eastwards, we find similar issues in the Austrian *Bundesland* of Carinthia, which borders on Slovenia. Arguably, this borderland is bound up with even greater sociopolitical tensions than those along the Austrian-Italian border. The previously mentioned Treaty of Saint-Germain (following the First World War) stipulated vague provisions for linguistic minorities in Austria, but it was the 1955 *Österreichischer Staatsvertrag* that set up rather clear arrangements for the Slovene as well as the Croat linguistic minorities as regards the rights to bilingual education and signage. As in South Tyrol, issues linked to minority rights

Figure 9.16 Sign designating hiking trails in Dorf Tirol, South Tyrol, Italy
Photo: Kristine Horner

in Carinthia became increasingly visible in the early 1970s, since much of the bilingual signage foreseen by the Treaty had never been erected. This was rather expediently rectified in 1972, only to be met with what is referred to as the *Ortstafelsturm*, which entailed the symbolically and physically violent act of ripping down the newly erected bilingual German-Slovene signs.

The dispute over bilingual topographic signs persisted through the following decades, and the debate escalated again in 2001, when Austria's Constitutional Court declared unconstitutional the numerical threshold according to which the minority group (that is, the Slovenes in this instance) needed to constitute at least 25 per cent of the population to warrant bilingual signage. Minority rights became the focus of heated debates that involved the Carinthian provincial government and its then right-wing governor, Jörg Haider, during the period between the accession of Austria (1995) and Slovenia (2004) to the EU. In Carinthia, it was the Slovene linguistic minority who were the target of debate, as illustrated by a press release in which Haider calls for Ludwig Adamovich, then President of Austria's Constitutional Court, to step down as well as framing his personal viewpoint on bilingual signs as consensual. He is quoted as saying:

> Zweisprachige Ortstafeln seien kein geeignetes Mittel der Volksgruppenpolitik, sondern "ein Steckenpferd der Nationalslowenen". Sie würden von den meisten Angehörigen der slowenischen Minderheit gar nicht gewünscht.
>
> (*Der Standard*, 18 December 2001, www.ots.at/presseaussendung/ OTS_20011217_OTS0192/der-standard-bericht-haider-will-zahl-slowenischer-ortstafeln-in-kaernten-reduzieren-er-verlangt-den-ruecktritt-von-praesident-adamovich-erscheinungstag-18122001)

Figure 9.17 Screenshot of 'Haček (k)lebt!' website
Source: www.unikum.ac.at/hacki_FI/hacki_karte.html

In 2002, a campaign was launched by the Universitätskulturzentrum Klagenfurt (UNIKUM) in response to the polarised nature of the debates on bilingual signs in Carinthia. The campaign entailed the distribution of adhesive stickers displaying the haček **diacritic** (in **graphemes** such as č and š) that could be affixed to topographic signs, such as those indicating German place names – most provocatively, perhaps, on the <r> in Klagenfurt, the Carinthian capital, a bold example of transgressive emplacement (see section 9.2). The haček is probably the most strikingly visible feature of the use of Slovene in the Carinthian linguistic landscape due to the fact that it is not part of the German orthographic system. The graphic on the activist website shown in Figure 9.17 provides a striking visual display portraying the multiplication of hačeks.

• Can you find other examples of signs in the public space that have been transformed, and, if so, what were the reactions to these modified signs?

The *Ortstafelfrage* in Carinthia shows how sociolinguistic issues may be rooted in conflict. While this broader trend of shifting boundaries affects various research sites in a changing

Europe, this is happening in different ways and may or may not be overtly politicised. For example, the town of Sopron, Hungary, which lies just east of the Austrian border, has an ethnic German minority population which is linguistically completely assimilated (that is, its members are either bilingual or monolingual in Hungarian). Bilingual signs in the town therefore serve different purposes: for the local ethnic German community, they have a purely symbolic function, while for the frequent Austrian visitors, eager to take advantage of keenly priced local goods and services, they provide both necessary information and a signal of welcome (see Figures 1.1 and 1.2 in Chapter 1). Interestingly, the town sign facing visitors on arrival is bilingual (Sopron/Ödenburg), but its counterpart facing the other way is only in Hungarian. The linguistic landscape in this borderland therefore reflects a local accommodation to changing economic conditions rather than political tensions.

9.5 Conclusion

This chapter has explored some of the ways that the material use of language on public signs forms a central part of our sociolinguistic environment. We discussed key concepts such as symbolic vs. instrumental functions of language and top-down vs. bottom-up signs. In our discussion of language and place, we considered how place semiotics provides us with helpful tools to conduct multimodal discourse analysis. Finally, we observed the importance of the historical context for an understanding of how certain aspects of the linguistic landscape can become the focus of public debate and conflict as well as reflecting changing economic conditions.

Tasks and suggestions for research

Reflective task

Consider the role of the historical context in relation to how we 'read' signs. Provide examples, if you can, and decide to what extent it is helpful to know who commissioned or designed the signs and who decided on their emplacement.

Research tasks

1 Photograph a number of linguistic landscape items (remember to note the emplacement of each sign). Analyse the images with reference to Scollon and Scollon's three systems of place semiotics: code preference, inscription and emplacement. Consider whether or not it is feasible to distinguish between top-down and bottom-up signs and whether this distinction supports or detracts from the analysis.
2 Collect a number of multilingual advertisements, which could be photos of advertising billboards or ads in newspapers or magazines, on the radio or TV, or on the internet. Analyse both visual and verbal text. Try to account for language choice and consider the use of different linguistic varieties. Distinguish between aspects of symbolic vs. instrumental use of language and consider the potential relevance of this.

Project ideas

1 Explore how features of the linguistic landscape in a German-speaking country, or in a country where German is used as a minority language, are perceived. Choose multilingual

signs and/or monolingual signs in a minority language or non-standard variety and conduct interviews with people who are the readers and/or viewers of these signs. How do they interpret the signs? How do they react to the choice of languages used on the signs? Consider interviewing people from the minority and majority groups. Are there any differences between their readings? How can these differences be accounted for?

2   The German-speaking countries are surrounded by countries in which languages other than German predominate. Find out to what extent and in what ways German is present in the linguistic landscape in these contact zones and compose a comparative analysis. This could be done as a written report, as a PowerPoint presentation or as a poster.

Annotated further reading

Bogatto and Hélot (2010) explore the linguistic landscape of Strasbourg in Alsace, France and find the use of many languages, primarily French (as is mandated), English and, to a lesser extent, German. Alsatian appears even less frequently and is primarily used to denote a beer or wine café.

Burdick (2012) complements and extends upon the findings of Bogatto and Hélot (2010). It provides an analysis of the commodification of language, in particular Alsatian, and considers transitory or mobile texts as part of the linguistic landscape.

Busch (2013), Chapter 3, discusses the *Ortstafelfrage* along the Austrian-Slovenian border and shows how people engage with debates on bilingual signage in various ways.

Carl (2014) investigates the role of memories of place in interviews with ethnic Germans in Sopron, Hungary about their town and the languages that they speak, as well as how their accounts relate to the linguistic landscape in their town, which is situated on the Austro-Hungarian border. The analysis shows how people conceive the social and geographical spaces that are created by different languages.

Dal Negro (2009) explores how the linguistic landscape in South Tyrol, in the north of Italy, contributes to the construction of the public space. Issues of language and power are shown not to be fully linked to officiality, revealing the complexity inherent to the use of German and Italian in the public space in this borderland zone.

Gerst and Klessmann (2015) provide an investigation of the linguistic landscape of the twin cities Frankfurt (Oder) and Słubice along the German-Polish border. The relationship between language and the construction of borders is a key point of exploration.

Gully (2011) provides an analysis of the conflict on bilingual German-Slovene signs in Carinthia, Austria. It considers the *Ortstafelstreit* as an example of the 'performative' character of national languages, as well as the broader destabilisation of national languages marking the contemporary period.

Hoelscher (1998) is based on an in-depth cultural geographic and ethnographic study of ethnic Swiss heritage in New Glarus, Wisconsin, US. It illustrates how a constellation of broad changes and individual acts transformed the town into a tourist destination.

Horner (2011) takes an ethnographically grounded geosemiotic approach to the analysis of Luxembourgish linguistic and cultural heritage displays in Belgium, Wisconsin, US. Similar to Hoelscher (1998), it shows how localised practices are being renegotiated in relation to global processes, and it underlines the role of language.

Papen (2015) offers a detailed analysis of the semiotic landscape in the Prenzlauer Berg district of Berlin, showing the role of commercial signs and street art in the reconstruction of this gentrified neighbourhood.

Rasinger (2014) provides a linguistic landscape analysis of locales in Carinthia, Austria, with reference to the civic, the commercial and the church contexts. Although the findings show a tendency towards monolingual German, the church context constitutes an exception due to its relatively balanced use of both German and Slovene.

Reershemius (2011) analyzes the public display of Low German and the self-presentation of the community in tourism brochures in East Frisia, Germany. It shows that top-down and bottom-up approaches to implementing Low German in public language display reveal a remarkable homogeneity, thus creating a regional 'brand'.

Soukup (2016) provides an overview of the EllViA project, which investigates meaning-making through the choice of English on signs in the linguistic landscape of Vienna, Austria. The project deals with reception and considers the process of anticipation, interpretation and negotiation between language 'producers' and 'recipients'.

Ziegler (2013) provides a brief overview of a project on the visual multilingualism of the Ruhrgebiet in Germany. It is concerned with acts of identity, alterity, multiculturalism and belonging. The linguistic landscape research will focus on the cities of Duisburg, Essen, Bochum and Dortmund.

Part 3

Sociolinguistic controversies

10 Linguistic purism

10.1 Introduction

A key aspect of the study of *socio*linguistics is the investigation of the emotional value speakers attach to their language. In many societies, not just German-speaking ones, we encounter widespread feelings that a particular (variety of a) language is very warm or homely, while others are seen to be cold or even a threat. In addition, language change, or the perception of change, is often viewed as negative or damaging (see Chapters 6 and 7). In particular, instances of lexical **borrowing** in German through language contact have triggered very negative reactions by speakers since the seventeenth century. This is in some respect surprising since borrowing has been evident throughout the history of the German language.[1]

• Which of the following German words were borrowed from other languages? Find out which languages they were borrowed from and roughly when this occurred.

Tisch	Pizza	Straße	Karaoke
Kiosk	Hand	Büro	Wald
Musik	Wasser	Streik	Bruder

This list demonstrates very clearly that borrowing is a normal feature of the German language and that many words borrowed from other languages are no longer recognisable as 'foreign'. Over time, some **loanwords** are more deeply assimilated than others: for example, words like *Mauer*, *Bischof* or *Käse* are **etymologically** just as 'foreign' (they were all borrowed from Latin) as *Telefon*, *Computer* or *Auto*, but the **orthography** and **morphology** of the first three examples make them look much more German than the latter three.

To distinguish between different degrees of **assimilation**, some linguists distinguish between the terms *Fremdwort* (for all loanwords) and *fremdes Wort* (for words that still look or 'feel' foreign). However, as regards their assimilation in terms of **phonology** or morphology, there is no clear, predictable difference between *Fremdwörter* and *fremde Wörter*. In other words, the distinction isn't really about a difference within the language itself but rather about the *perception* of a word as foreign or native. In our discussion of attitudes towards language, though, this distinction between the two types of words becomes very useful. In the context of lexical borrowing, for example, complaints about the 'corrupting influences' of language contact only ever really apply to *fremde Wörter*.

Such complaints often suggest that borrowing, or rather 'too much' borrowing, can damage the integral feel, nature or structure of a language. Some would then argue that to prevent such damage to a language, it is important to remove foreign influences from it and hence restore its 'purity'. Such thinking and activities are referred to as **linguistic purism**, and in this chapter we will review the history of the long 'complaint tradition' about the state of the German language and show how particular patterns continually emerge and re-emerge at particular historical moments.

   Linguistic purism does not only take issue with the use of foreign words, however. Complaints about 'poor language use' can be found with regard to the use of particular **sociolects**, for example, words or constructions used by young people such as the emphasis marker *krass* in German (see Chapter 7) or the hesitation marker *like* in English, or particular regionalisms or non-standard features, such as the use of the double perfect (*ich habe etwas gesehen gehabt*) in German or multiple negation (*he never said nothing*) in English. And just as with regard to linguistic purism towards foreign words and structures, the key weakness of such complaints is that they make very *general* claims about the state of a language but only look at a very *specific* time, overlooking the fact that in all stages of their history German and English have been full of foreign, regional and sociolectal influence. There was never a time when either language was 'pure'. Indeed, all languages evolve through complex processes of internal adjustment and external contact.

10.2   The complaint tradition and the emergence of linguistic purism in Germany

Linguistic purism is not about language as such but about what speakers feel about language. Historical sociolinguists have argued, however, that purism constitutes an important part of the history of a language since this in turn is integral to the history of the society in which it is used. Some argue that the emergence of purism is closely linked with the existence of a **standard variety**, while others have found examples of purism in languages which have not been standardised.

   While linguistic borrowing is a continuous part of the history of German, there are certain phases when waves of borrowing can be found, at least as regards the written language. Such phases include borrowing from Greek and Latin in Old High German (in the language of the church and public administration), from French in Middle High German (in the language of literature) and from Italian in Early New High German (in the language of banking and music). But there are no accounts of vocal objections to these borrowings at the times when they occurred. Similarly, we find early references to the general linguistic diversity of German, for example, in this medieval quotation in Hugo von Trimberg's *Renner* (1300):

1 Swâben ir wörter spaltent,	Schwaben	spalten, zerteilen
2 Die Franken ein teil si valtent,	Franken	falten, biegen, teilen
3 Die Beier si zezerrent,	Bayern	auseinander zerren
4 Die Düringe si ûf sperrent,	Thüringen	aufsperren, öffnen
5 Die Sahsen si bezückent,	Sachsen	überlisten
6 Die Rînliute si verdrückent,	Rheinland	unterdrücken
7 Die Wetereiber si würgent,	Wetterau	würgen, sich quälen
8 Die Mîsener si vol schürgent,	Meißen	schieben, stoßen
9 Egerlant si swenkent,	Egerland	schleudern
10 Oesterrîche si schrenkent,	Österreich	schräg stellen
11 Stîrlant si baz lenkent,	Steiermark	biegen, wenden
12 Kernde ein teil si senkent.	Kärnten	senken, zu Fall bringen

This demonstrates that different dialects have been perceived in particular ways for many centuries, but there is not any one dialect that is identified as being 'better' than the others. This changes with time, however, and at least since the emergence of a standard variety of German from the sixteenth century onwards there have been debates about 'the state of the language'. The central questions for us are to what extent cases of linguistic purism are triggered by certain sociolinguistic circumstances and to what extent purism aimed at foreign words is qualitatively different from purism aimed at **regiolects** or sociolects.

As we have seen in Chapter 5, the Early Modern Period (Renaissance and Baroque) produced a significant amount of discussion on what a high-quality, prestigious German should look and sound like. Grammarians in the seventeenth century argued that German was one of the 'original' languages surviving after the fall of the tower of Babel and that its ancient pedigree put it on an equal footing with the holy languages Greek, Hebrew and Latin. Justus Georgius Schottelius, one of the most influential protagonists in this debate, argued that German is *naturally*, that is by nature, perfect and uses its **onomatopoeic** qualities to make the case:

> Zum Exempel nehme einer nur diese Wörter: Wasser fliessen/gesäusel/sanft/stille/etc. wie künstlich ist es/wie gleichsam wesentlich fleust das Wasser mit stillem Gesäusel von unser Zungen? Was kan das Geräusch des Fliessenden Wassers wesentlicher abbilden?
>
> (Schottelius 1663: 59; as cited in Gardt 1999: 97)

Because – according to Schottelius! – the words for flowing water (*fliessendes Wasser*) sound exactly like the object they describe, a language that mirrors nature so exactly has to be closer to the original language, the language of paradise. While this line of argument seems a little alien to a twenty-first-century reader, it was completely legitimate scholarly argumentation in the seventeenth century, when, for example, the Bible was still considered an accurate represention of ancient history.

The task of promoting the status of German was triggered at that time by a general sense that it was undervalued. The language of education and the church had always been Latin, but with the arrival of the Reformation, the Lutheran position that a believer should access divine inspiration *directly* – that is, not through the mediation of a priest – and in the **vernacular** – that is, not through Latin – fundamentally changed the perceptions of language in Germany. However, the high-status language of the aristocracy had become French, as France had been the leading cultural nation during the seventeenth century. In addition, the Thirty Years War (1618–1648) brought many foreign soldiers to the battlefields in central Europe, and it became very fashionable for young German aristocrats to travel to France to learn the arts of dancing, fashion and fencing.

The conservative reaction in Germany to the popularity of French culture was one of rejection and despair, very similar to modern reactions of parents about the musical taste and fashion sense of their teenage children. Importantly for our purposes, this concern about the import of foreign cultural traits also applied to language matters, and throughout the seventeenth and eighteenth centuries we find extensive evidence of anti-French views. The concern was that a language must be kept pure from foreign influence:

> Ueber dis stehet es auch sehr unsauber/wenn allerley Grichisch=Lateinisch=Französisch und andere Sprachen Wörter eingeschoben werden.
>
> (Butschky 1659)

A major result of such concerns over the status and shape of the German language was the foundation of language societies, similar to developments in Italy, the Netherlands and

France. The most famous of these societies, the Fruchtbringende Gesellschaft (Fructifying Society), was founded in 1617 and congregated over its lifetime some 800 aristocrats as well as bourgeois grammarians, translators, poets and lexicographers (see also Chapter 5). In its statutes, it explicitly states that one task of the society is to protect the German language from foreign influences:

> Fürs ander/daß man die Hochdeutsche Sprache in jrem rechtem wesen und standt/ohne einmischung frembder außländischer Wort/auffs möglichste und thunlichste erhalte/ und sich so wol der besten aussprache im reden/als der reinesten art im schreiben und Reimen=dichten befleissige.
>
> (statute of the Fruchtbringende Gesellschaft, cited in Schmidt 2000: 122)

Such efforts to promote the purity of the German language by rejecting foreign influences were closely tied to the creation of a prestige variety of the language. As discussed in Chapter 5, the **standardisation** of German referred to very similar mechanisms as lexical purism. George Thomas (1991) defined purism as follows:

> Purism is the manifestation of a desire [. . .] to preserve a language from, or rid it of, putative foreign elements or other elements held to be undesirable (including those originating in dialects, sociolects and styles of the same language).
>
> (Thomas 1991: 12)

The objection to certain dialects or sociolects is thus just as purist as objections to foreign words. But it is lexical purism that is most widespread in the history of German, though different waves of purism have different motivations. The efforts of Baroque language societies were primarily aimed at raising the value of German as a literary and prestige language. In contrast, Johann Heinrich Campe (1746–1818) promoted the use of German rather than foreign words because he felt that these would be more comprehensible to the general German population. Witnessing the French Revolution, he was amazed how ordinary French citizens would discuss high politics, and he embarked on translating some 11,500 foreign words into German, resulting in his two-volume *Wörterbuch zur Erklärung und Verdeutschung der unserer Sprache aufgedrungenen fremden Ausdrücke* (1801). His purism was not xenophobic or nationalist but emancipatory, and as many as 300 of his 3000 translations have become part of everyday German: a remarkable feat!

- The following list contains **neologisms** suggested by Campe (with **synonyms** in brackets). Use a modern dictionary to work out which ones have survived in modern German. Can you work out why some have been successful while others were not?

herkömmlich (konventionell)
Dörrleiche (Mumie)
Hochschule (Universität)
Lehrgang (Kursus)
Scheidekunst (Chemie)
Zwischenstille (Pause)
Stelldichein (Rendezvous)
Streitgespräch (Debatte)
tatsächlich (faktisch)

Zwangsgläubiger (Katholik)
Freigläubiger (Protestant)

The next milestone in the history of purism relates to the activities of the Allgemeiner Deutscher Sprachverein (ADSV), founded in 1885 at the height of German imperialism during the Wilhelmine Empire. The society, which lasted until the 1940s and had to up 35,000 members, largely from the middle classes, set itself the following targets:

1   die Reinigung der deutschen Sprache von unnötigen fremden Bestandtheilen zu fördern,
2   die Erhaltung und Wiederherstellung des echten Geistes und eigentümlichen Wesens der deutschen Sprache zu pflegen – und
3   auf diese Weise das allgemeine nationale Bewusstsein im deutschen Volke zu kräftigen.

•   Consider these aims and compare them with what you read about the Fruchtbringende Gesellschaft and J. H. Campe. What elements are different?

The mottos of the ADSV were: 'Kein Fremdwort für das, was deutsch gut ausgedrückt werden kann' and 'Gedenke auch wenn Du sprichst, daß Du ein Deutscher bist'. Foreign words were considered unnecessary, and their use was classified as disloyal to the German cause. The society formed branches across Germany, Switzerland and Austria-Hungary and engaged in a number of public and scholarly activities, for example, the publication of *Verdeutschungswörterbücher*, that is, dictionaries that provided handy translations for foreign words in particular domains. Ernst Lößnitzer's *Deutsche Speisekarte. Verdeutschung der in der Küche und im Gasthofswesen gebräuchlichen entbehrlichen Fremdwörter* (1900) offered translations for foreign words used in restaurants and kitchens, and similar publications exist for words related to transport.

   With the rise of nationalist and imperialist thinking in the late nineteenth and early twentieth century, the activities of the ADSV, which had originally been aimed at Greek and Latin, as well as French, now focused on words from languages spoken by the enemy, that is, French and English. Just as was the case in the seventeenth century, purist efforts were not concerned with the 'damaging' influence of *all* languages: only languages which were associated with cultures or countries perceived to be a threat to the cultural integrity of the German people were identified as dangerous or objectionable. Within the context of nineteenth-century imperialism, the British Empire and France were considered as the main competitors and threats, and hence, in the eyes of language purists, the use of words from French and English was portrayed as bordering on treason.

10.3   Purism in Germany today

Linguistic purism is not restricted to the past, and examples of people complaining about the current state of the language can easily be found in most societies. Where British people complain about the threat of Americanisms, Germans complain about the dangers associated with using English, members of the Danish minority in Schleswig-Holstein are concerned with the damaging effect of borrowing from northern German, while there is a vocal debate in Austria about the increasing use of German German (*Piefkedeutsch*). This not only shows that language contact is a common linguistic phenomenon but also that linguistic purism is a widespread sociolinguistic practice. It is noticeable that commentators are always concerned with the *current* state of their language and ignore the fact that borrowing and language change are part of a continuous process. Instead they argue that the language is in danger *now* and that urgent action is required to help save its integrity or purity, as illustrated by the following quotation:

> Jede Zeit sagt, daß derzeit die Sprache so gefährdet und von Zersetzung bedroht sei wie nie zuvor. In unserer Zeit aber ist die Sprache tatsächlich so gefährdet [. . .] wie nie zuvor. [. . .] Der Journalismus ist schuld, der geschriebene Journalismus und der gesprochene des Radios und des Fernsehens.
>
> (Weigel 1974)

There is, of course, a striking irony here in that the author suggests that at his time of writing in 1974, the German language was truly threatened, as compared to previous stages when this may simply have been a perception of threat. Given that the quotation is more than 40 years old, we can say with the benefit of hindsight that Weigel's view was also only a perception, since we know that the German language has survived and appears to be in a fit and healthy state now.

And yet, views that German is under threat by careless usage and needs to be protected by a mindful speaker community continue in the same vein as in the past. The most famous and successful commentator on the poor state of modern German today is the *Spiegel* journalist Bastian Sick, a graduate of history and French, whose contributions in print, in blogs, on TV shows and in front of thousands in sold-out concert halls have turned the lay-linguistic landscape on its head. His best-selling *Der Dativ ist dem Genitiv sein Tod* claims to fight 'gegen falsches Deutsch und schlechten Stil' (Sick 2004: 9) and targets the perennial enemies of language preservationists across the ages: 'abgedroschene Phrasen, unerträgliche Modewörter, lästige Anglizismen und Unwörter aus dem Journalisten- und Politikerjargon' (ibid: 9–10). The secret of Sick's success is likely to lie in the combination of his light-hearted style, the brevity of his chapters, and the punchy and provocative formulation of his worries: he's not shy to express his disgust about the language use of other people.

Reading his columns closely, and studying his seemingly hands-on approach to improving the language use of Germans, we find that his books contain little that will be of help to anyone who does not already have a good level of formal education and command of standard German. In his four-page chapter on verbs governing the genitive case, for example, Sick devotes more than two pages to sentences from newspapers containing the dative, rather than the genitive case, before illustrating with the example of *Vergissmeinnicht* (as opposed to *Vergiss*mich*nicht*) that, indeed, language does change over time. He ends his column with a table of verbs which – in formal, written, standard German – still govern the genitive case. No mention is made of register differences or the real significance of the *Vergissmeinnicht* example (namely that language change is an ever-present reality!). So, in the end, the reader is left with nothing more than a table which can be found in any reference grammar. Sick's commentary adds nothing of real substance, offering only examples of current language change in progress, or, as he would see it, language in a process of decay.

Books such as *Der Dativ ist dem Genitiv sein Tod* or *Deutsch für Profis* (Schneider 2001) sell in high numbers and enjoy considerable popularity, although they are not sanctioned in any official way by the state or educational authorities. Their phenomenal success tells us something about the status of standard German in modern society and the importance of knowing its rules and proscriptions in order to be professionally successful. The readers of such books are rarely people who are not already competent in most aspects of standard German, and who have obtained the highest school leaving qualification or university degrees.

The popularity of these books is thus due not to actual lack of linguistic competence amongst their readership but to the recognised value of knowing the prescribed rules of standard German in order to demonstrate educatedness and enable or, perhaps, *prevent* social mobility.

- Maitz and Elspaß (2007) argue that Sick's position represents a *Spracharistokratie.* What do you think they mean by this term? What does it suggest to you about the potential influence of such prominent language commentators?

Apart from the writing of journalists, there is also a more organised way of fighting the (perceived) decay of the German language: the Verein Deutsche Sprache (VDS), founded in 1997 as the Verein zur Wahrung der deutschen Sprache and boasting some 36,000 members. It defines its purpose as follows:

VDS in Kürze

Wir schätzen unsere deutsche Muttersprache, die „Orgel unter den Sprachen", wie Jean Paul sie nannte. Um sie als eigenständige Kultur- und Wissenschaftssprache zu erhalten, weiterzuentwickeln und vor dem Verdrängen durch das Englische zu bewahren, gründeten wir im Jahr 1997 den Verein Deutsche Sprache e. V. [. . .]

Wir wollen der Anglisierung der deutschen Sprache entgegentreten und die Menschen in Deutschland an den Wert und die Schönheit ihrer Muttersprache erinnern. Die Fähigkeit, neue Wörter zu erfinden, um neue Dinge zu bezeichnen, darf nicht verloren gehen.

Dabei verfolgen wir keine engstirnigen nationalistischen Ziele. Wir sind auch keine sprachpflegerischen Saubermänner. Fremdwörter – auch englische – sind Bestandteile der deutschen Sprache. Gegen *fair, Interview*, *Trainer*, *Doping*, *Slang* haben wir nichts einzuwenden. Prahlwörter wie *event, highlight*, *shooting star*, *outfit*, mit denen gewöhnliche Dinge zur großartigen Sache hochgejubelt werden, lehnen wir ab. [. . .]
http://vds-ev.de/allgemein/vds-in-kuerze/ (last accessed February 2017)

- What is the principal interest of this society?
- Discuss the third paragraph. What is the difference between *Interview* and *event* in the view of the VDS?

The Verein identifies three principal motivations for its existence: to preserve German as a language of cultural and academic writing, to further the language's development and to prevent its replacement by English. These aims carry a number of presuppositions, such as that German is currently threatened in the linguistic domains of culture and academia, that is, rather high registers, and that this threat is exercised by English in particular. This sounds very similar to concerns about the German language from the past when, however, the perceived threat came from French, not English.

In its publications, the VDS discusses the status of German as a language in Germany and as an international language of science and academia. In addition, significant space is dedicated to iterating the importance of teaching German to recent and established migrants, arguing that a lack of German language skills prevents successful participation in German society and culture. The society sees its vocation in playing an active part in the protection of the German language, for example, by lobbying politicians, companies and representatives of the media who have been found to be using English words in 'undesirable' ways. Its *Anglizismen-Index*,[2] which contains some 7500 words used in the *deutsche Allgemeinsprache*, aims to offer German alternatives for English borrowings which have recently entered the German language. It excludes Anglicisms which have already been assimilated to such a degree that their English origin is no longer recognisable, for example, *Streik*, *Sport*, *Keks* or *Partner*. It classifies English borrowings into three categories:

„Ergänzend"

sind Anglizismen, die eine Wortlücke schließen und dadurch neue Ausdrucksmöglichkeiten eröffnen, darunter auch solche, deren Status bereits dem von Lehnwörtern gleich kommt, obwohl sie phonetisch und grammatisch (noch) nicht voll assimiliert sind. [. . .] Beispiele: Baby, Boiler, Clown, fair, Interview, Sport.

„Differenzierend"

gegenüber existierenden deutschen Wörtern sind Anglizismen, die einen neuen Sachverhalt bezeichnen, für den eine deutsche Bezeichnung noch zu bilden und/oder wieder einzuführen ist. [. . .] Beispiele: E-Post für e-mail, Prallkissen für air bag

„Verdrängend"

wirken Anglizismen, die statt existierender, voll funktionsfähiger und jedermann verständlicher deutscher Wörter und Wortfelder in zunehmendem Maße verwendet werden, dadurch die Verständigung erschweren und den sprachlichen Ausdruck verflachen, oder deren Verwendung für moderne Sachverhalte das Entstehen einer deutschen Bezeichnung und dadurch die Weiterentwicklung der deutschen Sprache verhindern. Beispiele: keeper (Torwart), shop (Laden), slow motion (Zeitlupe), ticket (Fahr-, Eintritts-, Theater-, Kino-, Flugkarte, Strafzettel) bzw. all-inclusive (Pauschalangebot), bad bank (Auffangbank)

On this basis, the VDS reports the following distribution of the Anglicisms listed in the index: 3 per cent are *ergänzend*, 18 per cent are *differenzierend* and 79 per cent are *verdrängend*.

- Discuss the criteria for the three categories. Find five examples of borrowing from either (a) French, Latin or Italian into German or (b) American English into British English and attempt to classify them using the categories of the *Anglizismen-Index*. What challenges do you face in doing this?

In its overarching principles (*sprachpolitische Leitlinien*), the VDS states that the pressures of globalisation are causing a loss of identity amongst Europe's languages and cultures (see also Chapter 3). The society observes that new linguistic developments and technical terms are almost exclusively in English, as demonstrated by the declining importance of languages other than English in the administration and political bodies of the EU, and that this weakens the linguistic and cultural independence of European countries. The VDS makes the specific point that this development is *particularly* advanced ('besonders weit fortgeschritten') in the German-speaking countries, which is explained by the following claim:

Die Geringschätzung der Muttersprache, der Mangel an Sprachloyalität und die schwach ausgeprägte Förderung der deutschen Sprache von staatlicher Seite gefährden in diesen Ländern die Funktion der Sprache als Verständigungsmittel. Gleichzeitig (v)erklären Wissenschaftler, Meinungsführer und Politiker den Einfluss des Englischen zu einer begrüßenswerten Folge der Globalisierung. Aus der häufigen Verwendung englischer und scheinenglischer Ausdrücke, die als „modern" gilt und mit der man zu imponieren trachtet, ergeben sich Verständigungs- und Eingliederungsprobleme bis hin zur sprachlichen Diskriminierung.

It is argued that the use of English in such contexts is due to its status as a 'modern' language which can be used to impress other speakers, and it is suggested that this use of a fashionable language can cause a breakdown of communication and a consequent discrimination against those speakers who don't understand English. This applies in particular to older speakers of German who may have no or only little knowledge of English. The VDS states that the current situation cannot be compared with similar phases of lexical borrowing in the past since the use of French and Latin in previous centuries was reserved for the educated elites, whereas the use of English, for example, in advertising, can be seen by everyone.

What the VDS fails to recognise is, of course, that the use of language in advertising is *very* deliberate and that the placing of English words or phrases will always serve a particular purpose, for example, to emphasise the international standing of a company or the technological advancement of a product. This *specific* use of foreign languages in advertising is not restricted to English but can also be seen in the use of Italian when promoting coffee or pizza or French when promoting cheese or cars. In the English-speaking world, Volkswagen (*Das Auto.*) and Audi (*Vorsprung durch Technik*) use German to emphasise that they are German car-makers, even though very few members of their target audiences will understand what the precise words mean. Where advertising promotes products aimed at people less likely to understand (or like) the use of English, for example, pension funds or German delicatessens, the marketing companies are not very likely to use English. Thus where the VDS complains about the use of English in advertising, it appears not to be sufficiently aware of different strategies for different types of products.

Its general appeal to protect and promote cultural diversity across Europe can hardly be challenged, and it is explicit in distancing itself from nationalist claims rejecting all foreign influences. In this way, the VDS is very different from the ADSV 100 years earlier. However, while the precise formulations in rejecting English are rather more mild than those expressed by the ADSV, both societies are built on fundamental misconceptions on the relationship between words and meaning. Both the VDS and the ADSV assume a greater degree of transparency and ease of use for indigenous German words than for English words, when, in fact, there is no evidence for this. Is it easier to understand the word *Rechner* than the word *Computer*? Ease of comprehension has to do with frequency of use, not etymology.

But is the VDS as neutral as it claims to be? Its sole focus on Anglicisms (rather than words from *any* foreign language which may be difficult to understand) reveals a bitter taste that would suggest that its purpose is really about a general anti-American sentiment. Its emphasis on the importance of *European* cultures and languages appears to demonstrate that the principal differences between the ADSV and the VDS are not so much to do with quality but rather that while the ADSV thought Germany was in need of protection from uncivilised neighbours *within* Europe, the VDS is concerned with the broader perceived threat of cultural influences from beyond its shores.

10.4   Conclusion

This chapter explored the notion of linguistic purism in the history of German. It showed that purism is part of the complaint tradition whereby certain changes or perceptions of change are interpreted as symptoms of decline or decay. These trigger reactions of protest, aimed at particular foreign words, regiolects or sociolects. The chapter ended with a discussion of the foremost purist society in modern Germany, the Verein Deutsche Sprache, which focuses on a single issue, the threat of English to the integrity of the German language. It was shown how the society's aim is not in fact so much about a linguistic phenomenon but instead addresses a much more general perception of cultural decay, driven by globally dominant American cultural and economic influences.

Tasks and suggestions for research

Reflective task

'Purism fights language decay': what would happen to languages if they weren't 'protected from decay'? What would a 'damaged' language look like?

Research tasks

1   Conduct a straw poll by asking native speakers of German how they know if something is 'correct' German. Where would they look for the information? When did they last look something up? Why do they accept the judgements of the sources they refer to?
2   Read one of Sick's commentaries on a linguistic feature (available here: www.spiegel. de/thema/zwiebelfisch/) and explain who uses the linguistic feature. What is the 'problem' with its usage, what alternatives does he propose and what is the authority on which he bases the 'correct' use?

Project idea

Linguistic purism is not confined to the German-speaking countries: compare the complaint tradition in Germany with that in another country such as the UK or France. Try to incorporate concrete examples of specific targets or objects of complaint in different countries at different times (including the present).

Notes

1   We don't know, of course, when German 'began', but when we examine the oldest surviving documents in German, we see plenty of evidence of language contact from e.g. Latin and Greek.
2   There appears to be no conscious irony that the Verein chose to use foreign words to name this dictionary!

Annotated further reading

Bauer and Trudgill (1999) offer a very enjoyable collection of short essays on various myths from all areas of language use and perception.
Cameron (1995) explores popular attitudes towards language and discusses a number of case-studies of 'verbal hygiene', i.e. examples of where particular language uses are stigmatised or advocated.
Gardt (1999) is a textbook history of the discipline of linguistics in the German-speaking context.
Langer and Davies (2005) provide a collection of scholarly chapters on examples of linguistic purism in various Germanic languages from different centuries.

Langer and Nesse (2012) provide a comprehensive account of the concept of linguistic purism, with examples from German and other languages.

Maitz and Elspaß (2007) provide a very critical discussion of the usefulness of Sick (2004) for the teaching of German to non-native speakers.

McLelland (2009) is an important chapter for our understanding of the link between linguistic purism and political and cultural nationalism in northern Europe.

Milroy and Milroy (1999) provide a classic textbook on language standardisation, including a discussion of the term *complaint tradition*, which they coined in the original 1985 edition.

Pfalzgraf (2009) is a comprehensive exposition of most prominent discourses in the history of German purism.

Thomas (1991) is still a key contribution to our fundamental understanding of the processes of linguistic purism, using the term in a wider sense than many contemporary works.

11 Language and education

11.1 Introduction

A generally acknowledged role of school education is to equip students with good communicative skills. First and foremost this applies to the teaching of basic reading and writing skills – though normally only in the standard variety – and it extends to areas such as oral presentation skills or essay writing. While these skills are taught in all subjects in German schools, the subject of German itself, as well as the teaching of foreign languages such as English, French or Latin, will involve more advanced skills in written text analysis, for example, in the form of commentaries on literary texts. Being able to use language in a way that conforms to general social expectations is thus a key objective for students, and consequently achieving this aim has profound effects for the future prospects of school leavers. In this chapter we will discuss some key sociolinguistic issues affecting formal education. In particular, we will examine the application of the **standard language ideology** and the single-language ideology ('German only') in the context of contemporary Germany's multilingual society. We will then consider foreign language teaching in relation to the EU's '1+2 model' and implications for the promotion of regional and minority languages.

11.2 Language norms in the classroom

We learn our home language(s) from our immediate environment as we grow up, and for some German-speaking children this might be the local dialect or a more regional variety. For others, it may be the standard variety, but often exposure to standard German comes later, at school, where not just reading and writing skills in general are taught but, importantly, the reading and writing of texts in (and only in) standard German. It is generally taken for granted that the norms of written German are the basis for German lessons in schools. This is confirmed by the education authorities in many *Bundesländer*, who stipulate in the school curricula that students not only need to be able to communicate 'appropriately' in speech and writing but also need to use the standard variety. The national guidelines set the following targets:

> Die Schülerinnen und Schüler bewältigen kommunikative Situationen in persönlichen, beruflichen und öffentlichen Zusammenhängen situationsangemessen und adressatengerecht. Sie benutzen die Standardsprache.
>
> (KMK-Beschluss 2003, cited in Davies and Langer 2014: 301)

The intention is that through exposure to printed texts in standard German, and the importance placed on the teaching and learning of reading and writing, students will learn that printed texts represent 'good language use', and thus that the standard variety is to be seen as the authoritative form of the language (see also Chapter 5). Consequently, school lessons play an important role in the transmission of linguistic **norms**, and, by implication, teachers can be seen as 'norm transmitters' of standard German. But what do we know about teachers' own linguistic perceptions and their pedagogical practices?

In a number of recent studies teachers were asked about what they consider 'good German' (here: grammar and **lexis**) and what reference works they use as authorities on 'good' usage. Wagner (2009) interviewed 16 teachers from *Hauptschulen* – the type of school that focuses on practical and vocational education and whose students typically take up manual occupations – and 12 teachers from *Gymnasien* – where students work towards the equivalent of A-Levels and usually go on to study at university. Only three of the 28 teachers named the *Duden Grammatik* as a reference work they consult, though 18 listed the *Duden* spelling dictionary – which, however, does not contain any grammatical information (again, see Chapter 5). Thus, the standard language norm actually used by these teachers does not appear to be consciously based on the rules set out in standard reference works such as the *Duden.* Does this mean that what teachers think is standard German differs widely, or do they agree on the norms they teach to their pupils?

The teachers were shown a number of sample sentences, such as: 'Ich bin während dem Konzert in der 1. Reihe gestanden'.

- Before reading on, ask yourself: Is this sentence standard German? Which features, if any, strike you as non-standard?

Somewhat unsurprisingly, all but one of the 28 participants said that they would correct the use of *bin* to *habe*, and some noted – quite appropriately – that the use of *sein* with *stehen* is typical of southern German. In this respect, the teachers' views conformed to the rules prescribed by authoritative reference works. However, while these same works prescribe the use of the genitive after *während*, only two of the teachers corrected *dem* to *des*. Examples such as this suggest that teachers' perceptions of what constitutes standard German are not uniform or consistent (although their actual practices may be different again).

- Look at the maps for pencil case ('Behältnis für Schreibutensilien')/meat ball ('gebratener Fleischkloß')/*wegen mir* in the *Atlas der deutschen Alltagssprache* (www.atlas-alltagssprache.de/ – see Chapter 4) and compare them with what you find in your dictionary of standard German. What are the standard forms and where in the country are they used in everyday speech?

There therefore seems to be a tension between the schools' obligation to presume the norms of standard written German as a basis for all teaching and the more diverse actual use of German amongst both students and teachers. That the language students' use often doesn't conform to the standard norm is a well-known issue and one that continues to provide headlines about the supposedly poor education of children today. What research has shown, however, is that the teachers, too, have varying understandings of what the codified norm is. This is not to say that the teachers are uncertain in their judgement, as most report with confidence that they will correct what they consider non-standard (some of them would say 'incorrect') language use by their students. But a particular word or construction may be viewed as 'correct' by one teacher and as a 'mistake' by another.

- What was your experience at school? Did teachers ever correct your language use? Can you remember any particular 'errors' that were pointed out to you?

This section showed that schools play an important part in shaping people's understanding of what 'correct', 'standard' or 'prestigious' German looks like. By disseminating the codified norms found in the *Duden* and other authoritative reference books, teachers and schools become *norm transmitters*. However, because teachers, as experienced and confident users of normative language, appear largely to trust their own judgements on what constitutes 'correct' usage and may not always support these judgements by consulting reference works, they also become *norm authorities*. In this way, schooling plays a fundamental role in the promotion of the standard language ideology.

11.3   Multilingual classrooms

The exclusive emphasis on the standard variety for teaching and learning reading and writing skills in the classroom means that children's linguistic background at home will have a significant impact on their chances of success at school. In the 1970s and early 1980s, educationalists and linguists issued a number of short books (*Dialekt/Hochsprache – kontrastiv*) aimed at teachers, with dialect and standard German texts side-by-side. The aim of these booklets was to equip teachers with the necessary knowledge of local dialect features so that they understood with less prejudice why students made particular 'errors' in their use of standard German.

However, there is another set of students whose family language doesn't correspond to the language of schooling: children with migrant family backgrounds. Of course, this will have been an issue ever since the introduction of general schooling in the nineteenth century, but the public discussion of how to manage multilingual classrooms only really took off in the 1970s when the children of *Gastarbeiter* began to attend schools in significant numbers, and the debate has intensified as a result of the greater social and linguistic diversification of German society through rapidly increasing migration since 1989. The key concerns have revolved around the issues of how children from non-German-speaking backgrounds ('SchülerInnen nichtdeutscher Herkunftssprache' or *ndH*) could reasonably be expected to follow lessons in German schools and the effect a large group of non-German-speakers would have on the educational progress of the German children in the same classroom.

These issues gained urgent headline status after the publication of the PISA (Programme for International Student Assessment) results in 2001. This study, comparing educational achievements by school students across the world, ranked children in Germany as performing well below average, and this caused a shockwave through the country, which had always prided itself on its high educational standards (see www.oecd.org/edu/school/2960581.pdf for the executive summary of the report). Commentators were quick to point out that one of the reasons for the poor overall performance appeared to be the large number of children with a migration background (*Migrationshintergrund*), that is, children and grandchildren of immigrants, and the ensuing debate highlighted the need to reflect on the inequality in German society, not least with regard to educational opportunities.

The consensus of all interested parties appears to be that it is important for everyone to have a high level of proficiency in standard German, in both reading and writing. The controversy revolves around the practicalities of achieving this in a multilingual classroom. The principal opposition is between those who favour incorporating, rather than suppressing, the bilingual repertoires of the pupils and those who favour a German-only approach. That this debate is not principally about bilingualism versus monolingualism, but rather about larger issues to do with a perceived threat to cultural identity, is shown by the fact that nobody appears to argue against German-Danish or German-French bilingualism, nor, indeed, the introduction of English in primary schools.

The objections are about the presence of less prestigious (or less 'legitimate') languages, such as Turkish or Russian, and the real issue has to do with the cultural practices and traditions associated with these languages, not the languages themselves: in other words, some types of bilingualism are considered better than others. The counter-argument is that through the acknowledgement of home languages other than German in schools children will handle their first language with confidence and hence cope with the challenges of learning or improving their second language, German, more easily. Research has shown very clearly that bilingualism is not cognitively challenging for children but rather offers potential for more reflective linguistic analysis and consequently more highly developed linguistic capabilities. Where social problems coincide with bilingual communities, the problems have nothing to do with bilingualism but with more general problems of social disadvantage (especially high unemployment or poverty).

In 2006, the Herbert-Hoover Schule, a secondary school in the inner-city district of Wedding in Berlin, where some 90 per cent of students have an L1 other than German, made national headlines by adding the following statement to its statutes (*Schulordnung*):

> Die Schulsprache unserer Schule ist Deutsch, die Amtssprache der Bundesrepublik Deutschland. Jeder Schüler ist verpflichtet, sich im Geltungsbereich der Hausordnung nur in dieser Sprache zu verständigen.[1]
> (www.hhs-berlin.de/index.php/104-schulportrait/137-schulordnung, 7 March 2016)

This declaration created a wave of discussion on the importance of confirming and protecting the status of German in education. It meant that throughout the school grounds, no other languages were permitted, not even in the playground during breaks. The school further stated:

> Gute Deutschkenntnisse sind nicht nur eine Grundvoraussetzung für die Verständigung von Kindern und Jugendlichen untereinander, sie stellen auch eine bessere Bildung sicher.
> (cited in Buselmeier 2008: 147)

• Why do you think the school felt the need to make this declaration and what kind of responses do you think it received amongst the public, the media and the students themselves? (You will find many relevant comments online.)

The reactions to this rule were replete with accusatory terms such as *Zwangsgermanisierung* or *Weddinger Sprachverbot*, and heated discussions took place on talk shows and in print media. While no one disputed the importance of learning German, the key concern was the effect the *Sprachverbot* might have on the perception of the value of languages other than German and, by implication, of their speakers.

Outside this more political dimension of the debate, the key issue in terms of language learning and educational development is not how many languages you speak but whether they are used in normal conversation and whether the acquisition of literacy skills is supported in the family. Where such support does not exist, pupils from both German *and* migrant backgrounds will be at a disadvantage with regard to the standard language skills expected at school. This is a message articulated by the head teacher of a Berlin *Gymnasium* in the following interview excerpt:

> Also, die Probleme, die wir haben, liegen in der Schriftsprache. Die Probleme, die wir haben, liegen in der Wissenschaftssprache, wo wir am Gymnasium irgendwann hinkommen wollen. Wenn ich in der Oberstufe in Philosophie-Kursen mich mit Kant-Texten beschäftige, dann komme ich, wenn ich eine Zusammensetzung in meinen Lerngruppen rein deutscher Herkunft habe, relativ zügig ins Philosophieren. Wenn man das mit Lerngruppen macht, wo 75 Prozent Kinder nicht deutscher Herkunft sind, dann muss ich erst mal mir den deutschen Text erschließen. Und das ist dann ein anderes Philosophieren.
> (Interview with Michael Wüstenberg, head teacher, Lessing-Gymnasium Berlin)

- Read the rest of this interview with Michael Wüstenberg and language acquisition expert Professor Rosemary Tracey (www.deutschlandradiokultur.de/stoerfall-oder-gluecksfall-das-mehrsprachige-klassenzimmer.954.de.html?dram:article_id=281220). What are the main arguments? What advantages of multilingualism are mentioned?

11.4 Promoting foreign languages: the EU 1 + 2 model

It is a widespread but puzzling observation that multilingual competence in, say, German and Turkish or English and Urdu is seen to be a problem for school students, yet knowing a foreign language such as Spanish or French is considered very desirable and as enriching the general cognitive abilities of the learner. The educational strategy of the EU includes the expectation that every EU citizen should have competence in two foreign languages, in addition to their first language.

1 + 2 Modell

> Die Mehrsprachigkeit ist nach Ansicht der EU ein wichtiges Element europäischer Wettbewerbsfähigkeit. Zu den Zielen der EU-Sprachenpolitik gehört deshalb, dass jeder europäische Bürger zusätzlich zu seiner Muttersprache zwei weitere Sprachen beherrschen sollte.
> (www.europarl.europa.eu/atyourservice/de/displayFtu.html?ftuId=FTU_5.13.6.html)

This statement doesn't actually specify any of the 'major' European languages (English, French, Spanish, German), but it is fair to say that English is the most widely taught foreign language in schools and universities throughout Europe and that French and German are seen – rightly or wrongly – as more important than, say, Estonian or Slovenian, and languages that are not officially recognised in any EU member state are usually ignored in this context. Importantly, the expectation is that a second foreign language will be learned, and the clear, though unstated, aim of this strategy is to ensure that learning a foreign language means more than simply learning English. Languages are considered a key cultural asset of the European landscape, and language learning is an important step towards understanding other cultures and countries. However, the strategy is clearly predicated on a conception of member states as essentially monolingual (or rather: only having official languages).

- What does 'multilingualism' appear to mean in the context of the EU language strategy? What seems to be driving the strategy? (Consider in particular the reference to '*Wettbewerbsfähigkeit*', competitiveness.)

As we have seen in Chapter 3, the EU also has firmly entrenched principles about language use within its institutions, and individual EU citizens have the right to communicate with these institutions in any one of the 24 official languages. In the next section of this chapter we will consider another aspect of exercising linguistic human rights at a more local level, specifically in the context of education in Germany, where individual *Bundesländer* can determine their own policies.

11.5   Teaching regional and minority languages: the *Handlungsplan Sprachenpolitik* in Schleswig-Holstein

Since the late 1960s and early 1970s, there has been a revalorisation of practices that are part of local and regional culture in German-speaking countries. This applies to foods, folk dance and poetry, the protection of historic buildings and ecological habitats, and – most importantly in our context – local and regional languages. This has led to a revival of the use of dialect and minority languages in various aspects of popular culture, amateur dramatic societies, newspaper columns and radio programmes, generally with great success but always viewed as entertainment and an aspect of cultural heritage, not as a means of protecting speakers of languages other than German (see also Chapters 4 and 7). More recently, Germany (1998) and Austria (2001) signed and ratified the European Council's Charter for Regional or Minority Languages (www.coe.int/t/dg4/education/minlang/default_en.asp) and thus committed themselves to supporting their listed regional and minority languages with special measures in education, administration, media presence and the law (see Table 11.1).

Table 11.1 Regional and minority languages in Germany and Austria, as recognised under the Charter for Regional or Minority Languages

	Regional languages	*Minority languages*
Germany	Low German (in Schleswig-Holstein, Hamburg, Lower Saxony, Mecklenburg-Vorpommern and parts of North Rhine Westphalia, Brandenburg and Sachsen-Anhalt)	Frisian (in parts of Lower Saxony and Schleswig-Holstein) Sorbian (in parts of Brandenburg and Saxony) Romani Danish (in parts of Schleswig-Holstein)
Austria		Croatian (in Burgenland) Slovenian (in Styria and parts of Carinthia) Hungarian (in Greater Vienna and parts of Burgenland) Czech (in Greater Vienna [Land Wien]) Slovak (in Greater Vienna) Romani (in Burgenland)

The signing of the Charter was perhaps more symbolic than practical, as many of the language support measures had already been in place for many years. The Charter requires countries to commit to a certain number of provisions in key areas, such as education, and then to report on achievements every three years. Certainly Low German, Frisian and Danish are fully accepted in the German cultural landscape, with no one seriously objecting to their visibility, though some would question the practical value of teaching minority languages for two hours per week to students who don't have any exposure to such languages outside of school.

The introduction of regional and minority languages to the curriculum of state-funded schools marks a significant departure from previous practices, since they had traditionally been excluded from the classroom on the same grounds as local and regional dialects, with the consequence that in multilingual regions such as the German-Danish borderlands they became marked as inferior to German. In the nineteenth century, the age of nationalism (see Chapter 2), some – mostly intellectuals – argued for the inclusion of such languages in the curriculum, but at no stage was it suggested that the standard variety should be replaced as the default language of instruction. This has not changed, but the teaching of regional and minority languages is taken very seriously in some *Bundesländer*. As an example, we will take a look at the *Handlungsplan Sprachenpolitik*, published by the regional government of Schleswig-Holstein in 2015 (see www.schleswig-holstein.de/DE/Fachinhalte/M/minderheiten/Downloads/152906_Handlungsplan_Sprachenpolitik.pdf?__blob=publicationFile&v=5).

Schleswig-Holstein is unique in Germany in that it is home to four of the five protected languages of the country: North Frisian, Danish, Low German and Romani (the fifth being Sorbian, spoken in Brandenburg and Saxony). Each of these languages has a very different geographical spread and linguistic status, and the *Handlungsplan* details the government's ambitions to put in place specific provisions for each of the languages suitable for its particular sociolinguistic context.[2]

The *Handlungsplan* outlines the government's principal positions as follows:

> Schleswig-Holstein ist ein Mehrsprachenland. Die Regionalsprache Niederdeutsch sowie die Minderheitensprachen Nordfriesisch, Dänisch und Romanes sind Teil unserer Identität. [. . .] Mit dem Handlungsplan Sprachenpolitik [. . .] formuliert [die Landesregierung] ein eigenständiges sprachenpolitisches Konzept, das in alle Bereiche des Regierungshandelns hineinwirkt. Grundlegend dafür ist unser Verständnis eines gleichberechtigten Nebeneinanders der Mehrheitssprache sowie der Regional-oder Minderheitensprachen bei uns im Land. Es muss daher für die Sprecher der Regional-oder Minderheitensprachen Möglichkeiten geben, ihre Sprachen im Alltag nutzen zu können. Das schließt sowohl die Möglichkeiten und Angebote des Erlernens und Vertiefens der Sprechfähigkeit (vom Kindergarten bis zu Universität) als auch ihre Verwendung im öffentlichen Raum (im Kontakt mit Behörden und Verwaltung, Präsenz in den Medien) mit ein.
>
> (Handlungsplan 2015: 3)

• What are the most likely practical problems confronting the government's ambitions to aim for a *gleichberechtigtes Nebeneinander* of the languages in Schleswig-Holstein?

Low German (see Figure 11.1)

Low German (Niederdeutsch or Plattdeutsch) is spoken all over northern Germany, and thus covers an area much larger than Schleswig-Holstein. It is most strongly represented in East Frisia (Lower Saxony), in Mecklenburg and on the west coast of Schleswig-Holstein, where you can hear the language spoken in the streets. A regional language, it has neither an ethnic nor a national base and nowadays has the sociolinguistic status of 'regional dialect' in the area; in other words, its use is largely restricted to the spoken domain, its speaker numbers are generally dwindling and it is used much more by older speakers in rural environments than by others. It is taught at several universities in the region, and any student of German at Kiel or Flensburg University has to do at least one module in Low German or Frisian. In 2014–2015, an initiative to teach Low German in 27 primary schools was launched, providing two hours of lessons per week, and it has been offered as an optional or extra-curricular activity in secondary schools since the 1970s, but these efforts are often dependent on the personal enthusiasm of individual teachers.

Danish (see Figure 11.2)

The autochthonous variety of Danish in the area is Sønderjysk, but it has declined rapidly over the last 30 years or so and has now all but disappeared south of the Danish-German border. The language used by the Danish minority is standard Danish (Rigsdansk), though the vast majority use German as their family language. The schools run by the Danish School Association (Dansk Skoleforening) use Danish as the sole language of instruction, with no explicit allowance for students who don't have Danish as a family language. In practice, attending Danish secondary schools presupposes that students will have attended Danish kindergarten and primary schools and thus acquired sufficient levels of Danish. In the German schools in the northern part of Schleswig-Holstein, Danish is offered as a second foreign

Figure 11.1 Bilingual place sign in German and Low German
Photo: Bergedorfer Zeitung

Figure 11.2 Bilingual place sign in German and Danish
Photo: Nils Langer

language. The *Handlungsplan* makes no mention of the provision of Danish in schools but emphasises the role of the universities of Flensburg and Kiel in contributing to the training of teachers of Danish.

North Frisian (see Figure 11.3)

North Frisian is restricted to the north-western coastline and islands in Nordfriesland, where it is still spoken by some 4,000–5,000 people. Apart from two small areas (on the island of Föhr and in Risum-Lindholm), you are unlikely to hear the language spoken in

Figure 11.3 Bilingual place sign in German and North Frisian
Photo: Nils Langer

the street, but it is a distinguishing part of Frisian identity and over the last 20 years or so, the language has become increasingly visible on street signs, stickers and names for cafés and restaurants (see also Chapters 4 and 9). Frisian was part of the school curriculum sporadically during the twentieth century. It is now taught at 11 state primary schools from year 1 onwards, another two from year 3, for two hours per week. Lessons are voluntary and will be provided if the parents request them, as long as a minimum number of 12 students can be found. In addition to the German schools, a number of schools of the Danish School Association also provide lessons in Frisian, although the Danish school in Risum-Lindholm is the only one where Frisian is used as a language of instruction (in addition to Danish).

The teaching of North Frisian and Low German faces three major obstacles:

•   The limited availability of teaching materials and textbooks;
•   The small number of teachers qualified, able and motivated to teach these languages; and
•   The diminishing numbers of speakers, both at school age and older.

While the first two points could feasibly be remedied by the state authorities and supportive cultural institutions – and the *Handlungsplan* demonstrates that this is indeed taking place – the third point can only be addressed by the speaker communities themselves, and the common wisdom is that the decline of Low German and North Frisian is unstoppable (a problem faced by regional and minority languages across Europe).

By contrast, the position of Danish is much stronger: in the Danish minority schools it provides the key linking element to mainstream Danish society. In these schools, it is generally accepted to be a good thing to learn the language of the northern neighbour, especially because of the importance of Danish tourists in Flensburg and the surrounding area and the high number of cross-border commuters who work in Denmark due to the higher wages but who continue to live in Germany because of the much lower living costs. In addition to such economic reasons, Danish is popular because it provides a link with Danish culture, which, like all Scandinavian culture, commands high prestige. In fact, it is a well-known phenomenon that many middle-class Germans – with no family connection to Denmark – send their children to Danish minority schools because they feel that they provide a better, more liberal and more attentive education. This development is not without problems, however, as members of the Danish minority rightly argue that their school system is intended for Danish nationals,[3] not just for anyone who likes Denmark. On the other hand, this popularity of Danish schools also means that student numbers are up, and hence difficult questions about the sustainability of the current system are less likely to be asked.

11.6   Conclusion

In this chapter we explored the role of language in education, with a particular focus on school teaching. We considered the controversial nature of the standard language ideology, weighing up the pedagogical benefits claimed by its proponents against the prejudice and discrimination it may entail for children growing up in a family using non-standard varieties of German or other languages; it is a part of the social injustice of many western societies that this applies most readily to groups already marginalised, especially those who are socially disadvantaged through poverty and recent immigration. We also discussed the teaching of languages other than German in schools, especially in the context of the importance attached at national and supra-national levels to learning 'important' foreign languages, such as English and French, and the challenges of providing education in the myriad languages, especially in urban schools, resulting from high levels of recent migration. However, we have also seen how through the recognition of regional and minority languages as a part of regional cultural heritage, the classroom in Germany can be multilingual, though with many different types of support and levels of acceptance.

Tasks and suggestions for research

Reflective tasks

1   In what ways, if at all, has this chapter helped you to think more critically about terms such as 'correct German' or 'minority languages' and the (dis)advantages of bilingualism?
2   Why do you think the European Charter excludes dialects and languages of recent immigrants? Consider this in the light of political and educational factors.

Research tasks

1   Review the media coverage on either (a) the promotion or protection of minority/ regional languages or (b) the issues associated with multilingual classrooms. What lines of argumentation are dominant and how plausible are they?
2   Compare the Official Reports on the Implementation of the European Charter for Regional or Minority Languages in Germany or Austria and another, non-German-speaking country, and identify similarities and differences with regard to the perception and status of lesser-used languages in these countries.

Project idea

Put yourself in the position of the education minister in Berlin or Schleswig-Holstein. Form a small working group on language policy and draw up a plan that seeks to balance an appropriate emphasis on the need for all school students to learn standard German with the opportunity to learn regional or minority languages (such as Frisian, Danish, Turkish or Russian).

Notes

1 The second sentence has been deleted in the most recent version of the statues but a statement on the school's website robustly defends the policy of insisting on the use of German in every aspect of life in the school (http://hhs-berlin.de/index.php/schulchronik/2016-17/464-deutsch-als-schulsprache-2).
2 Romani does not receive the same direct support as the other languages since the Romani-speaking community considers their language to be spoken-only and reserved for their community.
3 Most members of the Danish minority consider themselves to be part of the Danish *nation* but also German *citizens*. North Frisians are classified as a separate *Volksgruppe* (ethnic group), but most consider themselves German as well. Speakers of Low German simply see themselves as German.

Annotated further reading

Buselmeier (2008) is a critique of Siebert-Ott (1999) and provides a useful general overview of the key issues in relation to multilingual classrooms.

Davies and Langer (2014) offer a comprehensive discussion of the tensions faced by teachers who want to be sensitive to linguistic variation and diversity but who, due to their role as teachers, need to provide corrections to their pupils' performance.

The European Charter for Regional or Minority Languages has an official website (www.coe.int/t/dg4/education/minlang/default_en.asp) with plenty of documents, including lists of countries that signed and ratified the Charter and official reports from signatory countries.

Imo (2008) discusses the tensions between written and oral language use in the context of teaching linguistic norms in German lessons.

Leitfaden für den Niederdeutschunterricht an Grundschulen in Schleswig-Holstein (www.schleswig-holstein.de/DE/Landesregierung/III/Service/Broschueren/Bildung/Niederdeutsch.pdf;jsessionid=547C93E8EE1D9F458126462F674CB063?__blob=publicationFile&v=2) provides guidelines for teaching Low German in primary schools in Schleswig-Holstein.

Siebert-Ott (1999) provides a still useful discussion of the issues of multilingual classrooms and should be read in conjunction with Buselmeier (2008).

Wagner (2009) is a doctoral thesis discussing the perception of 'good' or 'correct' German amongst pupils and teachers from two different types of schools in Rheinland-Pfalz.

Walker (2009) is a useful summary of the multilingual nature of Nordfriesland, the administrative district in the very north-west of Germany where five different autochthonous languages are spoken.

Weber and Horner (2012) include a number of case studies on the issue of minority languages and teaching.

12   Language and citizenship

12.1   Introduction

In the country where you are studying, and perhaps also where you were born or grew up if that was elsewhere, you may have come across statements (in the media, for example) that underline the necessity for newcomers to know or learn the language of the host country. For example, 'if you want to live in Germany, you should be able to speak German'.

- What kinds of rationale are provided to support these statements? They may seem to be stating the obvious, but in what ways might they be contentious in principle and problematic in practice?
- What are some of the difficulties that newcomers may experience when trying to learn the language of the host country?

In this chapter, we return to some of the questions we raised in Chapters 1 and 2 in connection with the relationship between language and nation (or language and state), this time exploring how language issues are linked to debates on migration, integration and citizenship. We focus here on Germany and Luxembourg, to examine the contrasting situations in different German-speaking countries, as well as on the broader European context.

12.2   Language ideologies and migration

Despite the fact that it is subject to a great deal of current debate in Europe, migration is by no means a new phenomenon – it has been part of European life for centuries. Even if we limit our perspective to the relatively recent past, we can see that at various points in the twentieth century political upheavals and related reconfigurations of boundaries triggered significant population movements, most dramatically following the World Wars (see Chapter 1). In the direct aftermath of the Second World War, in particular, population displacement and migration flows added to the critical shortage of the (male) workforce in Germany – East and West – at the time, and the respective governments had to take measures to deal with this deficit.

The GDR government's response was to recruit large numbers of 'contract workers' (*Vertragsarbeiter*) from other socialist countries such as Vietnam, Cuba and Mozambique, most of whom stayed only for a relatively short time (although some, especially Vietnamese, were stranded there when the GDR ceased to exist in 1990). Similarly, the West German government entered into agreements with countries in southern Europe, as well as with Turkey and Morocco, to recruit predominantly manual labourers from the mid-1950s until 1973.

Although it was envisaged that these workers would only stay temporarily and were even referred to as *Gastarbeiter*, many of them stayed permanently, and, in many cases, their family members joined them to make a new home in various parts of West Germany, such as the industrialised *Ruhrgebiet*, and in West Berlin.

West Germany experienced high levels of economic growth in the decades after the war, which played a major role in transforming it de facto from a country of emigration to a country of immigration. Yet, there was no marked change in migration policies as a response to this situation. Official recognition of migration patterns in post-1990 unified Germany only began to take place at the turn of the twenty-first century, when the German *Staatsangehörigkeitsgesetz* was reformed and somewhat more inclusive citizenship provisions came into effect on 1 January 2000 (see also Chapter 2 on the concepts *nation* and *state*). A number of political events in the late twentieth century, including the fall of the Berlin Wall and collapse of the Soviet Union, the consolidation and expansion of the EU and the refugee crisis in the former Yugoslavia, as well as in parts of Africa and the Middle East, all contributed to new, more complex patterns of migration. Five factors of particular relevance to EU countries are the number of countries of origin, the number of people on the move, the diversity of motives for migration, family unification and, notably, the politicisation of migration. As a result of these and other factors, contemporary Germany is characterised by significant levels of linguistic and cultural diversity, which in turn has led to intense public debates on migration and diversity, including those focused on multiculturalism and the related concept of *Leitkultur*.

Related debates frequently portray **societal multilingualism** as a problem that needs to be solved (see also Chapters 7 and 11). Read the following statement by the conservative political party Christian Social Union (CSU), which was published in *Spiegel Online Politik* on 5 December 2014, as well as the #YallaCSU tweet on 6 December 2014 as one example of the responses:

> München – Die CSU hat in einem Leitantragsentwurf zum Parteitag in der kommenden Woche gefordert, dass sich Migranten auch zu Hause auf Deutsch unterhalten sollen. Das berichtet der "Bayerische Rundfunk", dem das Papier vorliegt. "Wer dauerhaft hier leben will, soll dazu angehalten werden, im öffentlichen Raum und in der Familie Deutsch zu sprechen", zitiert der BR aus dem Entwurf. "Ein gesellschaftliches Miteinander funktioniert nur, wenn alle dieselbe Sprache sprechen", heißt es laut BR weiter. Deshalb erwarte man von jedem Migranten, "dass er die deutsche Sprache lernt". Für Ausländer, die ohne Sprachkenntnisse einreisen oder hier bleiben dürfen, "bieten wir Sprachförderung in allen Lebenslagen an."
>
> (*Spiegel Online*, 5 December 2014, www.spiegel.de/politik/deutschland/csu-in-bayern-migranten-sollen-im-wohnzimmer-deutsch-sprechen-a-1006904.html)

> Zeigen wir der #CSU wie schön es ist, auch andere Sprachen zu sprechen. #YallaCSU.
> (Mohamed Amjahid @mamjahid, https://twitter.com/hashtag/yallacsu)

- What assumptions about language and society seem to lie behind the CSU statement?
- In what ways do #YallaCSU tweets, such as the previous one, potentially challenge the CSU statement and related beliefs about language and society? Why is the tag *Yalla* used? What arguments are put forward in other #YallaCSU tweets?

It is often taken for granted that the optimal form of societal organisation is based on monolingual norms. But what are the origins of these beliefs that prioritise a monolingual society? In Chapter 2, we discussed how the ideal of the homogeneous nation-state took strong hold in Europe during the long nineteenth century and also how language constituted a key ingredient in this formulation. In present-day debates on diversity we can see how these **language ideologies**, or deeply ingrained and institutionally supported beliefs about the way people think language and society should be organised, continue to be prominent and even come across as basic common sense in many contexts. The use of a particular language often functions as a means of signalling ('**indexing**') group membership in a nation-state and can even position speakers at different points on linguistic hierarchies. Being a 'native speaker' of German in Austria, for example, confers a higher status than speaking another European language such as Hungarian, which in turn, however, may be valued more positively there than speaking Arabic or Farsi. Consistent and repeated forms of indexing can make certain links appear so naturalised that they often meet with little or no challenge: for example, the idea that 'Germany is a German-speaking country'. This is what Irvine and Gal (2000) refer to as **iconicity**: **iconic** relationships between languages and idealised nation-states are a common feature of language ideologies, especially in the European context.

This historically deeply rooted 'one nation, one language' ideology still dominates language policy in Germany and many other European states (see Chapters 2 and 11). At the same time, however, the EU consistently promotes an ideal of European multilingualism:

> 'United in diversity', the motto of the European Union, first came into use in 2000. It signifies how Europeans have come together, in the form of the EU, to work for peace and prosperity, while at the same time being enriched by the continent's many different cultures, traditions and languages.
>
> (http://europa.eu/abc/symbols/motto/index_en.htm)

- Consider this statement in relation to policies that prioritise the role of the **national** and/or **official language** of individual EU countries.

This all suggests that there are competing perspectives on linguistic and social diversity in contemporary Europe. In the next section, we consider the impact this has on conceptions of citizenship and on public perceptions of the role of language knowledge and language use in fostering social integration.

12.3   Discourses on language, integration and social cohesion

In Chapter 2, we discussed how ideologies of nationalism fuse together the concepts of nation and state, with language playing a central role in the construction of this idealised homogeneous unit. This is linked to what Blommaert and Verschueren (1998: 194–195) call the 'dogma of homogeneism' or 'a view of society in which differences are seen as dangerous and centrifugal and in which the "best" society is suggested to be one without intergroup differences'. This view appears to underpin mainstream ideas on the relationship between language, migration and citizenship. It is frequently claimed that monolingual policies are necessary for social cohesion and, as a result, that people who speak 'other' languages are in need of integration. Many European countries now impose their national and/or official language upon these people through language testing procedures as part of recently modified forms of citizenship legislation. Behind such policies on integration and citizenship, there seems to lie not only a concern with social cohesion but also a deeper and more irrational fear of societal multilingualism and 'difference'. Therefore, we will first explore the discourse of integration before moving on to examine some of the policies on language testing and citizenship in German-speaking countries.

Integration, often co-occurring with the term *social cohesion*, has become a keyword in dominant discourse. It can refer to both European integration (that is, the harmonisation of member states' political and economic structures) and the integration of people categorised as 'migrants' or 'foreigners'. Here, we will look at how integration in the second sense is used in official policy documents and media discourse in Germany. First, consider the pivotal report by the 2001 Unabhängige Kommission 'Zuwanderung' that led to the eventual adoption of the 2004 Immigration Act, after more than three years of debates that did not fully subside even after the legislation came into effect in 2005. The following question is posed in the report: 'Wie können wir die Menschen anderer Herkunft und Kultur in unsere Gesellschaft integrieren?' And the report is full of compound nouns – such as *Integrationsangebot*, *Integrationsschulung*, *Integrationskurse* – that develop a complex discursive framework around a particular way of understanding 'integration'.

- How do you understand the question posed in the report? What does it seem to imply about what 'integration' means and how it can be achieved?
- Otto Schily, Federal Minister of the Interior at the time, controversially stated in an interview with the *Süddeutsche Zeitung* that 'die beste Form der Integration ist die Assimilierung'. Do 'integration' and 'assimilation' mean the same thing to you?

The focus on the difficulties of integration and how it requires hard work and effort is a core aspect of the discourse of integration. For example, an *Index zur Messung der Integration*, analysed by the Berlin-Institut in 2009, evaluated the degree of integration achieved by different migrant groups on the basis of 20 indicators, with an emphasis on the domains of education and the labour market. The so-called *Integrationswerte* (integration scores) were calculated for each group and placed on a scale ranging from 1 (unsuccessful) to 8 (successful integration). As a result, certain groups were perceived as, and implicitly blamed for, being poorly integrated. The authors of the report claimed that it was not their intention to blame certain groups. However, this is how the results of the report were portrayed in the media:

Migranten-Studie: Türken sind mit Abstand am schlechtesten integriert
(*Der Spiegel*, 24 January 2009, www.spiegel.de/politik/deutschland/migranten-studie-tuerken-sind-mit-abstand-am-schlechtesten-integriert-a-603294.html)

Warum Türken bei der Integration nicht mitspielen
(*Die Welt*, 25 January 2009, www.welt.de/politik/article3088721/Warum-Tuerken-bei-der-Integration-nicht-mitspielen.html)

Probleme türkischer Einwanderer: Integration ist mangelhaft
(*taz*, 26 January 2009, www.taz.de/!5168947/)

- What responsibility do you think report writers have in presenting research results?
- Read some of the articles covering the report and reflect critically on how the term *integration* is used. How is it linked to German language proficiency?

So language has become a key aspect in debates on migration, integration and citizenship in contemporary Germany and many other European countries. These debates are shaped by monolingual norms, despite the fact that the lived reality for many people is multilingual. It is often assumed that people who speak languages other than German – widely referred to as immigrant languages – have a deficit regarding their German language proficiency. The situation seems to be different, however, for people whose multilingual repertoires comprise languages with high market value, such as English (see Chapter 11).

•   Watch the following clip from the German comedy show *Ladykracher* with Anke Engelke: *Deutschkurs für türkische Mitbürger* (www.youtube.com/watch?v= mPH7ZIGZ4BE). Consider what a sketch with English-speaking students learning German might look like and also whether such people are commonly referred to as migrants. Discuss the potential of comic performance in challenging dominant discourse on migration, integration and citizenship (and see also Chapter 7).

12.4   Language testing regimes and citizenship legislation

Since the turn of the twenty-first century, a certain degree of harmonisation of policies on migration, asylum and citizenship has taken place within the EU and the so-called Schengen countries. A number of mechanisms that allow for the movement of EU passport holders, and restrict that of non-EU passport holders, have been implemented. For this reason, many scholars refer to the concept of *layered citizenship* in Europe that consists both of EU citizenship and that of the state. This is indicated by the naming of both the EU and the respective member state on the cover of passports in EU countries (see Figures 12.1 and 12.2 on the following pages).

It is in this context that citizenship legislation has been reformed in many European countries. These new laws, or amendments to existing laws, often include the introduction of formalised language and/or civics tests: the latter are frequently referred to as tests on the 'knowledge of society' (KoS) and simultaneously can function as a means of testing language proficiency. This significant and wide-ranging shift in policy has led a number of sociolinguists to explore the motivations and consequences of these language requirements and testing procedures that now form part of citizenship legislation in various European countries.

•   Does the country where you are studying require citizenship applicants to take a language test or a civics (KoS) test? If so, what level of language proficiency is required and what kind of 'knowledge of society' is tested?

In Chapter 1, we discussed the challenges in defining German-speaking countries. On the basis of official language policy, we indicated that we would refer to five countries in Europe as German-speaking: Germany, Austria, Liechtenstein, Switzerland and Luxembourg. We also noted that there is a continuum in terms of whether these countries are officially deemed to be monolingual or multilingual, with Germany, Austria and Liechtenstein on the former end of the continuum and Switzerland and Luxembourg on the latter end. This continuum provides the rationale for the focus of the remaining part of this chapter, which is a comparative discussion of policies in Germany and Luxembourg.

Before proceeding, it is interesting to note that citizenship policy in all of the German-speaking countries was shaped largely by the principle of *jus sanguinis* (citizenship by

Figure 12.1 German passport
Photo: Nils Langer

descent) during the greater part of the twentieth century. This has shifted towards (some) opening to the principle of *jus soli* (citizenship by place of birth), principally in the case of Germany. These countries also implemented formalised language testing requirements as part of citizenship legislation in the early part of the twenty-first century. It is this combination of relaxing certain parameters for access to citizenship and implementing new barriers such as language testing for citizenship that is crucial to bear in mind.

This combination of factors has been commented on in diverse ways. On the one hand, there has been a great deal of positive response to reductions in the required residence period and shifts towards the *jus soli* principle in relation to acquiring citizenship. On the other hand, the implementation of formalised language testing has met with more varied views.

Figure 12.2 Luxembourg passport
Photo: Kristine Horner

Much of the critical response has come from researchers working in the field of language policy. Key issues that have been raised pertain to the fairness and validity of the tests and also whether these policies actually promote social inclusion.

•   It may well seem reasonable to expect people applying for citizenship of a country to demonstrate some degree of proficiency in its official or national language(s). But what would constitute a fair test in this respect? For example, how would you decide what the appropriate level of proficiency is and how would you assess it?

As indicated at the beginning of this chapter, major reforms to citizenship legislation in Germany entered into effect on 1 January 2000. This allowed for children born in Germany of foreign parents to qualify for German citizenship as long as at least one of their parents had been living legally in the country for eight years or more, and adults were entitled to apply for citizenship after eight years' residence (instead of after 15 years, as had previously been the case). However, it was stipulated that applicants would be refused naturalisation if they did not provide evidence of German language proficiency which, following queries on the meaning of 'ausreichende Kenntnisse' (sufficient knowledge) in the initial legislation of 15 July 1999, led to the following amendment:

Ausreichende Kenntnisse der deutschen Sprache liegen vor, wenn sich der Ein-bürgerungsbewerber im täglichen Leben einschließlich der üblichen Kontakte mit Behörden in seiner deutschen Umgebung sprachlich zurechtzufinden vermag und mit ihm ein seinem Alter und Bildungsstand entsprechendes Gespräch geführt werden kann. Dazu gehört auch, dass der Einbürgerungsbewerber einen deutschsprachigen Text des alltäglichen Lebens lesen, verstehen und die wesentlichen Inhalte mündlich wiedergeben kann [. . .] Die Fähigkeit, sich auf einfache Art mündlich verständigen zu können, reicht nicht aus.

(Bundesministerium des Inneren, Allgemeine Verwaltungsvorschrift zum Staatsangehörigkeitsrecht [StAR-VwV], December 2000, www.bmi.bund. de/SharedDocs/ExterneLinks/DE/Juris_Links/S/StAR-VwV.html)

Reforms to citizenship legislation also came into effect in Luxembourg on 1 January 2002. Unlike the case of Germany, provisions had already existed for the naturalisation of all for-eigners. This new legislation reduced the residency period (from 10 to 5 years), and, like in Germany, it stipulated language requirements:

Naturalization will be refused to the foreigner [. . .] if he does not demonstrate suf-ficient integration, notably if he does not demonstrate sufficient active and passive knowledge of at least one of the languages [Luxembourgish, French, German] stipu-lated by the language law of February 24th 1984 and if he does not have at least a basic knowledge of the Luxembourgish language, accompanied by certificates or by official documents.

(Mémorial: Journal Officiel du Grand-Duché de Luxembourg/Memorial: Amtsblatt des Großherzogtums Luxemburg. Recueil de Législation. A – No 129, 26 October 2001: 2597–2604; translation from French in Horner 2009)

• What similarities and differences do you notice in the above extracts from legal policy documents in Germany and Luxembourg?

Based on the Common European Framework of Reference for Languages (CEFR; www. coe.int/t/dg4/linguistic/cadre1_en.asp), many European countries passed further forms of legislation stipulating the level of language proficiency that candidates for citizenship need to demonstrate. In this context, various controversies unfolded in individual coun-tries. There were two issues that complicated the implementation of standardised forms of testing in Germany. First, there were different categories of migrants, including ethnic German *Aussiedler* from central and eastern Europe who were permitted to apply for citizenship prior to the 2000 legislation and were subject to different procedures, because their migration had been governed by different laws linked to Cold War politics. Second, the initial versions of the *Einbürgerungstests* following from the new policy in 2000 were highly diverse as they were designed in different *Bundesländer* due to the federal structure of the German state.

Despite these various tensions, consensus was ultimately reached, and standardised KoS tests were introduced in 2008. The year before, the level of language proficiency required for German citizenship had been set at CEFR Level B1, which could be demonstrated by providing official documentation such as the *Zertifikat Deutsch*. These are the criteria for CEFR level B1:

B1 'Threshold' competencies: Common European Framework of Reference for Languages

- ○ Can understand the main points of clear standard input on familiar matters regularly encountered in work, school, leisure, etc.
- ○ Can deal with most situations likely to arise while travelling in an area where the language is spoken.
- ○ Can produce simple connected text on topics which are familiar or of personal interest.
- ○ Can describe experiences and events, dreams, hopes and ambitions and briefly give reasons and explanations for opinions and plans.

- • Consider how you might prepare for a test with knowledge-based questions that is administered in a language you started learning as an adult. Reflect on the B1 'Threshold' Competencies.

In Luxembourg, a new citizenship law was passed in 2008 that, amongst other things such as allowing broader provisions for dual citizenship, stipulated that applicants are required to pass a language test in Luxembourgish but not a KoS test. The CEFR level was set at B1 for listening comprehension and A2 for oral production. In addition to the broader controversies around this law, including debates on dual citizenship, there are two interrelated language issues to consider. First, Luxembourg is an officially trilingual country, with the use of Luxembourgish, German and French implemented in state schools. Second, Luxembourgish is first and foremost a language of spoken communication: it is widely used for informal and formal oral communication amongst a large segment of the population, but less so in writing (except in certain domains); in terms of the implementation of linguistic standardisation processes, Luxembourgish is therefore less fully developed than French or German, especially in the framework of the educational system (see Chapters 5 and 11).

The uncertainty around the 'linguistic authority' of Luxembourgish gave rise to disputes concerning the introduction of formalised language testing for citizenship. Considerable efforts had to be made to establish Luxembourgish in public discourse as the 'language of integration' in the years leading up to the 2008 law. Even after the introduction of the law, some individuals in Luxembourg challenged the language requirements, using the argument that Luxembourgish could not be seen as the 'generic' or default language of everyday life due to the widespread use of spoken and written French (especially in the capital) and also due to the relative lack of written materials in Luxembourgish in the public sphere.

- • Consider how you might prepare for a test in a language that is mainly spoken rather than written. Reflect on the relationship between this test and the official trilingual policy of Luxembourg.

There remain many controversies around language requirements and testing as part of citizenship policy, both in individual European countries and on a broader scale. One key point that we can note on the basis of our discussion is the diversity in the design of tests as well as levels of required language proficiency in different countries. The tensions between conceptions of citizenship at national and supra-national levels will be an important issue in the ongoing project of developing greater European integration, and an understanding of sociolinguistic principles and debates will provide you with a critical perspective on the ways in which ideas about language are incorporated into policies on citizenship.

12.5 Conclusion

In this chapter, we focused on how language issues have become central to debates on migration, integration and citizenship in German-speaking countries and across Europe. The discussion has shown how monolingual norms, linked to a deeply rooted 'monolingual mindset' (Clyne 2008), remain highly prominent in the early twenty-first century. We explored the discourse of integration as a means of uncovering the ways that monolingual norms are perpetuated despite, or perhaps even due to, high levels of linguistic and cultural diversity. We then considered recently implemented policies on language testing and citizenship as a poignant example of institutionalised monolingualism. Finally, we compared and contrasted policies on language and citizenship in Germany and Luxembourg to draw attention to some of the paradoxes and tensions inherent to these policies. It will be interesting to observe how these policies are maintained, challenged and potentially modified in the near and distant future.

Tasks and suggestions for research

Reflective task

There are various different ways of defining 'citizenship'. What do you think constitutes a 'good citizen' and what role (if any) should language play in this?

Research tasks

1   Gather historical data on migration to Germany (both East and West) between the mid-1950s and the mid-1970s. How does more recent migration to Germany post-1990 differ?
2   Look at the citizenship tests for Germany, Austria, Luxembourg, the UK and/or other countries online – and try them yourself. What kinds of knowledge do they require? What level of language proficiency would seem necessary to respond to such questions? Would you qualify for citizenship on the basis of your performance in these tests?

Project idea

Analyse recent debates on language, migration and citizenship in one or more of the German-speaking countries, based on academic and media sources as well as official policy documentation, and draw up a proposal for a language policy that would support a positive conception of citizenship in the interests of both individual and state in the twenty-first century.

Annotated further reading

Extra et al. (2009) and Hogan-Brun et al. (2009) offer wide-ranging discussions and case studies on various aspects of language testing and citizenship in Europe from a critical and language ideological perspective.

Flubacher (2013) provides a discussion of the role of language and the discourse of integration in relation to citizenship legislation with a focus on German-speaking Switzerland.

Hansen-Thomas (2007) takes a historically situated approach to unpacking the ways that language ideologies are linked to the German citizenship legislation of 2000 as well as the implementation of language requirements.

Horner (2015a) provides an analysis of official policy and media discourse on language, integration and citizenship in Luxembourg, exploring the controversies around shifting policies on official trilingualism and the role of Luxembourgish.

Laversuch (2008) provides an analysis of cross-regional differences in implementing policies in Bavaria and Saxony-Anhalt, following nationwide measures in Germany to move towards standardising language testing procedures for citizenship.

Möllering (2010) provides an account of some of the more recent developments regarding citizenship legislation in Germany, following Piller (2001) and Stevenson (2006).

Pfaff (2010) gives a critical overview of the role of language in relation to social policies in contemporary Germany, including recent forms of citizenship policy.

Piller (2001) is a landmark article in the scholarship on ideological approaches to language testing and citizenship, which focuses on the situation in Germany in 2000.

Stevenson (2006) offers a discussion of the relationship between discourses on citizenship and national identity, with a focus on the role of language in citizenship legislation in early twenty-first-century Germany and Austria.

Keywords

(Note: this list is intended only as a brief guide to the ways selected concepts are used in this book. In many cases, the terms are open to a wide range of definitions and interpretations.)

accommodation   The practice of adapting your speech to be similar to, or different from, that of the person you are talking to.

acronym   A word formed by combining the initial letters of other words, e.g. 'LOL' for 'laugh out loud'.

affricate   A stop sound followed immediately by a fricative sound, e.g. [tʃ].

allochthonous   Not native or does not originate from the place in which it is currently found.

Alltagssprache   The language used in everyday life.

Amtssprache   Official language (i.e. one that has official status and/or function in a particular country or region).

Anglicism   An originally English word that has been borrowed (either unaltered or adapted) by another language.

Anglizismus   See Anglicism.

Arbeitssprache   Working language, i.e. a language used for everyday business within a multinational organisation such as the European Commission or the United Nations.

assimilation   The influence of one sound on an adjacent one, e.g. *geben* pronounced as [ge:bm].

Austriacism   A word that is only found in Austrian German or an Austrian German word that has been borrowed by another language.

autochthonous   Resident in a particular place from earliest recorded times.

auxiliary (verb)   A verb used in conjunction with the main verb of a clause in order to indicate tense, mood, etc., e.g. 'have' in the sentence 'Have you done your homework?'

borrowing   A word belonging to one language is adopted by another, either unaltered or adapted, e.g. *Schadenfreude* in English.

Central German   Referring to a collection of High German dialects spoken in a belt that crosses the middle of Germany from the Rhineland in the west to Berlin and surrounding areas in the east.

code-mixing   Blending two speech varieties (languages, dialects, etc.) together within a single utterance.

code-switching   Changing from one speech variety (language, dialect, etc.) to another during a conversation.

codification   The stage in the process of language standardisation in which a systematic account of its forms (especially grammar and vocabulary) is developed.

colloquial speech   A general term for speech forms that differ less markedly from standard German than dialects and are used over a wider geographical area.

communicative competence   The knowledge of the norms or conventions governing the use of different forms of language according to the social situation in a given speech community.

complementary distribution   (In this context) a relationship between two language varieties in which each is used exclusively for one set of functions (or in one set of domains).

computer-mediated communication (CMC)   A general term referring to all forms of digital communication (i.e. conducted on computers and other digital devices such as tablets and smartphones).

concord   When two lexical items 'agree' with or 'match' each other. In German, nouns and adjectives must agree in number, case and gender; the person and number of subjects and verbs must also match.

conjunction   A word used to link two ideas or clauses in a sentence, e.g. *and, but, since*, etc.

coronalisation   The production of sounds by raising the tongue blade towards the teeth or the hard palate, e.g. /n/, /d/, or the realisation of a sound like /s/ as /ʃ/ (e.g. *ist* pronounced as *ischt*).

covert prestige   A non-standard variety of a language is viewed as having more prestige than the standard variety only by those who speak it.

desemantisation   Referring to the broadening of a word's meaning to such an extent that it becomes generic.

Deutsch als Fremdsprache (DaF)   German as a foreign language, referring to the study and use of German by speakers for whom German is not their first language.

diachronic   Referring to the historical development of a phenomenon (such as language).

diacritic   A mark added to a written symbol to alter the way it is pronounced.

dialect   Definitions vary, but the term is used here to mean any non-standard speech form that differs significantly from standard German at all linguistic levels and is associated with a particular geographical (usually rural) location.

Dialekt   See dialect. Note though that *Dialekt* is generally used with a more restrictive sense than the English *dialect*, which can also refer to any (not only geographical) non-standard variety of a language.

diglossia   A particular form of societal multilingualism in which the two languages or language varieties are said to be in complementary distribution (see above).

diphthong   A vowel sound in which there is an audible change during its production, e.g. [ai], [au].

diphthongisation   The process of producing a vowel sound which combines two single vowel sounds. See diphthong.

discourse   Refers (a) to the organisation of language use above the level of the sentence and (b) to language use as a form of social practice or a way of articulating a particular stance, e.g. 'the discourse of homeopathy' versus 'the discourse of medical science'.

discourse marker   Word or phrase used to connect and organise what we say or write. Can also be used to express an attitude or opinion, e.g. *frankly, but*, etc.

discursive practice   A common communicative behaviour, or manner of speaking, which is based on and, in turn, shapes social norms, values and ideologies, e.g. patterns of personal address.

domain   A social setting such as school, home, church or workplace.

elision The omission of sounds or syllables in connected speech, e.g. *sie ist 'ne alte Bekannte von mir.*

empirical Based on experiment and observation rather than theory.

enregister(ment) The process in which a particular use or type of language becomes associated with certain social identities and those who participate in these customs.

epistemic Referring to the degree of certainty expressed in an utterance, based on the knowledge that is stated in that utterance.

ethnolect (primary, secondary, tertiary) A variety of language that is associated with a specific cultural or ethnic group. Often used to demarcate a particular identity or group identity.

etymology The study of (or an account of) the origin and history of a word.

finite verb The conjugated form of a verb, i.e. the form that agrees with the subject in number, tense, mood, etc. For example, the verb forms in *I do, you do, he does* and so on.

fremdes Wort A word taken from a foreign language. See loanword. Similar to ***Fremdwort***, but often used to refer more narrowly to a more obviously 'foreign' word (e.g. one that has not been adapted orthographically). For example, *Manager* might be considered a *fremdes Wort*, while *Streik* might be seen as a ***Fremdwort***.

fricative A consonant produced by forcing air through a narrow gap in the vocal tract, causing audible friction, e.g. [f], [s].

front vowel Vowel produced with the tongue at or near the front of the mouth, e.g. [i:].

gender-neutral Not referring or specific to any gender, e.g. *es* in German.

generic Refers to a class of word that denotes a class of items, e.g. *bird*, which subsumes *eagle, sparrow*, etc., or *the reader of this book*, meaning *all readers of this book*.

genre Referring to the type of text a discourse can be categorised as, based on its form, function and meaning, e.g. recipe, lecture, joke.

glottal stop Referring to the consonantal sound that is produced by completely closing the glottis and then opening it, as when e.g. 'water' is pronounced without a /t/ sound. The IPA symbol is /ʔ/.

grapheme Smallest unit in a writing system; in alphabetical systems, this is the letter, e.g. <h>, <ü>.

Hauptsatz See main clause.

Helveticism A word only found in Swiss varieties of German.

High German An umbrella term referring to all German dialects spoken in the south of Germany, Austria and Switzerland, e.g. *Bairisch* or Bavarian. 'High' refers to the fact that southern Germany is mountainous. In non-academic usage used to refer to standard German (which was originally based on central/southern varieties of German).

Hochdeutsch See High German.

hyponymy A semantic relationship between two words, in which the more specific term is included in the more general, e.g. 'cat' and 'dog' are both hyponyms of 'animal'; in this example, 'animal' is said to be the 'superordinate' term.

hypotactic Refers to sentence structures in which one component is dependent on, or subordinate to, another, e.g. *Wir sind alle in die Kneipe gegangen, nachdem wir unsere Aufsätze eingereicht hatten.*

iconic(ity) Referring to the relationship between the form of a sign and its meaning.

index (as verb) To identify the relationship between two items or categories, as when a word or linguistic variety clearly relates to or indicates a place, behaviour pattern or social category, e.g. 'the use of traditional dialect indexes a rural way of life'.

indexical(isation) (Process by which a word or linguistic variety becomes considered to be) clearly indicative of a place, behaviour pattern or social category. See index.

individual multilingualism The ability of an individual to use more than one language (variety).

inflecting Refers to a language (e.g. Latin) in which words often contain more than one grammatical component, but where each component cannot necessarily be identified as a separate item, e.g. in 'in den Wolken', *den* contains the elements 'definite article', 'plural' and 'dative'.

isogloss A line on a map indicating the boundary of an area in which a particular linguistic feature is used.

language ideology Any set of beliefs or values pertaining to the use of language, e.g. which language (variety) should be used, in what context and by whom.

language maintenance An outcome of situations in which two or more languages are in contact, whereby both (or all) of the languages continue to co-exist.

language shift An outcome of language contact situations whereby one of the languages displaces the other(s).

lenition Process by which a sound becomes less strongly articulated, e.g. when 'writer' is pronounced like 'rider'.

levelling A process through which language varieties become more similar to one another.

lexeme A word or lexical item that functions as a unit, e.g. 'turn round'.

lexicography The compiling and writing of dictionaries.

lexicon The inventory or repertoire of words possessed by a particular language, individual, etc.

lexis Vocabulary.

lingua franca Any language (variety) used to facilitate communication between speakers of different native languages.

linguistic relatedness A principle used in determining whether two or more linguistic 'varieties' may be considered forms of the same language: do they share certain grammatical structures and vocabulary?

linguistic resources The set or range of languages, varieties or words, styles and registers within a certain language (variety) that a person has access to.

liquid A type of consonant such as [1] and [r].

literacy The ability to read and write.

loanword A word borrowed from one language into another.

Low German Denotes all dialects spoken in the north of Germany (where it is not mountainous), e.g. *Plattdeutsch*.

main clause A clause that can stand alone as a simple sentence.

marked form A lexical form that is altered (usually by adding either a prefix or a suffix) in order to show that it is different from the 'base' form, e.g. *unfair* is the marked form of *fair*. Also the 'less expected' or 'less general' form of a word, e.g. *male nurse* is a marked form, whereas *nurse* is an unmarked form.

metalinguistic (discourse) Referring to language that is used to talk about language itself, e.g. metalinguistic debates are debates about language.

monoglot Someone who speaks only one language.

monophthong A single, steady vowel sound, e.g. [o:], [Y].

morphology The branch of grammar that deals with the structure of words.

morpho-syntax Referring to the relationship between the morphological and syntactic properties of an utterance, e.g. in *meine Schwestern studieren Germanistik* the feature 'plural' is marked both by the form of the word *Schwestern* and by the agreement between subject and verb.

multiethnolect   A variety used by multiple ethnic minority groups, drawing on and combining forms from two or more languages. See also new urban vernacular.

Mundart   See *Dialekt*.

national language   A language that is regarded as a symbol of national identity; it may or may not also be an official language.

Nationalsprache   See national language.

Nebensatz   See subordinate clause.

neologism   A word that has been newly coined.

new urban vernacular   A non-standard variety, drawing on different languages, that is used in highly diverse urban communities. See also multiethnolect.

Niederdeutsch   See Low German.

norm   A standardised set of rules that prescribe the use of language in social contexts. There is often pressure placed on speakers by official institutions (such as schools) not to deviate from the norm.

North Frisian   A West Germanic language spoken in Schleswig-Holstein (northern Germany).

Oberdeutsch   See Upper German.

official language   The language used by the government of a particular country or region and stipulated for use in certain domains and contexts. It is usually accorded special status and more provisions than non-official or minority languages.

onomatopoeic   A word that resembles the sound it is trying to replicate, e.g. 'bang!'

orality   The use of spoken language.

orthography   The spelling and punctuation systems of a language.

paralinguistic   Referring to features of speech that are not describable in normal linguistic terms, e.g. voice quality ('breathy' or 'creaky' voice, etc.); may also include body language, e.g. gestures, facial expressions.

paratactic   Refers to constructions in which two components are juxtaposed without a linking conjunction, e.g. *Der Krieg ging zu Ende, die Überlebenden waren erschöpft.*

periphrastic possessive   The use of separate words rather than inflection to indicate the grammatical relationship between two items, e.g. 'the house of my mother' rather than 'my mother's house'.

phonetics   The study of the production and perception of speech sounds.

phonology   (The study of) the sound system of a language.

place semiotics   The study of how the meaning of signs is conditioned or determined by their physical location and their broader social context of production and reception.

Platt(deutsch)   See Low German.

plosive   Consonants produced by a complete closure of the vocal tract, which is then opened with an audible release of breath, e.g. [p], [t].

pluricentric   Referring to languages that have two or more standard varieties, each typically associated with a particular centre of influence, e.g. a major city.

polyglot   Knowing or using more than one language.

pragmatics   The study of meaning in context.

reduction (of consonant clusters)   Reducing the number of consonant sounds in a group of sounds, e.g. pronouncing *zwei* as [svai] rather than [tsvai].

regiolect   A variety of language associated with a particular region or area.

register   Has many definitions; here, it is used in reference to those aspects of a text over which the writer/speaker has relatively little control and which are largely determined by the topic and the function of the text, e.g. law, sport, physics.

repertoire   The resources available to an individual in terms of what type of language they can use and knowing which context to use it in.

rounded vowel   Vowel produced with rounded lips, e.g. [y:] as in *über*.

rule   A law governing the structure of language, describing what can be done rather than prescribing what should be done. See norm.

Schriftsprache   Literary language. A type of language that tends to be highly stylised and standardised for use in particular situations. Sometimes used to mean standard German.

second sound shift   A systematic change in the consonantal sounds in certain West Germanic languages. This is the reason why English and standard German sound different from each other, despite both being Germanic languages. High German varieties underwent the second sound shift, while Low German and English did not.

semantics   The study of meaning.

semiotics   The study of signs (linguistic and non-linguistic) and their use.

societal multilingualism   The co-existence in one speech community of speakers of more than one language.

sociolect   A language variety spoken by or associated with a particular social group.

speech community   Used here in the very loose sense of a group of people who know and/or use the same language(s) or varieties, or who share similar linguistic repertoires.

speech event   A communicative exchange which can be analysed in terms of identifiable, culture-specific structural patterns, e.g. greetings, ordering a drink, telling a joke.

standard   A form or variety of a language that has been standardised through the writing of grammars, compiling of dictionaries, etc.

standardisation   The process of creating or determining a variety of a language that has relatively stable grammatical, lexical and orthographic forms.

stop   See plosive.

style   Has many different definitions; here, it is used in reference to those aspects of a text over which the writer/speaker has considerable control, and it is characterised in terms such as formal/informal, personal/ impersonal, serious/humorous.

subjunctive   A grammatical feature of verb forms typically used to express a wish, possibility or uncertainty and in reported speech.

subordinate clause   Dependent on the main clause of the sentence. Common subordinate clauses in German are introduced by *weil*, *obwohl*, etc.

superordinate   Also known as a hypernym. This is a word with a broader meaning that can contain within it several hyponyms with narrower meanings, e.g. *animal* is a superordinate of *mammal*, while *mammal* is a superordinate of *dog*.

synchronic   Referring to a particular point in time.

synonym   Word that has the same, or a similar, meaning as another word, e.g. *Wettbewerb* and *Konkurrenz* both mean 'competition' (but may have different connotations).

syntax   The rules and processes which govern the structure of a given language, specifically the ways in which words can be combined to form sentences.

talk   A term used to refer to speech as a form of patterned social behaviour.

territorial principle   (In this context) the principle that a particular language (or languages) has official status within a given territory and must be used in all dealings with official authorities.

Teutonism A word specifically found in varieties of German found in Germany, or a word loaned from German into another language.

text type A means of classifying individual texts (whether written or spoken) for the purpose of description and analysis, e.g. letter, interview, newspaper article.

transfer Referring to occasions when a speaker applies parts of their knowledge of one language to another. An example of this is when someone uses features from her first language when speaking in a second language.

translanguaging The use of multiple linguistic resources in social interaction, drawing in creative ways on different languages and varieties in highly diverse communities.

Überdachung The idea that a single standard language variety has an 'umbrella' effect enabling two or more non-standard varieties to be classified as belonging to the same language.

unmarked form The 'base' or unaltered form of a word, or referring to a 'more expected' or 'more general' category. See marked form.

unrounded vowel A vowel articulated without rounding the lips, e.g. /iː/ as in *feet*.

Upper German A group of High German dialects spoken in the southern area of the High German language region. Austrian German varieties are an example.

variable A linguistic feature that is subject to social or stylistic variation and can therefore be realised in two or more ways.

variant One of the possible realisations of a sociolinguistic variable.

variety A specific type of language, such as a dialect or sociolect.

vernacular Referring to a variety that is native or indigenous to an individual or group of people.

vernacular literacy The ability to read and write in one's first language.

verticalisation (of language varieties) Historical process by which different language varieties become perceived as being in a hierarchical relationship to each other.

vocalise/vocalisation A change in the pronunciation of a consonant so that it becomes more like a vowel, e.g. pronouncing the final sound in *hotel* as [u] rather than [l].

voiced consonant A consonant sound that is accompanied by vibration of the vocal cords, e.g. /d/, /g/, etc.

voiceless (or unvoiced) consonant A consonant produced without vocal cord vibration, e.g. /t/, /k/, etc.

Zweite Lautverschiebung See second sound shift.

Bibliography

Agha, Asif (2003) 'The social life of cultural value', *Language and Communication* 23: 231–273.

Agha, Asif (2006) *Language and Social Relations*, Cambridge: Cambridge University Press.

Ammon, Ulrich (2015) *Die Stellung der deutschen Sprache in der Welt*, Berlin: De Gruyter.

Ammon, Ulrich et al. (2004) *Variantenwörterbuch des Deutschen*, Berlin and New York: De Gruyter.

Androutsopoulos, Jannis (2001) '"Ultra korregd, Alder!" Zur medialen Stilisierung und Popularisierung von Türkendeutsch', *Deutsche Sprache* 4: 321–339.

Androutsopoulos, Jannis (2007) 'Ethnolekte in der Mediengesellschaft. Stilisierung und Sprachideologie in Performance, Fiktion und Metasprachdiskurs', in Christian Fandrych and Reinier Salverda (eds.) *Standard, Variation und Sprachwandel in Germanischen Sprachen: Standard/Variation and Language Change in Germanic Languages*, Tübingen, Germany: Narr, 113–155.

Androutsopoulos, Jannis (2010) 'Ideologizing ethnolectal German', in Sally Johnson and Tommaso M. Milani (eds.) *Language Ideologies and Media Discourse*, London: Continuum, 182–202.

Androutsopoulos, Jannis (2011) 'Die Erfindung des Ethnolekts', *Zeitschrift für Literaturwissenschaft und Linguistik* 41: 93–120.

Androutsopoulos, Jannis (ed.) (2014) *Mediatization and Sociolinguistic Change*, Berlin and Boston: De Gruyter.

Androutsopoulos, Jannis and Kasper Juffermans (eds.) (2014) 'Digital language practices in super-diversity', guest-edited special issue, *Discourse, Context and Media* 4–5: 1–6.

Androutsopoulos, Jannis and Katharina Lauer (2014) '"Kiezdeutsch" in der Presse: Geschichte und Gebrauch eines neuen Labels im Metasprachdiskurs', in Seyda Ozil, Michael Hofmann and Yasemin Dayiogly (eds.) *Jugendbilder – Repräsentationen von Jugend in Medien und Politik*, Göttingen, Germany: Vandenhoeck and Ruprecht, 67–93.

Appadurai, Arjun (1996) *Modernity at Large: Cultural Dimensions of Globalization*, Minneapolis: Public Worlds.

Arndt, Karl J.R. and May E. Olson (1976) *The German Language Press of the Americas* (3rd edition), Munich: Verlag Dokumentation.

Atlas zur deutschen Alltagssprache (2003-) www.atlas-alltagssprache.de [accessed 15 August 2016].

Auer, Peter (2003) '"Türkenslang". Ein jugendsprachlicher Ethnolekt des Deutschen und seine Transformationen', in Anne Häcki Buhofer (ed.) *Spracherwerb und Lebensalter*, Tübingen, Germany: Francke, 255–264.

Auer, Peter (2013) 'Ethnische Marker zwischen Varietät und Stil', in Arnulf Deppermann (ed.) *Das Deutsch der Migranten* (= *Jahrbuch des Instituts für Deutsche Sprache 2012*), Berlin: De Gruyter, 9–40.

Auer, Peter and Inci Dirim (2003) 'Socio-cultural orientation, urban youth styles and the spontaneous acquisition of Turkish by non-Turkish adolescents in Germany', in Jannis Androutsopoulos and Alexandra Georgakopoulou (eds.) *Discourse Constructions of Youth Identities*, Amsterdam: Benjamins, 223–246.

Auer, Peter and Susanne Günthner (2003) 'Die Entstehung von Diskursmarkern im Deutschen – ein Fall von Grammatikalisierung?', *Interaction and Linguistic Structures* 38: 1–29.

Auswärtiges Amt (no date) *Auswärtige Kultur- und Bildungspolitik*. www.auswaertiges-amt.de/DE/ Aussenpolitik/KulturDialog/01_Ziele_und_Aufgaben/ZielePartner_node.html [accessed 15 August 2016].

Barbour, Stephen and Cathie Carmichael (eds.) (2000) *Language and Nationalism in Europe*, Oxford: Oxford University Press.

Barbour, Stephen and Patrick Stevenson (1990) *Variation in German*, Cambridge: Cambridge University Press (Revised edition, in German, *Variation im Deutschen* published by De Gruyter, 1998).

Bauer, Laurie and Peter Trudgill (eds.) (1999) *Language Myths*, London: Penguin.

Besch, Werner (1996) *Duzen, Siezen, Titulieren*, Göttingen, Germany: Vandenhoeck and Ruprecht.

Betz, Ruth (2006) *Gesprochensprachliche Elemente in deutschen Zeitungen*, Radolfzell, Germany: Verlag für Gesprächsforschung.

Blommaert, Jan (ed.) (1999) *Language Ideological Debates*, Berlin: Mouton de Gruyter.

Blommaert, Jan (2010) *The Sociolinguistics of Globalization*, Cambridge: Cambridge University Press.

Blommaert, Jan and Ad Backus (2011) 'Repertoires revisited: "Knowing language" in superdiversity', *Working Papers in Urban Language and Literacies* 67: 1–26.

Blommaert, Jan and Jef Verschueren (1998) 'The role of language in European nationalist ideologies', in Bambi Schieffelin, Kathryn A. Woolard and Paul V. Kroskrity (eds.) *Language Ideologies: Practice and Theory*, Oxford: Oxford University Press, 189–210.

Bogatto, François and Christine Hélot (2010) 'Linguistic landscape and language diversity in Strasbourg: The *Quartier Gare*', in Elana Shohamy, Eliezer Ben Rafael and Monica Barni (eds.) *Linguistic Landscape in the City*, Bristol: Multilingual Matters, 275–291.

Burdick, Christa (2012) *Mobility and Language in Place: A Linguistic Landscape of Language Commodification*. Masters Dissertation, University of Massachusetts. http://scholarworks.umass.edu/cgi/viewcontent.cgi?article=1001andcontext=chess_diss [accessed 15 August 2016].

Busch, Brigitta (2013) *Mehrsprachigkeit*, Vienna: Facultas Verlags- und Buchhandels AG.

Busch, Brigitta (2016) 'Categorizing languages and speakers: Why linguists should mistrust census data and statistics', *Working Papers in Urban Language and Literacies* 189: 1–18.

Buselmeier, Karin (2008) 'Schulerfolg und Mehrsprachigkeit', *Muttersprache* 118: 146–155.

Butschky, Samuel (1659) *Erweiterte Hoch=Deutsche Kanzelley*, Breßlau, Germany: Trescher.

Cameron, Deborah (1995) *Verbal Hygiene*, Abingdon, UK: Routledge.

Carl, Jenny (2014) 'Multilingualism and space: Memories of place in language biographies of ethnic Germans in Sopron', in Kristine Horner, Ingrid de Saint-Georges and Jean-Jacques Weber (eds.) *Multilingualism and Mobility in Europe: Policies and Practices*, Frankfurt: Peter Lang, 247–263.

Castles, Stephen and Mark J. Miller (1998) *The Age of Migration: International Population Movements in the Modern World*, Basingstoke: Palgrave Macmillan.

Chambers, Jack and Peter Trudgill (1980) *Dialectology*, Cambridge: Cambridge University Press.

Clyne, Michael (1995) *The German Language in a Changing Europe*, Cambridge: Cambridge University Press.

Clyne, Michael (2008) 'The monolingual mindset as an impediment to the development of plurilingual potential in Australia', *Sociolinguistic Studies* 2: 347–365.

Clyne, Michael, Edina Eisikovits and Laura Tollfree (2002) 'Ethnolects as in-group markers', in Anna Duszak (ed.) *Us and Others: Social Identities Across Languages, Discourses and Cultures*, Amsterdam: Benjamins, 133–157.

Council of Europe (no date) *European Charter for Regional or Minority Languages*. www.coe.int/t/dg4/education/minlang/default_en.asp [accessed 15 August 2016].

Coupland, Nikolas (ed.) (2010) *The Handbook of Language and Globalization*, Malden and Oxford: Wiley-Blackwell.

Coupland, Nikolas (2014) 'Sociolinguistic change, vernacularization and broadcast British media', in Jannis Androutsopoulos (ed.) *Mediatization and Sociolinguistic Change*, Berlin and New York: De Gruyter, 67–96.

Dailey-O'Cain, Jennifer (2000) 'Competing language ideologies in Germany: When east meets west', in Patrick Stevenson and John Theobald (eds.) *Relocating Germanness: Discursive Disunity in Unified Germany*, Basingstoke: Macmillan, 248–266.

Dal Negro, Silvia (2009) 'Local policy modeling in the linguistic landscape', in Elana Shohamy and Durk Gorter (eds.) *Linguistic Landscape: Expanding the Scenery*, New York and Abingdon, UK: Routledge, 206–218.

Davies, Winifred (2000) 'Language awareness amongst teachers in a central German dialect area', *Language Awareness* 9: 119–134.

Davies, Winifred and Nils Langer (2014) 'Die Sprachnormfrage im Deutschunterricht: das Dilemma der Lehrenden', in Albrecht Plewnia and Andreas Witt (eds.) *Sprachverfall: Dynamik-Wandel-Variation*, Berlin and New York: De Gruyter, 299–323.

Denkler, Markus et al. (eds.) (2008) *Frischwärts und unkaputtbar: Sprachverfall oder Sprachwandel im Deutschen*, Münster: Aschendorff.

Deppermann, Arnulf (2007a) 'Playing with the voice of the other. Stylized "Kanaksprak" in conversations among German adolescents', in Peter Auer (ed.) *Style and Social Identities: Alternative Approaches to Linguistic Heterogeneity*, Berlin and New York: Mouton de Gruyter, 325–360.

Deppermann, Arnulf (2007b) 'Stilisiertes Türkendeutsch in Gesprächen deutscher Jugendlicher', *Zeitschrift für Literaturwissenschaft und Linguistik* 37/148: 43–62.

Deumert, Ana (2014) *Sociolinguistics and Mobile Communication*, Edinburgh: Edinburgh University Press.

Deumert, Ana and Wim Vandenbussche (eds.) (2003) *Germanic Standardizations*, Amsterdam: Benjamins.

Duden (2009) *Die Grammatik* (8th edition), Mannheim, Germany: Dudenverlag.

Durrell, Martin (1992) *Using German*, Cambridge: Cambridge University Press.

Ehrenreich, Susanne (2010) 'English as a business lingua franca in a German multinational corporation: Meeting the challenge', *Journal of Business Communication* 47/4: 408–431.

Eichinger, Ludwig et al. (2009) *Aktuelle Spracheinstellungen in Deutschland*, Mannheim, Germany: IDS.

ELLViA (no date) *English in the Linguistic Landscape of Vienna, Austria*. https://homepage.univie.ac.at/barbara.soukup/ellvia.html [accessed 15 August 2016].

Elon, Amos (1990) *The Pity of It All: A Portrait of Jews in Germany 1743–1933*, London: Penguin.

Ernst, Peter (2005) *Deutsche Sprachgeschichte*, Vienna: Wirtschaftsuniversität Verlag.

Extra, Guus, Massimiliano Spotti and Piet Van Avermaet (eds.) (2009) *Language Testing, Migration and Citizenship: Cross-national Perspectives on Integration Regimes*, London: Continuum.

Fagan, Sarah M.B. (2009) *German: A Linguistic Introduction*, Cambridge: Cambridge University Press.

Flubacher, Mi-Cha (2013) 'Language(s) as the key to integration? The ideological role of diglossia in the German-speaking region of Switzerland', in Jiří Nekvapil, Tamah Sherman and Petr Kaderka (eds.) *Ideological Conceptualisations of Language: Discourses of Linguistic Diversity*, Frankfurt: Peter Lang, 171–192.

Freywald, Ulrike (2010) 'Obwohl vielleicht war es ganz anders. Vorüberlegungen zum Alter der Verbzweitstellung nach subordinierenden Konjunktionen', in Arne Ziegler (ed.) *Historische Textgrammatik und Historische Syntax des Deutschen*, Berlin and New York: De Gruyter, 55–84.

Freywald, Ulrike, Leonie Cornips, Natalie Ganuza, Ingvild Nistov and Toril Opsahl (2013) 'Urban vernaculars in contemporary northern Europe: Innovative variants of V2 in Germany, Norway and Sweden', *Working Papers in Urban Language and Literacies* 113: 1–21.

Fuchs, Christian (2014) *Social Media: A Critical Introduction*, London: Sage.

Fuller, Janet M. (2012) *Bilingual Pre-Teens: Competing Ideologies and Multiple Identities in the U.S. and Germany*, Abingdon, UK: Routledge.

Gal, Susan (2012) 'Sociolinguistic regimes and the management of "diversity"', in Alexandre Duchêne and Monica Heller (eds.) *Language in Late Capitalism: Pride and Profit*, Abingdon: Routledge, 22–42.

Gal, Susan and Kathryn A. Woolard (2001) 'Constructing languages and publics: Authority and representation', in Susan Gal and Kathryn A. Woolard (eds.) *Languages and Publics: The Making of Authority*, Manchester: St Jerome Publishing, 1–12.

García, Ofelia and Li Wei (2014) *Translanguaging: Language, Bilingualism and Education*, London: Palgrave Macmillan.

Gardt, Andreas (1999) *Geschichte der Sprachwissenschaft*, Berlin and New York: De Gruyter.

Gardt, Andreas (2000) 'Sprachnationalismus zwischen 1850 und 1945', in Andreas Gardt (ed.) *Nation und Sprache: Die Diskussion ihres Verhältnisses in Geschichte und Gegenwart*, Berlin: De Gruyter, 247–271.

Georgakopoulou, Alexandra and Tereza Spilioti (eds.) (2016) *The Routledge Handbook of Language and Digital Communication*, London: Routledge.

Gerst, Dominik and Maria Klessmann (2015) 'Multilingualism and linguistic demarcations in border regions: The linguistic border landscape of the German-Polish twin cities Frankfurt (Oder) and Słubice', *Rhetorics and Communications E-Journal* 15: 1–31.

Gilles, Peter and Claudine Moulin (2003) 'Luxembourgish', in Ana Deumert and Wim Vandenbussche (eds.) *Germanic Standardizations*, Amsterdam: Benjamins, 303–331.

Glück, Helmut (1992) 'Aktuelle Beobachtungen zum Namen Deutsch', in Klaus Welke, Wolfgang Werner Sauer and Helmut Glück (eds.) *Die deutsche Sprache nach der Wende* (= *Germanische Linguistik 110–111*), Hildesheim, Germany: Olms, 141–171.

Glück, Helmut (2002) *Deutsch als Fremdsprache in Europa vom Mittelalter bis zur Barockzeit*, Berlin and New York: De Gruyter.

Glück, Helmut and Wolfgang Werner Sauer (1990) *Gegenwartsdeutsch*, Stuttgart: Metzler.

Goethe-Institut (2015) *Deutsch als Fremdsprache weltweit. Datenerhebung 2015.* www.goethe.de/resources/files/pdf37/Bro_Deutschlernerhebung_final2.pdf [accessed 15 August 2016].

Goethe-Institut. www.goethe.de/en/index.html [accessed 15 August 2016].

Gould, Robert (2000) 'Integration, Solidarität and the discourses of national identity in the 1998 Bundestag election manifestos', *German Life and Letters* 53/4: 529–551.

Grützmacher, Lena (2012) *Der Friesischunterricht an der Nis-Albrecht-Johannsen-Schule in Lindholm*, Leeuwarden, The Netherlands: Fryske Academie.

Guibernau, Montserrat (1996) *Nationalisms: The Nation-State and Nationalism in the Twentieth Century*, Cambridge: Polity Press.

Gully, Jennifer M. (2011) 'Bilingual signs in Carinthia: International treaties, the Ortstafelstreit, and the spaces of German', *Transit* 7/1: 1–14.

Gumperz, John J. (1982) *Discourse Strategies*, Cambridge: Cambridge University Press.

Günthner, Susanne (2008) '"weil – es ist zu spät". Geht die Nebensatzstellung im Deutschen verloren?', in Markus Denkler, Susanne Günthner, Wolfgang Imo, Jürgen Macha, Dorothee Meer, Benjamin Stoltenburg and Elvira Topalovic (eds.) *Frischwärts und unkaputtbar. Sprachverfall oder Sprachwandel im Deutschen*, Münster: Aschendorff Verlag, 103–128.

Günthner, Susanne, Dagmar Hüpper and Constanze Spieß (eds.) (2012) *Genderlinguistik: Sprachliche Konstruktionen von Geschlechtsidentität*, Berlin and New York: De Gruyter.

Haas, Walter (1982) 'Die deutschsprachige Schweiz', in Robert Schläpfer (ed.) *Die viersprachige Schweiz*, Zürich: Benziger, 77–160.

Handlungsplan (2015) *Handlungsplan Sprachenpolitik der schleswig-holsteinischen Landesregierung im Kontext von Regional- und Minderheitensprachen*, Kiel: Der Ministerpräsident.

Hansen-Thomas, Holly (2007) 'Language ideology, citizenship, and identity: The case of modern Germany', *Journal of Language and Politics* 6/2: 249–264.

Havinga, Anna (2015) 'Germanising Austria: The invisibilisation of East Upper German in 18th- and 19th-century Austria', in Anna Havinga and Nils Langer (eds.) *Invisible Languages in the Nineteenth Century*, Oxford: Lang, 257–281.

Hennig, Mathilde (2012) 'Was ist ein Grammatikfehler?', in Susanne Günthner, Wolfgang Imo, Dorothee Meer and Jan Georg Schneider (eds.) *Kommunikation und Öffentlichkeit. Sprachwissenschaftliche Potenziale zwischen Empirie und Norm*, Berlin and Boston: De Gruyter, 125–151.

Hinnenkamp, Volker (2000) '"Gemischt sprechen" von Migrantenjugendlichen als Ausdruck ihrer Identität', *Der Deutschunterricht* 5/2000: 96–107.

Hinnenkamp, Volker (2003) 'Sprachalternieren – ein virtuoses Spiel? Zur Alltagssprache von Migrantenjugendlichen', in Eva Neuland (ed.) *Jugendsprachen – Spiegel der Zeit. Internationale Fachkonferenz 2001 an der bergischen Universität Wuppertal*, Frankfurt: Lang, 395–416.

Hoelscher, Steven (1998) *Heritage on Stage: The Invention of Ethnic Place in America's Little Switzerland*, Madison: University of Wisconsin Press.

Hogan-Brun, Gabrielle, Clare Mar-Molinero and Patrick Stevenson (eds.) (2009) *Discourses on Language and Integration: Critical Perspectives on Language Testing Regimes in Europe*, Amsterdam: John Benjamins.

Horan, Geraldine (2016) '"Sprache der Heimat": Discourses of dialect and identity in modern-day Cologne', in Gijsbert Rutten and Kristine Horner (eds.) *Metalinguistic Perspectives on Germanic Languages: European Case Studies From Past to Present*, Oxford: Lang, 213–238.

Horner, Kristine (2009) 'Language, citizenship and Europeanization: Unpacking the discourse of integration', in Gabrielle Hogan-Brun, Clare Mar-Molinero and Patrick Stevenson (eds.) *Discourses on Language and Integration: Critical Perspectives on Language Testing Regimes in Europe*, Amsterdam: John Benjamins, 109–128.

Horner, Kristine (2011) 'Language, place and heritage: Reflexive cultural Luxembourgishness in Wisconsin', *Journal of Germanic Linguistics* 23/4: 375–400.

Horner, Kristine (2015a) 'Discourses on language and citizenship in Europe', *Language and Linguistics Compass* 9/5: 209–218.

Horner, Kristine (2015b) 'Language regimes and acts of citizenship in multilingual Luxembourg', *Journal of Language and Politics* 14/3: 359–381.

Horner, Kristine and Joanna Kremer (2016) 'Contesting ideologies of linguistic authority: Perspectives "from below" on language, nation and citizenship in Luxembourg', in Gijsbert Rutten and Kristine Horner (eds.) *Metalinguistic Perspectives on Germanic Languages: Past and Present*, Oxford: Peter Lang, 239–260.

Horner, Kristine and Jean-Jacques Weber (2008) 'The language situation in Luxembourg', *Current Issues in Language Planning* 9: 69–128.

Horner, Kristine and Jean-Jacques Weber (2011) 'Not playing the game: Shifting patterns in the discourse of integration', *Journal of Language and Politics* 10/2: 139–159.

Imo, Wolfgang (2008) 'Wenn mündliche Syntax zum schriftlichen Standard wird: Konsequenzen für den Normbegriff im Deutschunterricht', in Markus Denkler, Susanne Günthner, Wolfgang Imo, Jürgen Macha, Dorothee Meer, Benjamin Stoltenburg and Elvira Topalovic (eds.) *Frischwärts und unkaputtbar. Sprachverfall oder Sprachwandel im Deutschen*, Münster, Germany: Aschendorff Verlag, 153–179.

Irvine, Judith T. and Susan Gal (2000) 'Language ideology and linguistic differentiation', in Paul V. Kroskrity (ed.) *Regimes of Language: Ideologies, Polities, and Identities*, Oxford: James Currey, 35–83.

Jakob, Karlheinz (2010) '"Swâben ir wörter spaltent". Ein Überblick über die Dialektbewertungen in der deutschen Sprachgeschichte', in Christina A. Anders et al. (eds.) *"Perceptual Dialectology". Neue Wege der Dialektologie*, Berlin: De Gruyter, 51–66.

Johannessen, Janne Bondi and Joseph Salmons (2015) *Germanic Heritage Languages in North America: Acquisition, Attrition and Change*, Amsterdam: John Benjamins.

Johnson, Sally (2012) 'Orthography, publics and legitimation crisis: The 1996 reform of German', in Alexandra Jaffe, Jannis Androutsopoulos, Mark Sebba and Sally Johnson (eds.) *Orthography as Social Action: Scripts, Spelling, Identity and Power*, New York: Mouton de Gruyter, 21–42.

Johnson, Sally and Natalie Braber (2008) *Exploring the German Language* (2nd edition), Cambridge: Cambridge University Press.

Johnstone, Barbara (2011) 'Dialect enregisterment in performance', *Journal of Sociolinguistics* 15/5: 657–679.

Keim, Inken (2012) *Mehrsprachige Lebenswelten. Sprechen und Schreiben der türkischstämmigen Kinder und Jugendlichen*, Tübingen, Germany: Narr.

Keim, Inken and Ralf Knöbl (2007) 'Sprachliche Varianz und sprachliche Virtuosität von türkischstämmigen "Ghetto"-Jugendlichen in Mannheim', in Christian Fandrych and Reinier Salverda (eds.) *Standard, Variation und Sprachwandel in Germanischen Sprachen/Standard, Variation and Language Change in Germanic Languages*, Tübingen, Germany: Narr, 157–200.

Kelly-Holmes, Helen (2014) 'Linguistic fetish: The sociolinguistics of visual multilingualism', in David Machin (ed.) *Visual Communication*, Berlin: De Gruyter, 135–151.

Kloss, Heinz (1978) *Die Entwicklung neuer germanischer Kultursprachen seit 1800* (2nd edition), Düsseldorf: Schwann.

KMK-Beschluss (2003) Beschlüsse der Kultusministerkonferenz: Bildungsstandards im Fach Deutsch für den Mittleren Bildungsabschluss www.kmk.org/fileadmin/Dateien/veroeffentlichungen_ beschluesse/2003/2003_12_04-BS-Deutsch-MS.pdf.

König, Werner (1978) *dtv-Atlas Deutsche Sprache*, Munich: Deutscher Taschenbuch Verlag.

König, Werner, Stephan Elspaß and Robert Möller (2015) *dtv-Atlas Deutsche Sprache* (18th edition), Munich: dtv.

Kotthoff, Helga (2004) 'Overdoing culture. Sketch-Komik, Typenstilisierung und Identitätskonstruk-tion bei Kaya Yanar', in Karl H. Hörning and Julia Reuter (eds.) *Doing Culture. Neue Positionen zum Verhältnis von Kultur und sozialer Praxis*, Bielefeld: Transcript, 184–200.

Kroskrity, Paul V. (2000) 'Regimenting languages: Language ideological perspectives', in Paul V. Kroskrity (ed.) *Regimes of Language: Ideologies, Polities, and Identities*, Oxford: James Currey, 1–34.

Krotz, Friedrich (2009) *Mediatization: Concept, Changes, Consequences*, New York: Lang.

Krumm, Hans-Jürgen, Christian Fandrych, Britta Hufeisen and Claudia Riemer (eds.) (2010) *Deutsch als Fremd- und Zweitsprache. Ein internationales Handbuch*, 2 volumes, Berlin and New York: De Gruyter.

Kruse, Jan (2013) 'I don't understand the EU-Vorlage. Die Folgen der sprachenpolitischen Praxis in den Institutionen der EU für den deutschen Bundestag', in Karin Wiejowski et al. (eds.) *Vielfalt, Variation und Stellung der deutschen Sprache*, Berlin: De Gruyter. 309–324.

Kühn, Ingrid (1995) 'Alltagssprachliche Textsorten', in Gerhard Stickel (ed.) *Stilfragen*, Berlin: De Gruyter, 329–354.

Labov, William (1972) *Sociolinguistic Patterns*, Philadelphia: University of Pennsylvania Press.

Labov, William (1994) *Principles of Linguistic Change. Volume 1: Internal Factors*, Malden and Oxford: Oxford University Press.

Labov, William (2001) *Principles of Linguistic Change. Volume 2: Social Factors*, Malden and Oxford: Oxford University Press.

Labov, William (2006) *The Social Stratification of English in New York* (2nd edition), Cambridge: Cambridge University Press.

Langer, Nils (2003) 'Low German', in Ana Deumert and Wim Vandenbussche (eds.) *Germanic Stan-dardizations*, Amsterdam: Benjamins, 282–302.

Langer, Nils (2009a) 'Sociolinguistic changes in the history of Low German', in Geraldine Horan et al. (eds.) *Landmarks in the History of German*, Oxford: Lang, 211–232.

Langer, Nils (2009b) 'Sprachverfall in the New Germany', *Germanistik in Ireland* 4: 117–132.

Langer, Nils (2010) 'Sprechereinstellungen zur Zielsprache im britischen und irischen DaF-Unterricht', in Christina Anders et al. (eds.) *"Perceptual dialectology" – Neue Wege der Dialektologie*, Berlin and New York: De Gruyter, 409–431.

Langer, Nils (2014) 'Standard German in the eighteenth century: Norms and use', in Gijsbert Rutten et al. (eds.) *Norms and Usage in Language History 1600–1900*, Amsterdam: Benjamins, 277–302.

Langer, Nils and Winifred Davies (eds.) (2005) *Linguistic Purism in the Germanic Languages*, Berlin and New York: De Gruyter.

Langer, Nils and Robert Langhanke (2013) 'Metalinguistic discourses on Low German in the nine-teenth century', *Linguistik-online.de* 58: 77–97.

Langer, Nils and Agnete Nesse (2012) 'Linguistic purism', in Juan Hernandez-Campoy and J. Camilo Conde-Silvestre (eds.) *Blackwell Handbook of Historical Sociolinguistics*, Oxford: Wiley, 607–625.

Laversuch, Iman Makeba (2008) 'Putting Germany's language tests to the test: An examination of the development, implementation and efficacy of using language proficiency tests to mediate German citizenship', *Current Issues in Language Planning* 9/3: 282–298.

Linn, Andrew and Nicola McLelland (eds.) (2002) *Standard Germanic*, Amsterdam: Benjamins.

Lucht, Felecia (2007) *Linguistic Variation in a Wisconsin German Community*. Ph.D. Dissertation, University of Wisconsin-Madison.

Lucht, Felecia, Benjamin Frey and Joseph Salmons (2011) 'A tale of three cities: Urban-rural asymmetries in language shift?' *Journal of Germanic Linguistics* 23/4: 347–374.

Macha, Jürgen (2006) 'Sprachgeschichte und Kulturgeschichte. Frühneuzeitliche Graphien als Indikatoren konfessioneller Positionierung', *Zeitschrift für Germanistische Linguistik* 34: 105–130.

Maitz, Peter and Stephan Elspaß (2007) 'Warum der "Zwiebelfisch" nicht in den Deutschunterricht gehört', *Info DaF* 34/5: 515–526.

Manz, Stefan (2004) 'Constructing a normative national identity: The *Leitkultur* debate in Germany, 2000/2001', *Journal of Multilingual and Multicultural Development* 25/5–6: 481–496.

Markhardt, Heidemarie (2005) *Das Österreichische Deutsch im Rahmen der EU*, Vienna: Lang.

McLelland, Nicola (2009) 'Linguistic purism, protectionism, nationalism in the Germanic languages today', *Journal of Germanic Linguistics* 21: 93–112.

McNamara, Tim and Elana Shohamy (2008) 'Language tests and human rights', *International Journal of Applied Linguistics* 18/1: 89–95.

Milroy, James and Lesley Milroy (1999) *Authority in Language*, London: Routledge.

Möllering, Martina (2010) 'The changing scope of German citizenship: From "guest worker" to citizen?', in Christina Slade and Martina Möllering (eds.) *From Migrant to Citizen: Testing Language, Testing Culture*, Basingstoke: Palgrave Macmillan, 145–163.

Muhr, Rudolf (2007) *Österreichische Aussprachedatenbank*. www.adaba.at/ [accessed 16 August 2016].

Nekvapil, Jiří and Tamah Sherman (2009) 'Czech, German and English: Finding their place in multinational companies in the Czech Republic', in Jenny Carl and Patrick Stevenson (eds.) *Language, Discourse and Identity in Central Europe*, Basingstoke: Palgrave, 122–146.

Newton, Gerald (ed.) (1996) *Luxembourg and Lëtzebuergesch: Language and Communication at the Crossroads of Europe*, Oxford: Clarendon Press.

Österreichisches Wörterbuch (1951) (1st edition), Vienna: Österreichischer Bundesverlag.

Papen, Uta (2015) 'Signs in cities: The discursive production and commodification of urban spaces', *Sociolinguistic Studies* 9/1: 1–26.

Pastor, Eckart (1995) '"SEIT WANN SIEZEN WIR UNS EIGENTLICH?" Zur Geschichte der pronominalen Anredeformen im Deutschen. Ein Streifzug durch Literatur- und Sprachgeschichte', *Germanistische Mitteilungen* 42: 3–17.

Pautz, Hartwig (2005) 'The politics of identity in Germany: The *Leitkultur* debate', *Race and Class* 46/4: 39–52.

Pennycook, Alastair (2007) *Global Englishes and Transcultural Flows*, London and New York: Routledge.

Pfaff, Carol (2005) '"Kanaken im Alemanistan": Feridun Zaimoğlu's representation of migrant language', in Volker Hinnenkamp and Katharina Meng (eds.) *Sprachgrenzen überspringen*, Tübingen, Germany: Narr, 195–225.

Pfaff, Carol (2010) 'Multilingual development in Germany in the crossfire of ideology and politics', in Urszula Okulska and Piotr Cap (eds.) *Perspectives in Politics and Discourses*, Amsterdam: John Benjamins, 327–358.

Pfalzgraf, Falco (2009) 'Linguistic purism in the history of the German language', in Geraldine Horan, Nils Langer and Sheila Watts (eds.) *Landmarks in the History of the German Language*, Oxford, Bern, Nerlin: Peter Lang, 113–136.

Piller, Ingrid (2001) 'Naturalization, language testing and its basis in ideologies of national identity and citizenship', *International Journal of Bilingualism* 5/3: 259–277.

Praxis Deutsch (2009) Special issue (215): *Sprachwandel,* Friedrich Verlag. https://www.friedrich-verlag.de/sekundarstufe/deutsch/praxis-deutsch/

Pusch, Luise (1984) *Das Deutsche als Männersprache*, Frankfurt: Suhrkamp.

Rampton, Ben (2011) 'From "multi-ethnic adolescent heteroglossia" to "contemporary urban vernaculars"', *Language and Communication* 31: 276–294.

Ransmayr, Jutta (2006) *Der Status des österreichischen Deutsch an Auslandsuniversitäten*, Frankfurt: Peter Lang.

Rasinger, Sebastian M. (2014) 'Linguistic landscapes in Southern Carinthia (Austria)', *Journal of Multilingual and Multicultural Development* 35/6: 580–602.

Reershemius, Gertrud (2011) 'Reconstructing the past? Low German and the creating of regional identity in public language display', *Journal of Multilingual and Multicultural Development* 32/1: 33–54.

Reershemius, Gertrud (2016) 'Autochthonous heritage languages and social media: Writing and bilingual practices in Low German on Facebook', *Journal of Multilingual and Multicultural Development*, 38/1: 1–15.

Reershemius, Gertrud and Evelyn Ziegler (2015) 'Sprachkontaktinduzierte jugendkulturelle Stile im DaF-Unterricht: Beispiele aus dem Film Fack ju Göhte', in Wolfgang Imo and Sandro Moraldo (eds.) *Interaktionale Sprache im DaF-Unterricht*, Tübingen: Stauffenburg, 241–274.

Rosa, Don (2008) *Onkel Dagobert: Sein Leben, Seine Milliarden*, EHAPA Comic Collection, Copenhagen: Egmont Publishers.

Russ, Charles V.J. (ed.) (1990) *The Dialects of Modern German*, London: Routledge.

Salmons, Joseph (2012) *A History of German*, Oxford: Oxford University Press.

Scheuringer, Hermann (1992) 'Deutsches Volk und deutsche Sprache', *Muttersprache* 102: 218–229.

Schmidt, Wilhelm (2000) *Geschichte der deutschen Sprache*, Leipzig: Hirzel.

Schneider, Wolf (2001) *Deutsch für Profis. Wege zu gutem Stil*, Munich: Goldmann.

Schottelius, Justus Georg (1663) *Ausführliche Arbeit von der teutschen Haubtsprache*, Braunschweig: Zilliger. Reprint ed. W. Hecht, Tübingen: Niemeyer, 1967/1995.

Schüpbach, Doris (2009) 'Testing language, testing ethnicity? Policies and practices surrounding the ethnic German *Aussiedler*', *Language Assessment Quarterly* 6/1: 78–82.

Schwarzenbach, Ruedi (2011) 'JA zur Mundart im Kindergarten. Sprachbildung als Politikum: zur Zürcher Volksabstimmung vom 15. Mai 2011', *SchweizerDeutsch: Zeitschrift für Sprache in der deutschen Schweiz* 19: 3–7.

Scollon, Ron and Suzanne Wong Scollon (2003) *Discourses in Place: Language in the Material World*, London: Routledge.

Sick, Bastian (2004) *Der Dativ ist dem Genitiv sein Tod*, Cologne: Kiepenheuer and Wisch.

Siebert-Ott, Gesa Maren (1999) *Zweisprachigkeit und Schulerfolg. Die Wirksamkeit von schulischen Modellen zur Förderung von Kindern zugewanderter Sprachminderheiten*, Soest: Landesinstitut für Schule und Weiterbildung.

Soukup, Barbara (2016) 'English in the linguistic landscape of Vienna, Austria (ELLViA): Outline, rationale, and methodology of a large-scale empirical project on language choice on public signs from the perspective of sign-readers', *Views* 25: 1–24.

Spitzmüller, Jürgen (2013) *Graphische Variation als soziale Praxis: Eine soziolinguistische Theorie skripturaler 'Sichtbarkeit'*, Berlin and New York: Mouton de Gruyter.

Statistik Austria (2007) *Bevölkerung 2001 nach Umgangssprache, Staatsangehörigkeit und Geburtsland*. www.statistik.at/web_de/statistiken/menschen_und_gesellschaft/bevoelkerung/volkszaehlungen_registerzaehlungen_abgestimmte_erwerbsstatistik/bevoelkerung_nach_demographischen_merkmalen/022896.html [accessed 15 August 2016].

Steensen, Thomas (2002) 'Friesischer Schulunterricht in Nordfriesland im 20. und 21. Jahrhundert', *Nordfriesisches Jahrbuch* 38: 77–119.

Stevenson, Patrick (ed.) (1995) *The German Language and the Real World*, Oxford: Clarendon Press.

Stevenson, Patrick (2002) *Language and German Disunity: A Sociolinguistic History of East and West in Germany, 1945–2000*, Oxford: Oxford University Press.

Stevenson, Patrick (2006) '"National" languages in transnational contexts: Language, migration and citizenship in Europe', in Clare Mar-Molinero and Patrick Stevenson (eds.) *Language Ideologies, Policies and Practices: Language and the Future of Europe*, Basingstoke: Palgrave Macmillan, 147–161.

Stevenson, Patrick and Jenny Carl (2010) *Language and Social Change in Central Europe: Discourses on Policy, Identity and the German Language*, Edinburgh: Edinburgh University Press.

Stevenson, Patrick and Livia Schanze (2009) 'Language, migration and citizenship in Germany: Discourses on language and belonging', in Guus Extra, Massimiliano Spotti and Piet Van Avermaet (eds.) *Language Testing, Migration and Citizenship: Cross-national Perspectives on Integration Regimes*, London: Continuum, 87–106.

Stotz, Daniel (2006) 'Breaching the peace: Struggles around multilingualism in Switzerland', *Language Policy* 5: 247–265.

Takada, Hiroyuki (1998) *Grammatik und Sprachwirklichkeit von 1640–1700*, Tübingen: Niemeyer.

Tertilt, Hermann (1996) *Turkish Power Boys: Ethnographie einer Jugendbande*, Frankfurt: Suhrkamp.

Thomas, George (1991) *Linguistic Purism*, London: Longman.

Townson, Michael (1992) *Mother-tongue and Fatherland*, Manchester: Manchester University Press.

Trudgill, Peter (2004) *Dialects*, London: Routledge.

University of Leipzig (2016) *GeWiss – gesprochene Wissenschaftssprache kontrastiv.* https://gewiss.uni-leipzig.de [accessed 15 August 2016].

Vollstedt, Marina (2002) *Sprachenplanung in der internationalen Kommunikation internationaler Unternehmen. Studien zur Umstellung der Unternehmenssprache auf das Englische*, Hildesheim, Germany: Olms.

Wagner, Melanie (2009) *Lay Linguistics and School Teaching*, Stuttgart: Steiner.

Walker, Alastair (2009) 'Friesisch, Hochdeutsch und die Sprachenvielfalt in Nordfriesland', in Michael Elmentaler (ed.) *Deutsch und seine Nachbarn*, Frankfurt: Lang, 15–29.

Watts, Richard J. (1999) 'The ideology of dialect in Switzerland', in Jan Blommaert (ed.) *Language Ideological Debates*, Berlin: Mouton de Gruyter, 67–103.

Weber, Jacques and Kristine Horner (2012) *Introducing Multilingualism*, London: Routledge.

Weigel, Hans (1974) *Die Leiden der neuen Wörter*, Munich: Artemis.

Wiese, Heike (2012) *Kiezdeutsch. Ein neuer Dialekt entsteht.* 2nd, revised edition, München: Becksche Reihe.

Wiese, Heike (2013) 'From feature pool to pond: The ecology of new urban vernaculars', *Working Papers in Urban Language and Literacies* 104: 1–29.

Wiese, Heike (2014) 'Voices of linguistic outrage: Standard language constructs and the discourse on new urban dialects', *Working Papers in Urban Language and Literacies* 120: 1–25.

Zaimoglu, Feridun (1995) *Kanak Sprak*, Berlin: Rotbuch.

Ziegler, Evelyn (2009) '"Ich sag das jetzt so, weil das steht auch so im Duden!" Sprachwandel als Sprachvariation: *weil*-Sätze', *Praxis Deutsch* (36) *Themenheft Sprachwandel*, 45–51.

Ziegler, Evelyn (2013) 'Metropolenzeichen: Visuelle Mehrsprachigkeit in der Metropole Ruhr', *Zeitschrift für germanistische Linguistik (Forschungsnotiz)* 41/2: 299–301.

Index

German terms are in *italics*; linguistic terms explained in the list of keywords are in **bold**.